UNMOVABLE

SETTLING INTO THE TRUTHS FOR THESE LAST DAYS

HENRY CHA

TEACH Services, Inc.
P U B L I S H I N G
www.TEACHServices.com • (800) 367-1844

World rights reserved. This book or any portion thereof may not be copied or reproduced in any form or manner whatever, except as provided by law, without the written permission of the publisher, except by a reviewer who may quote brief passages in a review.

The author assumes full responsibility for the accuracy of all facts and quotations as cited in this book. The opinions expressed in this book are the author's personal views and interpretations, and do not necessarily reflect those of the publisher.

This book is provided with the understanding that the publisher is not engaged in giving spiritual, legal, medical, or other professional advice. If authoritative advice is needed, the reader should seek the counsel of a competent professional.

Copyright © 2022 Henry Cha
Copyright © 2022 TEACH Services, Inc.
ISBN-13: 978-1-4796-1445-5 (Paperback)
ISBN-13: 978-1-4796-1446-2 (ePub)
Library of Congress Control Number: 2022912638
Unless otherwise stated, all scriptures are taken from the King James Version of the Bible

THE HOLY BIBLE, NEW INTERNATIONAL VERSION®, NIV® Copyright © 1973, 1978, 1984, 2011 by Biblica, Inc.® Used by permission. All rights reserved worldwide.

The Holy Bible: International Standard Version. Release 2.0, Build 2015.02.09. Copyright © 1995-2014 by ISV Foundation. ALL RIGHTS RESERVED INTERNATIONALLY. Used by permission of Davidson Press, LLC.

The ESV® Bible (The Holy Bible, English Standard Version®). ESV® Text Edition: 2016. Copyright © 2001 by Crossway, a publishing ministry of Good News Publishers. The ESV® text has been reproduced in cooperation with and by permission of Good News Publishers. Unauthorized reproduction of this publication is prohibited. All rights reserved.

Contemporary English Version®
Copyright © 1995 American Bible Society. All rights reserved.

Scripture taken from the New King James Version®. Copyright © 1982 by Thomas Nelson. Used by permission. All rights reserved.

www.TEACHServices.com • (800) 367-1844

Table of Contents

Introduction — v

Present Truth

Chapter 1 The Apostle and High Priest of Our Profession — 11
Chapter 2 A Priest upon His Father's Throne — 23
Chapter 3 The Great Controversy Revisited — 33
Chapter 4 The Great Controversy Prolonged — 45
Chapter 5 The Great Controversy Settled — 59
Chapter 6 The Christian Experience Promised — 73
Chapter 7 The Christian Experience Put into Effect — 83
Chapter 8 The Christian Experience Consummated — 93
Chapter 9 The Cleansing of the Soul Temple Illustrated — 105
Chapter 10 The Day of Atonements — 119
Chapter 11 Investigating the Investigative Judgment — 131
Chapter 12 Justifying the Investigative Judgment — 147
Chapter 13 Facing the Investigative Judgment — 159

Present Duty

Chapter 14 Ye Shall Afflict Your Souls — 179
Chapter 15 Fear God, Give Glory to Him, and Worship Him — 191
Chapter 16 Thou Must Prophesy Again — 209

Present Dangers

Chapter 17 The Danger of Concession, Conformity, and Compromise — 221
Chapter 18 The Danger of Abandoning Once-cherished Light — 235
Chapter 19 The Danger of Indolence — 249

Present and Future Perfections

Chapter 20 The Three Levels of Human Perfection — 261

Bibliography — 276

Introduction

The Repository of Sacred Truth

To preserve sacred truth throughout the ages, God has had repositories placed all along the timeline of church history. Even during the Dark Ages, when there was a famine for the Word of God, faithful sentinels and guardians were divinely appointed to act as repositories of sacred truths.

In these last days, the Seventh-day Adventist Church is standing in the very place where Israel used to stand. Whether one realizes it or not, this church is in the same privileged status as ancient Israel was in relation to God. She is His repository of sacred truth for the time of the end. The three great truths that defined Judaism, thus making it unique, have been restored in the Seventh-day Adventist Church. They are the Sabbath, sanctuary, and spirit of prophecy.

Just as Israel was tasked with preserving the knowledge of the creation Sabbath, the Seventh-day Adventist Church has been commissioned to hold it up to the world as God's true day of worship. The knowledge of the atoning ministry of Jesus Christ in the sanctuary, which Israel preserved through the centuries, has also been restored in Adventism. This truth is, in fact, "the central pillar and foundation of the Advent faith."[1] Even the prophetic gift God had bestowed upon ancient Israel has been restored in the Seventh-day

---

[1] White, *The Great Controversy*, p. 409.

Adventist Church through Ellen G. White's ministry. Her writings testify to the genuineness of her calling to the prophetic office. Many of us do not stop to think that the Seventh-day Adventist Church has been truly blessed with the same divine favors given to Israel of old, if not more!

Sacred truths once committed to Israel have been restored to this church, including light that has been accumulating through the ages. "In these last days we have the accumulated light that has been shining through all the ages, and we shall be held correspondingly responsible."[2]

What Sacred Truth Means to Us

This perfect chain of truths brings out more fully and clearly the work and mission of Jesus, especially as they relate to the church and the world in the time of the end. These peculiar truths make the Seventh-day Adventist Church stand out like a light on a hill, beckoning those steeped in the errors, delusions, and false teachings proliferating these last days to come to that light. They act like walls that serve to protect the church against attacks from without and within. These advanced truths also give her the potential to attain to higher levels of character development because the more light received and assimilated in the soul, the higher the level of character developed. After all, truth sanctifies. Jesus said, "Sanctify them through thy truth: thy word is truth" (John 17:17).

Finally, these mighty truths are what make the church not only unique but strong as a people as well:

> We have nothing to fear for the future, except as we shall forget the way the Lord has led us, and his teaching in our past history. We are now a strong people, if we will put our trust in the Lord; for we are handling the mighty truths of the word of God. We have everything to be thankful for.[3]

---

[2] White, "Notes on Travel," *The Review and Herald*, November 25, 1884.
[3] White, *Selected Messages*, book 3, p. 162.

Introduction

To remain strong as a people, Seventh-day Adventists must never forget the way the Lord has led them in the past; they must always keep fresh His teachings in their past history. The "teachings" refer to the truths handed down to the church by the pioneers of the movement through diligent Bible study. To remain formidable as a people, the church must faithfully hold on to the truths entrusted to her, no matter how unpopular and unappealing these truths may appear to many. She must never abandon them by concessions, conformity, and compromise to gain acceptance and the favor of other denominations. In other words, to remain strong as a people, Seventh-day Adventists must hold on firmly to their theology and never forget their history.

Seventh-day Adventists are only as strong as their efforts are to elevate these truths before the world. They must never hide them under a bushel. If they do, they will be instantly reduced to the proverbial salt, which has lost its savor. It is not numbers that make the church strong as a people. Instead, it is the truths that are on the church menu that make it spiritually nourished, morally strong, and healthy. The question comes, "Is the Seventh-day Adventist Church, the new Israel of God, still strong as a people today?" Is it still *peculiar* (see 2 Peter 2:9*)*, or has it blended with the other churches? Has it become just another generic church?

Present Truth Only for the Past?

Unfortunately, many within the ranks of contemporary Adventism today say the church seems to have developed an "unhealthy" relationship with regards to "present truth." These entertain the idea that the light our pioneers received during their time (e.g., the cleansing of the sanctuary, 2,300-days prophecy, investigative judgment, three angels' messages, etc.) only applied for their time and were not meant to be treated as present truth forever. They maintain that these truths were not meant to be enshrined forever in the denominational psyche. They say it is wrong to keep hanging on to those truths as if there were no more truths to discover. Many have expressed the thought that rather than "stagnating" on those truths of bygone days, the church ought to dispense with them and discover new truths!

On the surface, that idea sounds bright and novel. However, reduced to its simplest terms, that sentiment, shared by many today in the church, is nothing but a subtle invitation to marginalize and minimize the original doctrines that have been committed to the church. It is an insidious attempt to bury the ancient landmarks and "forget His teaching in our past history." This kind of talk should immediately raise red flags because it is nothing but an effort to destabilize the church by abandoning the truths that make it strong as a people. It is nothing but an effort to betray sacred trusts. We have to decide in our minds whether the truths committed to our pioneers and handed down to us were of a transitory nature or designed to endure while time shall last.

Our Sacred Duty with Regards to Present Truth

We are not told to abandon the present truths God entrusted to us through the pioneers in an attempt to discover new truths. It is not God's will that we discard truths, no matter how old, but to treasure every ray of light He, in mercy, has shed on our pathway. Far from discarding the old, foundational truths laid down by the pioneers of this movement, we are instructed to build on and develop them until they appear clearer and brighter.

We are not to teach the same old truths year after year. Instead, we are to present the ancient truths in a new framework. We are to be continually advancing in the discovery of newer truths that reinforce the old fundamental truths as new light is discovered. We are to combine the old *and* the new, not discard the old *for* the new. In the words of the Master Himself, "Then said he unto them, 'Therefore every scribe which is instructed unto the kingdom of heaven is like unto a man that is an householder, which bringeth forth out of his treasure things new and old'" (Matt. 13:52). Johann Wolfgang von Goethe, the famous eighteenth-century German poet and writer, once said, "The most original modern authors are not so because they advance what is new, but simply because they know how to put what they have to say as if it had never been said before." This is our challenge and high calling: to present God's timeless truths as if they have never been presented before!

Introduction

Far be it that we as a people should think along the lines of giving up the truths "once delivered unto the saints" (Jude 3) or making them of no effect. On the contrary, we ought to be faithful to our trust as God's custodians of sacred truth. It is the sacred obligation of those who have the light of present truth to develop it until it shines like the light of noonday.

The Lord has made his people the repository of sacred truth. *Upon every individual who has had the light of present truth devolves the duty of developing that truth on a higher scale than it has hitherto been developed.* The Lord will hold us accountable for the influence we might have exerted, and did not because we did not earnestly try to understand our accountability in this world.[4]

The statement above clearly states that Seventh-day Adventists are not to abandon but rather develop "the light of present truth… on a higher scale than it has hitherto been done." This means cherishing the truths that have been committed to the church through the pioneers and clearing new paths and paving the way for a deeper and more precise understanding of these truths. This can only be done through diligent and prayerful study. Recall a previous quote: "We have nothing to fear for the future, except as we shall forget the way the Lord has led us, and his *teaching* in our past history. We are now a strong people, if we will put our trust in the Lord; for we are handling the mighty truths of the word of God."

Where Much Is Given, Much Is Also Required

Since much has been given to the Seventh-day Adventist Church, in terms of the amount of light and privileges received, much is also required of her. She is required to "develop the truth on a higher scale than it has hitherto been developed." She is "accountable for the influence" the truth is to exert upon the world at large.

---

[4] White, "Ye Are the Light of the World," *The Review and Herald*, September 21, 1897 (emphasis added).

At the end of the day, will God find this church faithful to her trust? Will He commend her with the words, "Come faithful servant, enter into the joy of the Lord" (see Matt. 25:31)? Or will she be found unfaithful? What will God do to the Seventh-day Adventist Church if she fails to measure up to the responsibilities He has placed upon her as the repository of sacred truth for this time? If God did not spare the natural branches that were broken off from the tree, how much easier it would be for Him to break off the wild branches that were grafted into it (see Rom. 11:21)?

> In the balances of the sanctuary the Seventh-day Adventist church is to be weighed. She will be judged by the privileges and advantages that she has had. If her spiritual experience does not correspond to the advantages that Christ, at infinite cost, has bestowed on her, if the blessings conferred have not qualified her to do the work entrusted to her, on her will be pronounced the sentence: "Found wanting." By the light bestowed, the opportunities given, will she be judged.[5]

---

[5] White, *Testimonies for the Church*, vol. 8, p. 247.

1

The Apostle and High Priest of Our Profession

Idea in Brief: This chapter explains why the work of Jesus Christ as High Priest in the heavenly sanctuary is just as essential to the plan of salvation as was His death upon the cross. It presents arguments to prove the work of redemption did not end when the Savior was offered up as an atoning sacrifice but continues in the sanctuary above. For this reason, believers are admonished to consider Jesus as "the Apostle and High Priest of our profession" (Heb. 3:1).

The Book of Hebrews

Hebrews occupies a unique and special place in the New Testament canon. It continues where the other books of the New Testament leave off. It sheds tremendous light on the ongoing work in which the Savior has been engaged in for the redemption of humanity since His death, resurrection, and ascension into heaven.

A quick survey of the New Testament is in order here. The four Gospels, Matthew, Mark, Luke, and John, highlight the life, teachings, death, and resurrection of Jesus. Acts begins with the account of Christ's ascension in the clouds of heaven and moves on to relate the amazing acts the Spirit-filled church accomplished during its early history. The epistles expound on the core Christian doctrines, such as baptism, righteousness by faith, sanctification, the Lord's supper, marriage and the family, the judgment, church order, spiritual gifts, repentance, and numerous others. Also included in the epistles are numerous pastoral counsels and exhortations to holy living. Revelation, the last book of the Bible, primarily addresses end-time events. This book concludes with a delineation of the prophetic events surrounding the glorious appearing of Jesus and the splendors beyond.

The astute Bible student will notice that although Jesus is mentioned by name constantly in the epistles, He is *personally* absent from view since His ascension in Acts. He does not appear again until His glorious return in Revelation. None of the New Testament writers really mentions anything regarding the activities in which Jesus has been engaged in, since He ascended to heaven—until one arrives at the book of Hebrews.

Of the twenty-seven books of the New Testament, only Hebrews mentions a sanctuary in heaven where Jesus ministers as High Priest (see 8:1, 2). Although there are references in Revelation to a sanctuary in heaven, they are not as explicit and unambiguous as those found in Hebrews, which fills a massive void within the New Testament canon by dwelling on the Savior's ongoing ministry in heaven before His return to earth. Drawing heavily from the typical Mosaic tabernacle and its services, the author of Hebrews (evidence points to Paul) masterfully explains the nature of Christ's high-priestly work in the heavenly sanctuary. There, He is portrayed as "a minister of the sanctuary, of the true tabernacle, which the Lord pitched, and not man" (8:2). He is the great "high priest over the house of God" (10:21).

The importance of Hebrews to Seventh-day Adventists cannot be overemphasized. Without this book, it would be difficult to defend the position that there is a sanctuary in heaven where Jesus ministers as High Priest after the order of Melchizedek (Note: KJV uses different spelling). Without this book, the Levitical economy that looms enormously in the Old Testament finds no projection in the New Testament. For this reason, Hebrews occupies the same level of importance as do the books of Daniel and Revelation in Adventist soteriology.[6]

---

[6] In 1845, O.R.L. Crosier, Hiram Edson, and F.B. Hahn, pioneers of the Seventh-day Adventist church, leaned heavily on the book of Hebrews to teach about the dual ministration of Jesus in the heavenly sanctuary. They used it to raise arguments prov-

Finding Rest and Assurance in Christ Our High Priest

With this thought in mind, Paul's admonition in Hebrews 3:1 to those who are "partakers of the heavenly calling" to "consider Jesus Christ as Apostle and High Priest of our profession" becomes timely and apropos.

A careful consideration and study of the high-priestly work of Jesus in the heavenly sanctuary cannot but build faith and patience in the Christian struggle. It assures one of present salvation and inspires confidence and hope for the future. It is a revelation of the tremendous, unrelenting love that God and His Son have for the church on earth.

When Jesus died on the cross, His disciples became faint and weary in their minds because they did not possess a clear understanding of His work and mission. Influenced by the Jews and rabbis, they thought Jesus had come to deliver the nation from the hated Roman government. Their faith spiraled downward as they felt their hopes dashed on account of the Savior's death. If they only had a clearer understanding of Christ's work as the Atoning Sacrifice and High Priest, their faith would have remained firm and steadfast, despite losing Him. They would not have been "scattered as sheep without a shepherd" during the night of their bitter trial.

As we go through life's many trials and difficulties, we are to "look unto Jesus the author and finisher of our faith." Our merciful and compassionate High Priest feels what we feel; He is "touched with the feelings of our infirmities"; He understands our weaknesses. The same Jesus who, while on earth, said, "Come unto Me all ye that labor and are heavy laden and I will give you rest" (Matthew 11:28), now bids His people from the heavenly sanctuary to "come boldly to the throne of grace that they might find grace to help in time of need" (Heb. 4:16).

When Jesus said, "Learn of me… and you will find rest unto your souls," He meant we need to study not only His life but His present work and mission—His closing work as High Priest in the heavenly

---

ing salvation was not finished at the cross but instead is an ongoing process in the sanctuary in heaven.

sanctuary, in particular. By doing so, we shall find rest and assurance for our souls.

A Seven-fold Rendition of Christ's High-priestly Role

The continuous high-priestly ministration of Jesus in the heavenly sanctuary brings a train of spiritual and temporal benefits not fully grasped by the mind or appreciated by the heart. As **Propitiator**, our merciful and compassionate High Priest offers gifts and sacrifices to make atonement for sins (see 2:17). He shows "compassion to those who are ignorant and to those out of the way" (5:2). He is "touched with the feelings of our infirmities" (4:15). As **Justifier**, Jesus pardons the sins of His people and reconciles them with His Father (see Rom. 4:25; 5:10; 1 John 1:9). As man's **Substitute**, Jesus presents His perfect righteousness before His Father to make up for the imperfections of His people. They are accounted "perfect in Christ" (Col. 1:28); they are "complete in Him" (2:10); they are "accepted in the Beloved" (Eph. 1:6).

The incense of Christ's perfect righteousness is combined with the impure prayers of the saints before being offered to God (see Rev. 8:3).

> All incense from earthly tabernacles must be moist with the cleansing drops of the blood of Christ. He holds before the Father the censer of His own merits, in which there is no taint of earthly corruption. He gathers into this censer the prayers, the praise, and the confessions of His people, and with these He puts His own spotless righteousness. Then, perfumed with the merits of Christ's propitiation, the incense comes up before God wholly and entirely acceptable. Then gracious answers are returned.[7]

As mankind's powerful **Intercessor**, Jesus pleads for the saints and even His enemies so they may not be treated as they deserve. His powerful appeals shield His people from the evil one and fortify them

---

[7] White, *Selected Messages*, book 1, p. 344.

against his relentless assaults. Jesus is also their **Advocate**, defending them from the accusations of Satan, the "accuser of the brethren" who hurls his accusations against them "before God day and night" (Rev. 12:10). Jesus is our tireless **Helper** who sends help from the heavenly sanctuary so we can "obtain grace to help in time of need" (Heb. 4:16). "Send thee help from the sanctuary, and strengthen thee out of Zion" (Ps. 20:2).

In Hebrews 8:6, Paul introduces yet another priestly role of Jesus: "But now hath he obtained a more excellent ministry, by how much also he is the mediator of a better covenant, which was established upon better promises." The role of Jesus as the **Mediator** of the New Covenant is crucial. As Mediator, Jesus dispenses the rich blessings contained in the promises of the new covenant.

Is It Finished?

One wonders why there is so much apathy among mainline Christians regarding Christ's work, which is going forward in the sanctuary in heaven, when they are admonished to "consider Christ as Apostle and High Priest of their profession." Could it be because of the understanding that everything needed for salvation had been accomplished at the cross? "Salvation is a finished work!" is the cry being echoed from many pulpits. This sentiment has done much to dampen the enthusiasm of many to deeply study and consider Christ's high-priestly work in the heavenly sanctuary.

Indeed, if salvation is a finished work, then whatever else our Lord Jesus is doing in the heavenly sanctuary is not nearly as crucial for our salvation as was His death on Calvary. This presupposition is based on an incomplete understanding of the dual nature of Christ's atoning

> "
> One wonders why there is so much apathy among mainline Christians regarding Christ's work, which is going forward in the sanctuary in heaven, when they are admonished to "consider Christ as Apostle and High Priest of their profession." Could it be because of the understanding that everything needed for salvation had been accomplished at the cross?
> "

ministry, namely His death (see Heb. 2:9, 14) and high-priestly ministration (see 2:17; 8:1–3).

When Jesus died in AD 31, His role as Atoning Sacrifice was finished. He then ascended to heaven, carrying His shed blood with Him into the sanctuary so He can offer it for sin (see 9:12). This is what priests do: offer gifts and sacrifices for sin (see 2;17; 5:1; 8:3, 4). Priests make atonement for sin, not the sacrifice. To minimize and ignore Christ's function as High Priest is to fail to "consider Jesus Christ as Apostle *and* High Priest of our profession."

A Betrayal of Sacred Trust

The understanding that everything was finished at the cross is a denial of the critical, all-powerful role of Jesus as High Priest. This teaching is a direct attack on Adventism's beloved sanctuary theology; when endorsed, it effectively diminishes the desire to consider the ministration going forward in the heavenly sanctuary. It makes the work of atonement Jesus is doing in the heavenly sanctuary of no consequence. Seventh-day Adventists cannot afford to fall into this deceptive theological trap, for it would mean giving up the truths that make the movement what it is. It would mean abandoning the doctrines that make Adventism unique, such as the cleansing of the sanctuary on the day of atonement in Daniel 8:14, the investigative judgment, and the three angels' messages of Revelation 14.

Without these foundational truths, Adventism becomes "salt that has lost its savor." She is reduced to a church with nothing but a generic message to offer to the world. It has no more reason to exist as a separate denomination. It becomes just another cog in the great wheel of ecumenism, making up the masses of mainline Christian communions today. To give up Adventism's beloved sanctuary theology to be more acceptable to the religious world is a betrayal of sacred trust!

Sit at My Right Hand

Paul wrote that after Jesus purged our sins on the cross and ascended to heaven, He "sat down at the right hand of God" (Heb. 1:3). Many readily assume this proves Jesus had finished His work of salvation at the cross. He had made the great sacrifice of Himself, redeemed humanity through His death, and therefore fully and completely accomplished the mission He had come on earth to do. Therefore, Jesus now sits at the right hand of God as Ruler and King. The editors of *The KJV Study Bible* expressed that very idea: "Being seated at God's right hand indicates that the work of redemption is complete and that Christ is actively ruling with God as Lord over all."[8]

Romans 4:25 comes as a surprise to those who believe mankind's salvation was finished at the cross: "Who was delivered for our offences, and *was raised again for our justification*" (emphasis added). If salvation had been completed at the cross, why was Jesus raised again for our justification? What more "justification" do Christians need beyond what Christ had already accomplished for them at the cross? This argument can only point to one conclusion: salvation was not finished at the cross. It could only mean the work of salvation had merely begun at the cross but was not finished there. Jesus went up to heaven and sat down at the right hand of God, not because His work of redemption is over, but to assume the role of a priest: offer gifts and sacrifices for sin. There, He is the High Priest upon His Father's throne, continuing the work He began on earth (see Heb. 8:1–3).

Paul clearly stated that the sinner's justification is a benefit or result of the work of intercession by our Lord Jesus Christ at the right hand of God. "Who shall lay any thing to the charge of God's elect? *It is* God that justifieth. Who *is* he that condemneth? *It is* Christ that died, yea rather, that is risen again, who is even at the right hand of God, who also maketh intercession for us" (Rom. 8:33, 34).

In Hebrews 7:25, Paul substituted "justification" with being "saved to the uttermost," maintaining it is a benefit obtained from Christ's work of intercession in the heavenly sanctuary. "Wherefore, He is able to *save to the uttermost* them that come to God by Him seeing He ever liveth to makes intercession for them" (emphasis added).

---

[8] *The KJV Study Bible*, p. 2490.

Again, if everything humanity needs for salvation had been obtained exclusively at the cross, this verse will make no sense. What further "saving" work needs to be accomplished on behalf of humanity beyond what had already been obtained through the death of Jesus on the cross? This observation proves salvation and justification were not obtained for mankind at a specific point in time at Calvary; instead, they are benefits derived from the ongoing work of atonement in the sanctuary above.

Thus, it is clear the work of salvation is accomplished as a result of Jesus assuming two roles: Atoning Sacrifice and High Priest. As a "minister of the sanctuary" in heaven, Jesus applies the merits of His shed blood and functions as Savior, Intercessor, Justifier, Mediator, Advocate, Helper, and High Priest. The application of the merits of Christ's atoning death by a priest in the sanctuary is what produces justification, pardon, and salvation "to the uttermost" for those who exercise faith in Him.

The statement from the Spirit of Prophecy below affirms what the Bible teaches regarding Christ's dual role as sacrifice and priest: "The intercession of Christ in man's behalf in the sanctuary above is as essential to the plan of salvation as was His death upon the cross. By His death He began that work which after His resurrection He ascended to complete in heaven."[9]

Justification by faith in Christ is the essence of salvation and serves as the basis of the Christian's peace with God (see Rom. 5:1; 8:1). Again, it must be emphasized that the blessed experience of righteousness through faith is not something obtained exclusively at the cross for believers; rather, it needs to be seen as a benefit of the continuous ministration of Jesus as High Priest in the heavenly sanctuary. To minimize the work of Jesus as High Priest is to lose sight of the active role He plays at the present time for humanity's ongoing redemption.

---

[9] White, *The Great Controversy*, p. 489.

A Priest upon the Father's Throne

Hebrews 8:1–2 explains what active role Jesus plays while sitting at the right hand of God: "Now of the things which we have spoken this is the sum: We have such an high priest, who is set on the right hand of the throne of the Majesty in the heavens; A minister of the sanctuary, and of the true tabernacle, which the Lord pitched, and not man." Jesus officiates as High Priest, "a minister of the sanctuary," at the right hand of God. With this, the words of the prophet agree: "Even he shall build the temple of the LORD; and he shall bear the glory, and shall sit and rule upon his throne; and *he shall be a priest upon his throne*: and the counsel of peace shall be between them both" (Zech. 6:13).

Hebrews 1:13 is worth considering. This verse is important because it tells us Jesus will not always be sitting at the right hand of the Father's throne and performing priestly functions. "But to which of the angels said he at any time, Sit on my right hand, until I make thine enemies thy footstool?" According to this passage, Jesus' place on the right hand of God is a temporary arrangement. "Sit at my right hand only *until* I make Your enemies Your footstool." When Christ's enemies are subjugated, He will no longer sit at the Father's right hand. When Christ's enemies acknowledge His supreme authority, worship Him at His footstool, and are defeated, then His priesthood ends and He assumes the role of King.

The Efficacy and Power of Christ's Intercession

We need to become familiar with the power and efficiency of Christ's work as Intercessor so we do not become easily weary and faint in our minds. In Hebrews 5:6–7, we see a glimpse of the power and passion involved in Christ's mediatorial work in the heavenly sanctuary: "As he saith also in another place, 'Thou art a priest for ever after the order of Melchisedec,' who in the days of his flesh, when he had offered up prayers and supplications with strong crying and tears unto him that was able to save him from death, and was heard in that he feared."

There is a very good reason why Paul inserted the account of Christ's gut-wrenching experience in Gethsemane when explaining

His work as High Priest in the heavenly sanctuary in Hebrews 5. It is to help us grasp with our frail intellects and dull senses just what that work of intercession involves. Ellen White's account of what transpired in Gethsemane is powerful: "As the substitute and surety for sinful man, Christ was suffering under divine justice. He saw what justice meant. *Hitherto He had been as an intercessor for others; now He longed to have an intercessor for Himself.*"[10]

At Gethsemane, Jesus longed for someone to intercede on His behalf. The pain of that ordeal was so great that He felt His humanity was too frail to bear it. He wished His disciples would pray for Him, but they were found sleeping. No intercessor was found for Him. He was treading the winepress alone. Therefore, Jesus pleaded and interceded for Himself "with prayers and supplications and strong crying and tears unto Him who is able to save Him from death." His intercession for Self was so intense that blood oozed through the pores of His skin. According to the inspired record, his prayer was heard, and an angel was sent to strengthen Him.

Paul inserted Christ's excruciating Garden of Gethsemane experience in Hebrews 5 to help us understand His work as our Apostle and High Priest. It is a very powerful and passionate work. His intercession for His church today is no less powerful and passionate than when He interceded for Himself at Gethsemane.

Christ's work of intercession is not only powerful and passionate but *persistent* as well. The Gospels tell us Jesus often spent whole evenings on the mountain, praying and interceding for others. He once told Peter, "Simon, Simon, behold, Satan hath desired to have you, that he may sift you as wheat, but I have prayed for thee, that thy faith fail not" (Luke 22:31, 32). Satan had begged for the soul of Peter to destroy him, but Jesus interceded for him so his faith would not fail when Satan's darts were hurled at him. Peter's faith did endure as a result of his Master's intercession. The night he betrayed his Lord three times, he managed to pull back to seek the Lord by faith and repentance. Hence, the power and effectiveness of Christ's

---

[10] White, *The Desire of Ages*, p. 686 (emphasis added).

intercession on behalf of His followers is demonstrated. "Does Satan plead loudly against our souls, accusing of sin, and claiming us as his prey, the blood of Christ pleads with greater power."[11]

The Bible warns us that Satan, "like a roaring lion," is on the prowl, "seeking whom he may devour" (1 Peter 5:8). Whether we realize it or not, it is only through the continual intercession of Jesus in the heavenly sanctuary that we are kept safe and secure from his assaults. This is salvation at work! Satan has an accurate record of our sins and continuously accuses us before God, pointing out the sins he has tempted us to commit. He desires our ruin and pleads for our souls, that he may destroy us. Our sinful ways invite God's displeasure, and if it were not for Jesus' powerful work of intercession on our behalf, Satan would accomplish our ruin today. Is not this work of intercession in the heavenly sanctuary part of the process of salvation? "'His intercession is that of a pierced and broken body, of a spotless life. The wounded hands, the pierced side, the marred feet, plead for fallen man, whose redemption was purchased at such infinite cost."[12]

An Anchor to the Soul, Both Sure and Steadfast

Let us then become more intelligent in regards to the work going forward in the heavenly sanctuary. Let us by faith enter the door that leads to the Most Holy Place of the heavenly sanctuary—the door that Jesus has opened and no person can shut. With unwavering faith, let us go "within the veil, where the forerunner has entered, even Jesus, made an high priest for ever after the order of Melchisedec." There, "we have an anchor to the soul, both sure and steadfast" (Heb. 6:19, 20).

It is the knowledge of the powerful ministration of Jesus in the heavenly sanctuary that brings faith, assurance, comfort, and rest for the soul. Jesus demonstrates His unfailing love for His people daily by ever living to make intercession to save them to the uttermost.

---

[11] White, *Thoughts from the Mount of Blessings*, p. 8.
[12] White, *The Great Controversy*, p. 416.

2

A Priest Upon His Father's Throne

Idea in Brief: This chapter explains why the role of Jesus as High Priest at the right hand of His Father's throne is essential to salvation. Jesus does not receive His own throne, the promised throne of His father David, until His work as Priest and Intercessor to perfect the characters of His followers is finished.

An Interesting Prophecy

When the angel Gabriel spoke to Mary about the birth of Jesus, he prophesied that He would be great and God would give Him the throne of His father David. "And, behold, thou shalt conceive in thy womb, and bring forth a son, and shalt call his name JESUS. He shall be great, and shall be called the Son of the Highest: and the Lord God shall give unto him the throne of his father David: And he shall reign over the house of Jacob for ever; and of his kingdom there shall be no end" (Luke 1:31–33). This prophecy is full of meaning and needs to be studied carefully.

After Jesus accomplished His work on earth, ascended to heaven, and was "highly exalted and given a name which is above every name" (Phil. 2:9), one would assume Gabriel's words to Mary would then be fulfilled. One would think God the Father would give unto the Son the promised throne of David. Sitting upon that throne, Jesus would reign over the house of Jacob forever, as prophesied. Not so. Jesus was not yet given the throne of David.

In Hebrews 1:3, Paul informed us that after Jesus purged our sins on the cross and ascended to heaven, He sat down at the right hand of the Father. He repeated this sequence two more times: "But this man, after he had offered one sacrifice for sins for ever, sat down on the right hand of God" (10:12); "Looking unto Jesus the author and finisher of our faith; who for the joy that was set before him endured the cross, despising the shame, and is set down at the right hand of the throne of God" (12:2).

A Shared Throne

After Jesus overcame the world and "spoiled principalities and powers, [making] a shew of them openly, triumphing over them" (Col. 2:15), He was invited by the Father to sit with Him in His throne. "Sit on my right hand, until I make your enemies Your footstool" (Heb. 1:13). In other words, the Father shared His throne with His Son. The words of Gabriel to Mary at Christ's incarnation were not fulfilled. Jesus was not given the throne of His father David.

Given this rather unexpected development, it is natural to ask why God the Father asked His Son to sit at His right hand. Did the Father have a reason for not granting Jesus a throne of His own, the throne of His earthly father David, just as He promised He would do?

As mentioned in the previous chapter, Christians generally believe the fact that Jesus is sitting at God's right hand proves salvation is a finished work. Many believe Jesus is now coregent with His Father on His shared throne and reigning supreme over all creation. The truth is, at the right hand of the Father, Jesus only reigns over the angelic hosts that are loyal to God. The "authorities and powers being made subject unto Him" now do not include His enemies (1 Peter 3:22).

A Still-unanswered Question

Granted that this generally accepted postulation is correct, it remains to be seen why Jesus was not given the throne of David after accomplishing His mission on earth. It does not explain why the Father shared His throne with His Son. Are we to believe the throne of the eternal God the Father is the "throne of His father David,"

> "The fact that Jesus is not yet sitting on His own throne is convincing evidence that He did not complete His work on the cross. There is still work to be accomplished for the redemption of humanity from sin's power and presence."

about which Gabriel prophesied to Mary? That would hardly be the case.

When did David become a type of the heavenly Father? And when did David's throne become a type of the Father's throne? Never! David was a type of Christ, and his rule was a type of Christ's glorious reign. If Gabriel wanted to convey the idea that Jesus would sit at the right hand of the Father's throne, he would have plainly said so— "He shall be great and He shall sit on the right hand of His Father."

In AD 34, three years after Jesus ascended to heaven, He was seen by the martyr Stephen standing at the right hand of God (see Acts 7:55, 56). This observation tells us that at this point in time, Jesus still had not received the throne of David.

Eighteen centuries later, Ellen White penned the following words, showing that even then, Jesus still had not received the promised throne of David: "*I saw a throne, and on it sat the Father and the Son. I gazed on Jesus' countenance and admired His lovely person. The Father's person I could not behold, for a cloud of glorious light covered Him.*"[13]

Could it be that the reason Jesus is still sitting with the Father on His throne and not on His own throne, the throne of His father David, is because His work is not yet finished? Could it be that contrary to what is generally believed, Christ's work was not finished at the cross in AD 31? What other reason could there be to explain this mystery?

The fact that Jesus is not yet sitting on His own throne is convincing evidence that He did not complete His work on the cross. There is still work to be accomplished for the redemption of humanity from sin's power and presence.

---

[13] White, *Early Writings*, p. 54 (emphasis added).

He Shall Be Priest upon His Father's Throne

The reason why Jesus sat down at the right hand of the Father at His ascension is not because "the work of redemption is complete and Christ is actively ruling with God as Lord over all." He sat down at the right hand of the Father's shared throne to assume the role of a priest. "Now of the things which we have spoken this is the sum: We have such *an high priest*, who is set on the right hand of the throne of the Majesty in the heavens; A *minister* of the sanctuary, and of the true tabernacle, which the Lord pitched, and not man" (Heb. 8:1, 2). Jesus now officiates as High Priest, "a minister of the sanctuary," at the right hand of God.

The prophet foresaw this work when he wrote, "Even he shall build the temple of the LORD; and he shall bear the glory, and shall sit and rule upon his throne; and he shall be a *priest* upon his throne [the Father's throne]: and the counsel of peace shall be between them both" (Zech. 6:13, emphasis added).

Justification, a Benefit of Christ's Priestly Work

In Romans 4:25, Paul explained that Jesus was raised from the dead so sinners can be justified. This experience is made possible through the ministration of a priest. Justification by faith is a benefit of Christ's work as High Priest at the right hand of God. "Who shall lay any thing to the charge of God's elect? It is God that justifieth. Who is he that condemneth? It is Christ that died, yea rather, that is risen again, who is even at the right hand of God, who also maketh intercession for us" (8:33, 34).

"Wherefore he is able also to *save* them to the uttermost that come unto God by him, seeing he ever liveth to make intercession for them" (Heb. 7:25, emphasis added). Justification by faith and being "saved to the uttermost" point to the same experience. Salvation is an ongoing work. They are the result of Christ's continuous ministration as High Priest at the right hand of God and His throne. As our High Priest, Jesus is still working out mankind's salvation and justification, even after He began that work about 2,000 years ago through His death and resurrection!

To him that worketh not, but believeth on him that justifieth the ungodly, his faith is counted for righteousness. Even as David also describeth the blessedness of the man, unto whom God imputeth righteousness without works, Saying, Blessed are they whose iniquities are forgiven, and whose sins are covered. Blessed is the man to whom the Lord will not impute sin. (Rom. 4:5–8)

The blessed Christian experience, theologically known as righteousness (or justification) by faith, is nothing but a benefit of the ministry of Christ as High Priest in the heavenly sanctuary. As High Priest at the Father's throne, Jesus makes atonement with His shed blood so sins may be pardoned and justification may be brought within reach of all—in place of condemnation and the sentence of the second death. "For this reason, he had to be made like them, fully human in every way, so that he might become a merciful and faithful high priest in service to God, and that he might make atonement for the sins of the people" (Heb. 2:17, NIV).

Therefore, it comes as no surprise that the Spirit of Prophecy speaks of the role of Christ as High Priest as being just as crucial as was His death on the cross. Salvation is predicated on both the atoning death of Christ (see vs. 9, 14) and His intercessory work in the heavenly sanctuary (see v. 17): "The intercession of Christ in man's behalf in the sanctuary above is as essential to the plan of salvation as was His death upon the cross. By His death, He began that work which after His resurrection He ascended to complete in heaven."[14]

A Temporary Arrangement

The questions that need to be settled at this point are these: How long is Jesus going to sit at the right hand of His Father? Is it a permanent arrangement? Is the right hand of the throne of the Father Christ's final destination? Will the words of Gabriel to Mary ever be fulfilled?

---

[14] White, *The Great Controversy*, p. 489.

The fact is, Gabriel's prophecy assures us Jesus will not always be sitting at the right hand of His Father's throne. At some point, He will receive the symbolic throne of His earthy father, David, and rule over his house forever and ever, just as the angel declared.

In Hebrews 1:13, the Father Himself has set a time limit to the duration in which He will share His throne with His Son. "Sit thou at my right hand *until* I make thine enemies thy footstool" (emphasis added). Jesus is to sit with the Father on His throne until His enemies are subjugated and their kingdoms on earth are dismantled. In other words, as long as evil persists, Jesus must remain at the right hand of His Father and officiate as High Priest.

Hebrews 1:13 painfully reminds us that Christ's enemies did not become His footstool after He died at Calvary and ascended to heaven. The great controversy did not end even though Jesus cried "It is finished" on the cross. The ungodly kingdoms of this world, governed by Satan's corrupt principles, still remain intact. Sin and evil still reign in people's hearts. Satan's minions on earth are still active, and he himself remains alive and well.

Only after Christ's enemies are brought to naught, their dominions are taken away, and the rule of sin is crushed, will Jesus vacate His place at the right hand of His Father's throne and cease His work of priestly intercession. Gabriel's prophecy will then be fulfilled, and Jesus will be given the throne of His father David.

David's Kingship, a Type of Christ's

One might ask, What does the Davidic throne have to do with the kingship of Jesus Christ? David, who comes from the tribe of Judah, serves as a type of the kingship of Jesus Christ, the "Lion from the tribe of Judah." The reigns of the Davidic kings point to the ultimate establishment of Christ's kingdom of glory and never-ending reign as the King of kings and Lord of Lords. "The scepter shall not depart from Judah, nor a lawgiver from between his feet, until Shiloh come; and unto him shall the gathering of the people be" (Gen. 49:10). This means the Davidic line would continue reigning until Shiloh (Jesus), the greater David, comes.

There is more to David as a type of Jesus. Just as David was anointed king three times, so was Christ.[15] Even though he was anointed king, David did not assume kingly power immediately. He did not and could not assume kingly power until Saul, his enemy, died. Likewise, Jesus did not immediately assume kingly power after He ascended to heaven. His coronation as King waits until His enemies become His footstool. Jesus will assume the role of King after His function as High Priest at the right hand of His Father is finished. In other words, Jesus will receive the throne of His father, David, only after His work in the heavenly sanctuary is completed. The statement below lines up with what the Bible teaches regarding the matter:

> He "shall sit and rule upon His throne; and He shall be a priest upon His throne." Not now "upon the throne of His glory;" the kingdom of glory has not yet been ushered in. *Not until His work as a mediator shall be ended will God "give unto Him the throne of His father David,"* a kingdom of which "there shall be no end." ... As a priest, Christ is now set down with the Father in His throne.[16]

Sitting with Christ and the Father in Heavenly Places

The Bible teaches that believers in Christ of all ages have had the wonderful privilege of sitting with Jesus and the Father, by faith, in heavenly places. "But God, who is rich in mercy, for his great love wherewith he loved us, even when we were dead in sins, hath quickened us together with Christ... And hath raised us up together,

---

[15] David's first anointing was by the prophet Samuel in the presence of his brothers (see 1 Sam. 16:13). David was anointed the second time by the men of Judah (see 2 Sam. 2:4). He was anointed the third time by the elders of Israel (see 5:3). Christ, on the other hand, received His first anointing at His baptism. He was anointed as Priest-King the second time after He ascended to heaven (see White, *The Acts of the Apostles*, p. 38). The third and final anointing/coronation of Christ takes place in the New Jerusalem after the Millennium, in the presence of the redeemed host and the onlooking universe (see *The Great Controversy*, p. 666).

[16] White, *The Great Controversy*, p. 416 (emphasis added).

and made us *sit together in heavenly places* in Christ Jesus" (Eph. 2:6, emphasis added).

This spiritual truth has tremendous implications for daily Christian living. The call to holy living in the Scriptures is based on the idea that the believer has been exalted to the level of Christ's position at the right hand of God. It is only fitting, therefore, that one's conduct in this world should reflect such honored status.

> If ye then be risen with Christ, seek those things which are above, where Christ sitteth on the right hand of God. Set your affection on things above, not on things on the earth. For ye are dead, and your life is hid with Christ in God. When Christ, *who is* our life, shall appear, then shall ye also appear with him in glory. Mortify therefore your members which are upon the earth; fornication, uncleanness, inordinate affection, evil concupiscence, and covetousness, which is idolatry. (Col. 3:1–5)

Sitting with Jesus on the Davidic Throne

Members of the church of Laodicea, the last church, on the other hand, are more privileged than were those of previous churches when it comes to sitting on the throne. They are given a privilege not accorded to any previous generation of believers. The overcomers in Laodicea are granted the special privilege of sitting with Jesus on His own throne, the throne of His father David. "To him that overcometh will I grant to sit with me in *my throne*, even as I also overcame, and am set down with my Father in *his throne*" (Rev. 3:21, emphasis added).

Jesus sat with His Father in His throne (the Father's throne) because He was victorious. While on earth, Jesus encouraged His disciples with the words, "Be of good cheer, I have overcome the world" (John 16:33). He "spoiled principalities and powers" and "made a shew of them openly, triumphing over them" (Col. 2:15). As a result of His great accomplishment and victory, Jesus was exalted upon His ascension to heaven and made to sit at the right hand of His Father's throne.

The 144,000 are Laodicea's finest. They are those who will overcome as Christ overcame: by overcoming the beast, his image, mark, and the number of his name (see Rev. 15:2). They are described as being "faultless," or without sin, and having "no guile in their mouth" (14:5)

The words used to describe the 144,000 echo the words Peter used to express Christ's sinless perfection: "For even hereunto were ye called: because Christ also suffered for us, leaving us an example, that ye should follow his steps, who *did no sin* [faultless], *neither was guile found in his mouth*" (1 Peter 2:21, 22, emphasis added).

This demonstrates that this select group of end-time believers attain the perfection of Christ's sinless character and overcome as He overcame. Jesus will honor this group by allowing them to sit with Him on His throne, the throne of His father David, just as God the Father honored Him by placing Him at His right hand.

A Time of Greatest Eschatological Opportunity

Those who live in the time of the end live in a time of the most incredible eschatological opportunity! From the church of Laodicea is to arise the last generation of believers who will become part of the 144,000 sealed saints. God will be able to point to this faithful class of end-time believers, often referred to fondly as the "remnant," and say, "Here are they that keep the commandments of God and have the testimony of Jesus" (Rev. 12:17).

The following words of inspiration serve as an appeal to strive to become a part of this distinguished group. "Let us strive with all the power that God has given us to be among the hundred and forty-four thousand."[17]

What do we need to do to be counted among the 144,000? We are not left guessing on this fundamental question. To be part of that group, we must reflect the character of Christ. To reflect the righteousness of Christ, we are to "buy of [Christ] the gold tried in the fire, the eye salve, and the white raiment" (Rev. 3:18). The white

---

[17] White, *The Seventh-day Adventist Bible Commentary*, vol. 7, p. 970.

raiment is Christ's perfect character, which is offered to Laodicea as a gift—a benefit of Christ's final ministration in the heavenly sanctuary.

Jesus, the Faithful and True Witness, will provide what is required to be counted among the 144,000. "This robe, woven in the loom of heaven, has in it not one thread of human devising. Christ in His humanity wrought out a perfect character, and this character He offers to impart to us. 'All our righteousnesses are as filthy rags.'"[18]

It is the privilege of those who are members of the Laodicean church to be the recipients of the full display of Christ's power, as High Priest, to "save to the uttermost" at the time of the end. To the last generation of believers, Christ wants to manifest the full power of His priesthood to the extent that it becomes possible to overcome even as He overcame.

The Throne of His Glory

When Jesus appears the second time, He will sit on "the throne of His glory," the throne of His father David. He will no longer be sitting at the right hand of God, as His high-priestly work is done (see Matt. 25:31). When Jesus appears with kingly authority and sits on the Davidic throne, He will "gather the nations and like a shepherd, and He will divide His sheep from the goats" (v. 32). How we relate to the truths that speak about Christ's atoning ministry, which began on the cross and continues in the sanctuary above, will determine whether we are grouped with either the sheep or goats. Let us listen to the words of Jesus again as we close this chapter. "To him that overcometh will I grant to sit with me in *my* throne, even as I also overcame, and am set down with my Father in his throne" (Rev. 3:21, emphasis added).

---

[18] White, *Christ's Object Lessons*, p. 311.

3

The Great Controversy Revisited

Idea in Brief: This chapter explains why Jesus has not returned to earth and evil is tolerated in this world. Satan's execution is postponed until God has demonstrated that his claim that the law cannot be kept is false. Christ's example of a sinless life is to be demonstrated in the lives and characters of an end-time community of believers.

The Great Controversy Revisited

Paul taught that Jesus does not end His work as High Priest and assume kingly role until His enemies become His footstool (see Heb. 1:13). These words painfully remind us that the cosmic battle that began in eternity past between Michael and Satan (see Rev. 12:7–9) has not waned. It is still very much in progress on this planet today. This battle, evidently, did not end when Jesus cried "It is finished" on the cross. The truth is the great controversy will not end until Christ's enemies are subjugated and made to worship at His feet. Therefore, the ultimate goal of the sanctuary service is to bring the great struggle between good and evil to an end. The work of Jesus in the heavenly sanctuary, especially His final ministration, is designed to bring this about.

Satan's Execution Postponed

Failing to achieve his objective to usurp God's throne and finding himself cast out of heaven with his angels, Satan understood he would eventually have to face the grim consequences of his rebellion. The Bible mentions "an everlasting fire, prepared for the devil and his angels" (Matt. 25:41). Additionally, "the angels which kept not their first estate, but left their own habitation, he hath reserved in everlasting chains under darkness unto the judgment of the great day" (Jude 6).

To postpone his execution indefinitely, Satan came up with a novel plan. He took the heat that was upon him and placed it on God by accusing Him of being *unfair* for putting a yoke on the necks of His creatures that is impossible to bear. In short, he accused Him of demanding obedience to a law that cannot be kept. Lastly, he accused Him of being *unjust* for intending to hold responsible those who break that law that is impossible to obey in the first place. "Satan represents God's law of love as a law of selfishness. He declares that it is impossible for us to obey its precepts."[19]

What did Lucifer, the fallen angel, hope to gain personally by putting forth these irreverent accusations against God before the entire heavenly host? It boils down to one simple thing: self-preservation. By putting God on the defensive side, Satan hoped to gain time. Until God can prove his claims to be wrong beyond a shadow of a doubt, he cannot be thrown into the lake of fire, for that would cast a shadow on God's integrity.

For this very reason, Satan and his angels were not immediately cast into the lake of fire after they were expelled from heaven. Instead, they were cast to the earth (see Rev. 12:9). If God had destroyed Satan and his supporters as soon as they were cast out of heaven, the results would have

> **"**
> If God had destroyed Satan and his supporters as soon as they were cast out of heaven, the results would have been disastrous. It would have cast a shadow upon His just character and created doubts in the minds of the unfallen angels.
> **"**

---

[19] White, *The Desire of Ages,* p. 24.

been disastrous. It would have cast a shadow upon His just character and created doubts in the minds of the unfallen angels.

Ever since he persuaded the first pair in the Garden of Eden to transgress God's command, Satan has been emboldened to push further his claim that God's law is impossible to keep. His modus operandi is simple: Either through coercion or deception, he causes men and women to break God's commands. He then taunts God with the words, "I told you so! Your demands are impossible to satisfy."

> To deceive men, and thus lead them to transgress God's law, is the object which he has steadfastly pursued. Whether this be accomplished by casting aside the law altogether, or by rejecting one of its precepts, the result will be ultimately the same. He that offends "in one point," manifests contempt for the whole law.[20]

Continuous human sinning bolsters Satan's claim that it is impossible to obey God's law. It supports his argument that God is unreasonable and unfair in demanding perfect compliance to His holy law.

Satan's Sentiments Echoed by Religious Teachers

Satan has had great success in causing the religious world to side with him in the great controversy. His enmity against the law of God is revealed through the various sentiments expressed by those in the churches who profess loyalty to God while attacking His law. The just demands of the law are either minimized or denied altogether. An example of this is found in the teaching that the law had been abolished at the cross. Therefore, its demands, particularly that which enjoins all to reverence His Sabbath, is supposedly no longer binding. This has led men and women throughout the ages to transgress the fourth commandment.

There is another teaching that is universally accepted as infallible truth in the churches that are professedly loyal to God. When

---

[20] White, *The Great Controversy*, p. 582.

examined, however, it is nothing but an echo of Satan's argument that the law of God is impossible to keep. It is the teaching that says perfect obedience to the law is impossible because humanity is so hopelessly corrupt and morally weak. In short, sinning is unavoidable. Therefore, the only thing God can do is keep forgiving sins until Jesus comes. The idea that it is possible to live sinless lives in sinful flesh, as Jesus did, is dismissed by many as nothing short of a far-fetched fairytale. Hence, the very churches that should be foremost in honoring and upholding the law of God are giving people license to transgress it.

Jesus warned against unscrupulous religious teachers that make light of the demands of His law:

> Whosoever therefore, shall break one of these least commandments, and shall teach men so, he shall be called the least in the kingdom of heaven: but whosoever shall do and teach them, the same shall be called great in the kingdom of heaven. Matthew 5:19.
>
> Since "the law of the Lord is perfect," every variation from it must be evil. Those who disobey the commandments of God, and teach others to do so, are condemned by Christ.[21]

Wickedness on Earth Tolerated

The long, untrammeled reign of evil in this world can only be attributed to one reason: the continuous transgression of God's law. The parable of the wheat and tares is an illustration of how the wicked are allowed to grow and even prosper alongside God's people (see Matt. 13:24–30).

When the councils of heaven determine the cup of iniquity is full, God will turn the tables around and demonstrate there is no excuse for sinning. He will raise a people, the 144,000, who will vindicate His character and show that Satan's claims are incorrect—that by God's grace, His law can be kept. When this happens, the curtain will come down on the kingdoms of this world governed by Satan's evil

---

[21] White, *The Desire of Ages*, pp. 308, 309.

principles. Power will be taken away from them, and Christ will then establish His kingdom, which will last forever. "Until the Ancient of days came, and judgment was given to the saints of the most High; and the time came that the saints possessed the kingdom.... And the kingdom and dominion, and the greatness of the kingdom under the whole heaven, shall be given to the people of the saints of the most High, whose kingdom is an everlasting kingdom, and all dominions shall serve and obey him" (Dan. 7:22, 27).

Once again, we need to take a serious look at the work of Christ in the heavenly sanctuary, especially His closing ministration, because it is the very means by which His character will be reproduced in the 144,000.

The Whole of Creation Groaneth

Paul explained that "the whole creation groans and travails in pain together until now" (Rom. 8:22). This sad state of affairs is but the result of Satan's failed experiments in this world. In verses 19–21, Paul states that creation waits earnestly for the "manifestation of the sons of God" so it can be delivered from the bondage of corruption. Here is scriptural evidence confirming it is the revelation of godliness in His children that will deliver the earth from the bondage and corruption Satan's rebellion has introduced. This final demonstration will disprove his hoary claim, believed even by the churches, that obedience to the law of heaven is impossible. Thus, God will be justified in uprooting all the rebellious elements of this world once and for all: Satan, the root; his supporters, the branches.

The Coming of Jesus Waits

The appearance of the 144,000, a perfected and sealed company of saints on the stage of action at the time of the end, answers to Paul's "manifestation of the sons of God." They are brought in with the announcement, "Here are they that keep the commandments of God and the faith of Jesus" (Rev. 14:12).

After introducing the 144,000, the next scenario presented in Revelation 14 is the coming of the Son of Man to harvest the earth (vs. 14–16). "The harvest of the earth is ripe."[22] The full development of the characters of God's people is compared to the ripening of the crop for harvest. "The harvest of the earth is at the end of the world" (Matt. 13:39).

Jesus comes *only* when the harvest of the earth is "ripe," not before. That is, He returns when His people are perfected and their robes of character have "no more spot or wrinkle or any such thing." on them (Eph. 5:27). When they are "conformed to the image of His Son" (Rom. 8:29) and have grown "unto a perfect man, unto the measure of the stature of the fullness of Christ… speaking the truth in love, grown up into him in all things, which is the head, even Christ" (Eph. 4:13, 15), Jesus comes to claim them as His own. Jesus Himself said, "When the fruit is brought forth, immediately he putteth in the sickle, because the harvest is come" (Mark 4:29).

> "When the fruit is brought forth, immediately he putteth in the sickle, because the harvest is come." Christ is waiting with longing desire for the manifestation of Himself in His church. *When the character of Christ shall be perfectly reproduced in His people, then He will come to claim them as His own.*[23]

Jesus Proved Perfect Obedience Is Possible

Jesus came into this world more than 2,000 years ago, bearing the garb of sinful, fallen humanity, as any son or daughter of Adam would inherit it. He was made in the likeness of men (see Phil. 2:7). He was made of a woman, under the law (see Gal. 4:4). He was made "of the seed of David according to the flesh" (Rom. 1:3). "Forasmuch then as the children are partakers of flesh and blood, he also himself likewise took part of the same…" (Heb. 2:14).

Jesus kept His Father's commandments despite being cumbered with a fallen, weakened, hereditary nature. He challenged His enemies to accuse Him of any sin: "Can any of you prove me guilty

---

[22] "The harvest of the earth is over-ripe." (RV, BBE); "The harvest of the earth is fully ripe." (ESV, ISV).
[23] White, *Christ's Object Lessons*, p. 69 (emphasis added).

of sin?" (John 8:46, ISV). Jesus is our sinless High Priest: "For such an high priest became us, who is holy, harmless, undefiled, separate from sinners, and made higher than the heavens" (Heb. 7:26).

Jesus did not come to this earth to prove the law can be kept with a *sinless* nature. The unfallen angels who possess sinless nature are already demonstrating that. It would have been redundant and unnecessary for Him to undertake that task. Jesus came to earth and clothed His divinity with fallen humanity to demonstrate the law of God can be kept even in dilapidated, degraded, sinful flesh. He showed it is possible to obey the precepts of the law entirely, irrespective of whether one possesses sinless nature or sinful nature—even if that nature has been weakened by 6,000 years of sin.

Using only the same spiritual weapons available to any human being in the struggle against temptation, namely, faith and prayer, Jesus overcame sin in sinful flesh. "He condemned sin in the flesh that the righteousness of the law might be fulfilled in us, who walk not after the flesh, but after the Spirit" (Rom. 8:3, 4). Jesus showed that notwithstanding the weaknesses inherent in fallen nature, humanity could fulfill the law's demands and prove Satan's claims to be false if aided by the mighty agency of the Holy Spirit. If Christ's example of a sinless life cannot be emulated, Peter did not know what he was saying when he admonished believers to follow that example. "For even hereunto were ye called: because Christ also suffered for us, leaving us an example, that ye should follow his steps: Who did no sin, neither was guile found in his mouth" (1 Peter 2:21, 22).

> The Saviour's life of obedience maintained the claims of the law; it proved that the law could be kept in humanity, and showed the excellence of character that obedience would develop. All who obey as He did are likewise declaring that the law is "holy, and just, and good."[24]

---

[24] White, *The Desire of Ages*, p. 309.

We now come to the most critical questions in this chapter: Can Christ's example of a sinless life in sinful flesh be duplicated in the lives of His followers? Can an entire generation of professed believers, which is naturally more prone to being selfish, ambitious, covetous, and prideful than previous generations of believers, reflect the character of Jesus? To answer this formidable challenge is the rationale for the closing ministry of Jesus Christ in the heavenly sanctuary. "Unto two thousand and three hundred days then shall the sanctuary be cleansed" (Dan. 8:14). This passage has not been accorded the attention it deserves. Properly understood, this passage holds the definitive answer to Satan's challenge.

Character Perfection Through Christ's Priestly Ministry

The purpose of Christ's priesthood is to bring perfection to the worshippers. "If therefore perfection were by the Levitical priesthood, (for under it the people received the law,) what further need was there that another priest should rise after the order of Melchisedec, and not be called after the order of Aaron?" (Heb. 7:11). The perfection the Levitical priesthood could not give, Jesus will. The final cleansing of the sanctuary announced in Daniel 8:14 will result in the final purification of the characters of His people from all sin. It will result in the blotting out of the record of their sins from the books of heaven.

Jesus is longing for His character to be fully reproduced in His people so Satan's charges can be answered and the great controversy can be brought to an end. The amazing thing is, as members of the church of Laodicea, we are invited to be that people—the 144,000, to be exact. We can be those people if we take these truths seriously. Jesus offers Laodicea His perfect character in the invitation to "buy of me the white raiment!"

An Unpopular Truth

The idea that there will be a people living in the time of the end who will walk on the surface of this planet as Jesus walked, perfect and sinless in fallen flesh, is truly inspiring! One would think that since the possibility of living above sin is such a marvelous idea, Christianity as a whole would delight in that prospect and welcome it with open arms, but not so. That is the sad truth.

The notion of living above sin in this world by ordinary human beings is met with skepticism and disbelief. "How is this even possible," they ask? "Those who promote this foolish idea," they say, "have no understanding of the total depravity of the sinful heart." Thus, the very thought of achieving perfection of character in sinful flesh, demonstrated in perfect obedience to the commandments of God, is vehemently rejected by mainstream Christianity and given derogatory labels like "perfectionism," "extremism," "legalism," and "fanaticism."

We have already established that those who take the position that sinless living in sinful flesh is impossible echo Satan's claim that the law cannot be kept. It shows on which side of the great controversy they are.

> All who break God's commandments are sustaining Satan's claim that the law is unjust, and cannot be obeyed. Thus they second the deceptions of the great adversary, and cast dishonor upon God. They are the children of the wicked one, who was the first rebel against God's law. To admit them into heaven would again bring in the elements of discord and rebellion, and imperil the well-being of the universe. No man who willfully disregards one principle of the law shall enter the kingdom of heaven.[25]

Jesus once asked His hearers the following poignant question: "Nevertheless when the Son of man cometh, shall he find faith on the earth?" (Luke 18:8). "Whatever is not of faith is sin" (Rom. 14:23).

Come to think of it, unbelief on the part of God's professed people is mainly to blame for the delay in Christ's second coming and the harvest. After all, He cannot return until the harvest is ready. No farmers come to harvest their crops when they are not yet ripe. Hence, Jesus cannot return until His character is perfectly reproduced in His

---

[25] White, *The Desire of Ages*, p. 308.

people, for only then will the crop be ready for harvest. Because of the unbelief of God's professed churches, the great controversy is taking longer to settle.

Only those who have the same faith Jesus exercised will be able to keep God's commandments and be part of the 144,000. "Those only who through faith in Christ obey all of God's commandments will reach the condition of sinlessness in which Adam lived before his transgression. They testify to their love of Christ by obeying all His precepts."[26]

Two Opposite Case Studies of Faith

Zechariah, the father of John the Baptist, and Mary, the mother of Jesus, were both presented with the same impossible proposition: the birth of a child through supernatural means. The reply each gave followed the same line of reasoning: "What you're saying sounds good, but here's the problem…"

"And Zacharias said unto the angel, Whereby shall I know this? for I am an old man, and my wife well stricken in years" (Luke 1:18). For her part, Mary said, "How shall this be, seeing I know not a man?" (Luke 1:34). Zechariah was struck dumb by the angel while Mary was given a pass. What might account for the difference in outcomes? The Bible says Zechariah was struck dumb because of unbelief. "And, behold, thou shalt be dumb, and not able to speak, until the day that these things shall be performed, because thou believest not my words, which shall be fulfilled in their season" (Luke 1:20).

As for Mary, even though she did not quite understand how Gabriel's saying would come to pass, seeing she was a virgin, she nevertheless believed his words, "for with God, nothing shall be impossible," and humbly submitted

> *Zechariah was struck dumb by the angel while Mary was given a pass. What might account for the difference in outcomes?*

---

[26] White, *The Seventh-day Adventist Bible Commentary*, vol. 6, p. 1118.

by saying, "Behold the handmaid of the Lord; be it unto me according to thy word" (vs. 37, 38).

Zechariah's unbelief was inexcusable because he was a priest and should have known better what level of faith God expected of him. Besides, the proposition Gabriel presented to him was not as impossible as that which he presented to Mary. There were other women in the past who gave birth to children even though they were well-stricken in years. For example, Sarah, the wife of Abraham, was deemed too old to have a child when she had Isaac.

This fact should have made it easier for Zechariah to exercise faith. Virgin births, however, were unprecedented! It was more difficult for Mary to exercise faith given her circumstances, and yet she believed! Today, it is our privilege to pray for the same simple, unquestioning, childlike faith of Mary. "Lord, increase our faith" (17:5).

The point of bringing up the cases of Zacharias and Mary to the forefront is to show that unless we believe that God is able to do what is impossible with men, we can make no progress in the Christian walk. How can we become part of the sinless 144,000 if we say that it is impossible to live sinless lives?

On Which Side Are You?

On which side of the great controversy are we? At the end of the day, will we be counted worthy of being among the 144,000 faithful saints who have the seal of God on their foreheads, or will we be classed with the unfaithful, imperfect, disobedient inhabitants of earth who receive the mark of the beast?

Are we going to join hands with Satan by insinuating we will continue sinning until the cows come home because we are weak and hopelessly corrupt? Let us remember this whole great controversy issue is not about us and how weak and vulnerable we are. It is about God. Let us become thoroughly familiar with Christ's work in the heavenly sanctuary so we will no longer be skeptical and uncertain about how He will finish the work He has begun in our hearts until that day (see Phil. 1:6).

4

The Great Controversy Prolonged

Idea in Brief: This chapter explains how the cleansing of heavenly sanctuary will bring an end to the long and destructive reign of evil in this world. It cites evidence showing how the wicked are able to thrive and proliferate only because they are graciously made recipients of certain unconditional benefits from the sanctuary service, but only until the sanctuary is cleansed on the antitypical day of atonement. After that, those benefits are withdrawn.

Evil Tolerated

The great controversy between good and evil has raged for thousands of years on this planet. For God's people, it has been nothing but a never-ending rule of tyranny, intolerance, oppression, and persecution by a long line of kingdoms allied to Satan. Where is God in all this? How can a holy and righteous God tolerate for so long the cruelty and injustice done by the ungodly kingdoms of this world to His people?

David's Dilemma

In Psalm 73, David lamented over the fact that wickedness is rampant in this world, with God seemingly indifferent about the matter.

In verses 1–3, David confessed that even though he affirmed his trust in divine providence, his faith in God had almost *slipped* because of the demoralizing state of world affairs.

In verses 4–12, David explained that the wicked people prosper in this world and have no trouble; they live in abundance; they are proud and arrogant; they possess the earth.

In verses 13–14, David lamented that the righteous seem to toil for nothing and are afflicted and punished, while the wicked prosper, and their evil deeds seem to go unchecked.

In verses 14–16, David admitted he was despondent over the pathetic condition of society. He said, "When I thought to know this, it was too painful for me."

In verse 17, David finally saw the light. "Until I went into the sanctuary of God; then understood I their end." At first, David did not see how the reign of evil and oppression in this world could be brought to an end until he went into the sanctuary, and then he understood. David's understanding of the sanctuary helped him see how the long reign of sin and evil in this world will be brought to an end.

"How Long Shall the Host Be Trodden Underfoot?"

In the book of Daniel, the same dilemma in which David found himself is echoed. A question is posed: "How long shall be the vision concerning the daily sacrifice, and the transgression of desolation, to give both the sanctuary and the host to be trodden under foot?" (8:13). In short, "How long will the wicked powers of this world go after God's people?" It is the same question David asked in the Psalms. How long will God's people be tyrannized by the ungodly kingdoms, symbolized by the "daily" and the "transgression of desolation"? The desolating powers in view here are pagan Rome and papal Rome.[27]

The answer is given in the next verse: "Unto two thousand three hundred evenings and mornings then shall the sanctuary be cleansed" (v. 14). This passage teaches that it is through the cleansing of the sanctuary in heaven that God will make things right for His long-oppressed people. Hence, Christ's final ministration to cleanse the

---

[27] For a more thorough explanation of the meaning of the symbolic terms "daily" and 'transgression of desolation," see Uriah Smith, *Daniel and the Revelation*, p. 454.

sanctuary is the means by which the long-standing controversy between God and Satan is to be settled and brought to an end.

> The sanctuary in heaven is the very center of Christ's work in behalf of men. It concerns every soul living upon the earth. It opens to view the plan of redemption, bringing us down to the very close of time, and *revealing the triumphant issue of the contest between righteousness and sin.*[28]

"How Long... Dost Thou Not Avenge Our Blood?"

Likewise, in Revelation, the dilemma of the long reign of evil is raised with the question, "How long, O Lord, holy and true, dost thou not judge and avenge our blood on them that dwell on the earth?" (6:10). The souls of those who have been martyred in previous generations are seen in vision crying out for justice and vengeance. The answer to their question was the giving of "white robes to every one of them" (v. 11).

The "white robe" represents Christ's perfect character. It is given to the saints as part of His final ministration to purify them and cleanse the sanctuary. The final purification of God's people is an integral part of the cleansing of the sanctuary on the antitypical day of atonement. "For on that day shall the priest make an atonement for you, to *cleanse* you, that ye may be clean from all your sins before the LORD" (Lev. 16:30). Thus, the cleansing of the heavenly sanctuary in Daniel 8:14 and the giving of the "white robes" in Revelation 6:9–10 point to the same event.

The faithful ones who died in previous generations are the first to receive the "white robe" when the judgment is convened in heaven. This is the scenario John described. Wearing the "white robe" during the resurrection of the just, they rise from the grave bearing a likeness to the perfect character of Christ. The deformities of character they brought with them to the grave at death are gone!

---

[28] White, *Evangelism*, p. 222 (emphasis added).

The living believers who receive the "white robe" in the final cleansing will no longer possess the character defects that have marred their lives. These will have been taken away and replaced with the white robe of Christ's perfect character in the final atonement. Their sins, which have defiled the sanctuary, will have been blotted out. "And as the typical cleansing of the earthly was accomplished by the removal of the sins by which it had been polluted, so the actual cleansing of the heavenly is to be accomplished by the removal, or blotting out, of the sins which are there recorded."[29]

These last-generation believers in Christ will no longer sin. They will prove Satan's claims were false all along. Their faithfulness to God's commandments, even in the face of severe persecution and death threats, will show once and for all there is no excuse for breaking God's law.

Hence, in a nutshell, this is how the cleansing of the sanctuary in heaven solves the problem of evil. It results in the fall of the rebellious kingdoms of this world and the establishment of Christ's kingdom, which shall never end. "And the kingdom and dominion, and the greatness of the kingdom under the whole heaven, shall be given to the people of the saints of the Most High, whose kingdom is an everlasting kingdom, and all dominions shall serve and obey him" (Dan. 7:26, 27).

This joyous declaration is picked up in Revelation: "And the seventh angel sounded; and there were great voices in heaven, saying, 'the kingdoms of this world are become the kingdoms of our Lord, and of his Christ; and he shall reign for ever and ever'" (11:15).

Why the Sanctuary in Heaven Needs Cleansing

The fact that the sanctuary in heaven needs cleansing shows it had previously been defiled. If that were not so, then the proclamation in Daniel 8:14 would make no sense. The earthly sanctuary was cleansed with the blood of bulls and goats on the day of atonement, but the

---

[29] White, *The Great Controversy*, pp. 421, 422.

one in heaven is to be cleansed with "better sacrifices." Paul wrote, "It was therefore necessary that the patterns of things in the heavens should be purified with these; but the heavenly things themselves with better sacrifices than these" (Heb. 9:23).

How the Sanctuary Is Defiled

Sin pollutes the sanctuary. Wherever sin is found, defilement is present. "And I will set my face against that man, and will cut him off from among his people; because he hath given of his seed unto Molech, to defile my sanctuary, and to profane my holy name" (Lev. 20:3). "Moreover this they have done unto me: they have defiled my sanctuary in the same day, and have profaned my sabbaths" (Ezek. 23:38).

Sins waiting to be committed defile the sanctuary. In Matthew 5:28, Jesus taught that "anyone who looks after a woman with lust in his heart has already committed adultery with her." The lustful thought is not carried out for lack of opportunity. In confirmation, the Spirit of Prophecy states, "The books of heaven record the sins that would have been committed had there been opportunity."[30]

Sin-bearing Through the Sanctuary

The sanctuary was built so God might dwell with His people—His *sin-infested* people (Exod. 25:8). The building of the sanctuary itself was only a means to an end. The sanctuary was built primarily to be a receptacle for sins. The priesthood and the service conducted in the sanctuary were established so it might be possible for God to bear the sins of His people, lest they die in their sins "And the LORD said unto Aaron, Thou and thy sons and thy father's house with thee shall bear the iniquity of the sanctuary: and thou and thy sons with thee shall bear the iniquity of your priesthood" (Num. 18:1).

Whether or not sins are confessed and sinners are repentant, the sanctuary is defiled just the same. In mercy, God takes the sins from everyone, even before they confess them, so they might not be

---

[30] White, "A Perfect Law," *The Signs of the Times*, July 31, 1901.

> *The sanctuary service, which benefits even the undeserving, demonstrates God's unconditional love towards the wayward and erring. It shows He is longsuffering and abundant in mercy towards even the worst of His enemies.*

exposed to the wrath of His broken law and die. He does not wait until the sinner repents and brings a sin offering into the sanctuary before He will extend grace to the guilty. God provides *immediate* cover to him or her through the sanctuary because it is one's most urgent need. Then, God waits patiently to see if the sinner will acknowledge guilt in humble repentance before He extends the offer of forgiveness.

The sanctuary service, which benefits even the undeserving, demonstrates God's unconditional love towards the wayward and erring. It shows He is longsuffering and abundant in mercy towards even the worst of His enemies. "The Lord is not slack concerning his promise, as some men count slackness; but is longsuffering to usward, not willing that any should perish, but that all should come to repentance" (2 Peter 3:9). In the words of another prophet, "Have I any pleasure at all that the wicked should die? saith the Lord GOD: and not that he should return from his ways, and live?" (Ezek. 18:23).

Unconditional, Temporary Benefits for the Wicked Through the Sanctuary

The unconfessed sins of the wicked defile the heavenly sanctuary along with the confessed sins of the righteous. Through the continuous intercession of Jesus in the heavenly sanctuary, the unrighteous are allowed to exist along with the righteous. God compassionately tolerates their existence until the time the sanctuary should be cleansed and no longer bear sin.

In the meantime, the wicked are allowed to continue living out the course of their sinful, rebellious lives, having no fear of an imminent judgment and no dread of a future hellfire—*until judgment day*. The tares are allowed to exist with the wheat until the harvest. Hence, the benefits obtained by the wicked from the sanctuary may be unconditional, yet they are temporary.

Jesus tasted death for every human (see Heb. 2.9). As Mediator and Intercessor in the heavenly sanctuary, Jesus presents before the Father's throne the merits of His sinless life and atoning death. This work allows God to extend grace and mercy towards the undeserving (all of us). It enables Him to make the sun rise, not only on the good but also on the evil, and send rain, not only on the just but also on the unjust (Matt. 5:45).

Thanks to the sanctuary service, those who are ripe for destruction are spared even now and shielded from the outpouring of the wrath of an offended God. Christ's continuous work of atonement is the reason why the vials of God's wrath, the seven last plagues, are not falling on the heads of the wicked today. It explains why today, no one is burning in the lake of fire. The wicked do not realize it, but they owe their continued earthly existence to the work of Jesus as atoning Sacrifice and Intercessor in the heavenly sanctuary.

> It was impossible for the plagues to be poured out while Jesus officiated in the sanctuary; but as His work there is finished, and His intercession closes, there is nothing to stay the wrath of God, and it breaks with fury upon the shelterless head of the guilty sinner, who has slighted salvation and hated reproof.[31]

The cover God provides to the ungodly is unconditional. The wicked do not have to exercise "repentance toward God, and faith toward our Lord Jesus Christ" (Acts 20:21) to derive benefits from the sanctuary. The wicked are allowed to enjoy life to the fullest on this earth. The unjust continue enjoying the blessings of earthly life regardless of whether they experience baptism, the new birth, and conversion.[32] Many of the wicked prosper in this world, as David

---

[31] White, *Early Writings*, p. 280.
[32] This idea is not to be confused with the heresy of Universalism, which teaches that all people are saved regardless of whether Christ is accepted as Lord and Savior or not. Every person born into this world needs a Savior. Neither is this to be equated

noted in Psalm 73. Many are blessed with riches and temporal goods. Often, their prosperity is obtained at the expense of the just (see James 5:1–6).

A Special Service for Unconfessed Sins

A special service was instituted in the sanctuary to deal with the unconfessed sins of the impenitent and ungodly. This service was called the "morning and evening sacrifice." In Moses' time, the careless and indifferent in the camp managed to stay alive throughout the year unconditionally as a benefit of this service.

The morning and evening sacrifice allowed unconfessed sins to be deposited temporarily in the courtyard of the sanctuary so impenitent sinners could at least continue living until the day of atonement. Hence, the sanctuary mercifully continued bearing the sins of all, whether or not they were confessed. This morning and evening sacrifice consisted of a lamb to be offered day by day, one in the morning and one in the evening. This sacrifice was a burnt offering (see Exod. 29:38–42).

Below are some significant points regarding the morning and evening sacrifice:

- Moses received instructions from God about the offering of the morning and evening sacrifice for the congregation while he was still on Mount Sinai for forty days. The regulations and laws regarding private sin offerings were not given to Moses until after the sanctuary had been built (see Lev. 4).

- The morning and evening sacrifice was a *public* offering, meaning it was offered for the entire congregation, as opposed to the regular sin offerings, which were offered *privately* by individuals or groups of individuals.

---

with Universal Justification, which advances the idea that in Christ, all people have been justified unconditionally. Justification or the imputation of righteousness is a subjective experience and is always based on condition of faith and repentance. "*If we confess our sins, then he is faithful and just to forgive us our sins and to cleanse us from all unrighteousness*" (1 John 1:9, emphasis added).

- The morning and evening sacrifice was a *continual* burnt offering and followed the law of the burnt offerings in Leviticus 1:1–5.

- The blood of the morning and evening sacrifice did not atone for any specific sin but sin in general (see v. 4).

- The blood of the morning and evening sacrifice was not *sprinkled* on the horns of the altar of burnt offering in the courtyard, as in the case of the blood of private sin offerings. Instead, it was *splashed* in large quantity on the four sides of the altar below the horns. "Then he shall kill the bull before the LORD, and Aaron's sons the priests shall bring the blood and throw the blood against the *sides* of the altar that is at the entrance of the tent of meeting" (v. 5, ESV, emphasis added).

- The morning and evening sacrifice provided blanket atonement for the entire congregation, including those of the mixed multitude, the murmurers and complainers, and the impenitent. The Jews believed the morning sacrifice covered the congregation for sins committed the night before, whereas the evening sacrifice covered the congregation for the sins committed during the daytime.[33] Hence, the morning and evening sacrifice provided continuous, unconditional cover for the entire congregation day by day.

The True Morning and Evening Sacrifice

The offering of the morning and evening sacrifice in the courtyard of the sanctuary pointed to the death of Jesus at Calvary, the Lamb of God who takes away the sin of the entire world (see John 1:29). Jesus is the true morning and evening Sacrifice. Christ's sacrificial death on the cross benefitted not only the penitent and godly but the impenitent and ungodly as well. Jesus "tasted death for *every* man" (Heb. 2:9, emphasis added).

God demonstrated His love for us in that while we were yet His enemies—ungodly sinners without moral strength—Christ died for

---

[33] See Singer, *The Jewish Encyclopedia,* vol. 2, p. 277.

us (see Rom. 5:6–8). On the cross, Jesus prayed, "Father forgive them for they know not what they do" (Luke 23:34). *"That prayer of Christ for His enemies embraced the world.* It took in every sinner that had lived or should live, from the beginning of the world to the end of time."[34]

The offering of the morning and evening sacrifice showed God's unconditional love for sinners. To the death of Christ, all sinners and saints alike owe their earthly lives.

> To the death of Christ we owe even this earthly life. The bread we eat is the purchase of His broken body. The water we drink is bought by His spilled blood. Never one, saint or sinner, eats his daily food, but he is nourished by the body and the blood of Christ. The cross of Calvary is stamped on every loaf. It is reflected in every water spring.[35]

Evidence of Unconditional Sin-bearing in Daniel 8

The ungodly are alive today only because the sanctuary in heaven still bears their sins. If this were not so, none of the wicked would be alive today. There is evidence in Daniel 8 that confirms the sanctuary temporarily bears the iniquity of the wicked. In this chapter, objects belonging to the sanctuary are borrowed and used to represent the ungodly kingdoms of this world. In other words, these hostile kingdoms are clothed with ornaments borrowed from the sanctuary to show they are, for a time, allowed to reap benefits from its service.

The animal sacrifices offered in the sanctuary to make atonement for sin are used in Daniel 8 as symbols to represent the enemies of God's people.

- Medo-Persia was represented by a ram (see 8:3, 4). Rams were used in the sanctuary as trespass offerings (see Lev. 5:15). They were also sacrificed on the day of atonement (see Num. 29:7, 8).

---

[34] White, *The Desire of Ages*, p. 745 (emphasis added).
[35] White, *The Desire of Ages*, p. 660.

- Greece, under Alexander the Great, was represented by a goat (see Dan. 8:5–8). Goats were used as sin offerings (see Lev. 4:27–31). Two goats were also used on the day of atonement: one served as the Lord's goat and the other as the scapegoat (see 16:14).

- The horns on the altars in the sanctuary on which the blood of the atonement was sprinkled were also taken to represent ungodly powers. There were eight such horns: four on the altar of burnt offering and four on the altar of incense. All eight are used in Daniel 8. The first two horns are found on the ram's head to represent the allied kingdoms of the Medes and Persians. The notable horn found on the goat's head between the eyes, representing united Greece under Alexander the Great, is the third horn. Four more horns show up after the great horn of Alexander is broken. These four horns represent divided Greece under Alexander's four leading generals, Cassander, Lysimachus, Seleucus, and Ptolemy. The eighth horn is the little horn, representing Rome.

Hence, through the use of objects found in the sanctuary to represent the wicked kingdoms of this world, what inevitable conclusion can be drawn? It is that even the ungodly derive benefit from the work going forward in the sanctuary. Again, this speaks volumes of the wondrous love of God for sinners. "In the matchless gift of His Son, God has encircled the whole world with an atmosphere of grace as real as the air which circulates around the globe. All who choose to breathe this life-giving atmosphere will live and grow up to the stature of men and women in Christ Jesus."[36]

The Year-day Principle Associated with Sin-bearing

There is yet more evidence in Daniel 8 clearly showing how the sanctuary unconditionally bears the sins of the impenitent until the day of judgment. Let's focus our attention on the prophetic yardstick used to convert the 2,300 prophetic days of verse 14 to literal years.

---

[36] White, *Steps to Christ*, p. 68.

There is more to that yardstick, which Adventists fondly call the "year-day principle," than meets the eye. There is more to it than just a mechanism used to convert prophetic time to literal time. When used in familiar biblical passages like Numbers 14:34 and Ezekiel 4:4–6, the concept of bearing sin is always present. "After the number of the days in which ye searched the land, even forty days, each day for a year, *shall ye bear your iniquities*, even forty years, and ye shall know my breach of promise" (Num. 14:34). Here, the year-day principle is associated with sin-bearing—Israel to bear her iniquity for forty years, each year for a day they spied on the land of Canaan.

Ezekiel was commanded to lie on his left side to bear Israel's iniquity for 390 days. Then he was to lie on his right side to bear Judah's iniquity for forty days, with each day representing a year of apostasy.

> Lie thou also upon thy left side, and lay the iniquity of the house of Israel upon it: [according] to the number of the days that thou shalt lie upon it *thou shalt bear their iniquity*. For I have laid upon thee the years of their iniquity, according to the number of the days, three hundred and ninety days: so shalt thou bear the iniquity of the house of Israel. And when thou hast accomplished them, lie again on thy right side, and thou shalt *bear the iniquity of the house of Judah* forty days: I have appointed thee each day for a year. (Ezek. 4:4–6, emphasis added)

With this understanding in mind, it is easy to see the 2,300 days of Daniel 8:14 needs to be considered in connection with the concept of sin-bearing if it is to be understood properly. In effect, that verse says the heavenly sanctuary will continue bearing the sins of the rebellious world for 2,300 more years from Daniel's time, and then it will be cleansed. Once cleansed, the sanctuary in heaven will no longer be in the business of bearing sin and being defiled in the process. The wicked will then be made to bear their iniquity and suffer their dues unless they confess their sins while probation is still open.

God winks at the ignorance of the wicked, but only for a limited time. When the sanctuary is finally cleansed, the impenitent will be held responsible for defiling it with their unconfessed sins. "Wherefore, as I live, saith the Lord GOD; Surely, because thou hast defiled my sanctuary with all thy detestable things, and with all thine abominations, therefore will I also diminish thee; neither shall mine eye spare, neither will I have any pity" (Ezek. 5:11).

Duty to Warn the Wicked
As God's watchman, the church is tasked with sounding the warning message to the wicked today. The proclamation of the three angels' messages is all about this. "Fear God and give glory to Him for the hour of His judgment is come, and worship Him…" (Rev. 14:6). His unconditional love for sinners will be reflected by those who heed the mighty angel's call to "prophesy again before many peoples, and nations, and tongues, and kings" (10:11).

> So thou, O son of man, I have set thee a watchman unto the house of Israel; therefore thou shalt hear the word at my mouth, and warn them from me. When I say unto the wicked, O wicked *man*, thou shalt surely die; if thou dost not speak to warn the wicked from his way, that wicked *man* shall die in his iniquity; but his blood will I require at thine hand. Nevertheless, if thou warn the wicked of his way to turn from it; if he do not turn from his way, he shall die in his iniquity; but thou hast delivered thy soul. (Ezekiel 33:7–9)

5

The Great Controversy Settled

Idea in Brief: This chapter describes both the mechanics and timing of the cleansing of the sanctuary. The cleansing of the sanctuary in heaven is accomplished by the removal of the sins that have polluted it. In the process, God's people are forever cleansed of sin and able to demonstrate in their lives that the example of Christ's sinless life can be followed. This demonstration is what ends the great controversy.

As the Climax of the Great Controversy Approaches

As the great controversy approaches its climax, Satan and his hosts are astir. He will plunge the world into one great final crisis, and the last days will be a time of great peril for the church (see 2 Tim. 3:1). Her survival at that time will depend on whether her faith is anchored to the Forerunner, who has gone within the veil to engage in His final ministration (see

> "
> As the great controversy approaches its climax, Satan and his hosts are astir. He will plunge the world into one great final crisis, and the last days will be a time of great peril for the church (see 2 Tim. 3:1). Her survival at that time will depend on whether her faith is anchored to the Forerunner, who has gone within the veil to engage in His final ministration (see Heb. 6:19, 20). Her destiny will depend on whether or not she receives the benefit of that final work of atonement.
> "

Heb. 6:19, 20). Her destiny will depend on whether or not she receives the benefit of that final work of atonement.

It is extremely important that the faithful members of that church fully understand the means God has put in place to prepare for that terrifying ordeal. The mechanism He has implemented for her to safely navigate through the final crisis of this earth's history is contained in the message of Daniel 8:14: the cleansing of the sanctuary. A correct and thorough understanding of this subject is very much needed today by the church of Laodicea. It is, after all, "the central pillar and foundation of the Advent faith."[37]

The Significance of Daniel 8:14 to Laodicea

Daniel 8:14 puts the church of Laodicea on notice. It is an announcement that the great antitypical day of atonement has arrived and the time of the church's final purification has come. It is the time of her greatest eschatological opportunity, for it is the time for her to receive the body armor (the righteousness) she needs to prevail in the final conflict with the hosts of Satan. Her victory in this conflict settles the great controversy. "Clad in *the armor of Christ's righteousness*, the church is to enter upon her final conflict. 'Fair as the moon, clear as the sun, and terrible as an army with banners' (Song of Solomon 6:10), she is to go forth into all the world, conquering and to conquer."[38]

The experience about which we are talking in the final purification has nothing to do with being clothed with Christ's *imputed* righteousness, only. It means more than just being *accounted* righteous. It means having the character refined and made white to the extent that there are no more "spots or wrinkle or any such thing"— no more character blemishes or defects! It is to be perfect *like* Christ, not merely perfect *in* Christ. In fact, the mind is to be perfected to the extent that not even the slightest memory of past sins committed is to be found (see Jer. 50:20).

---

[37] White, *The Great Controversy*, p. 409.
[38] White, *Prophets and Kings*, p. 725 (emphasis added).

Daniel referred to this end-time scenario when he wrote, "Many will be purified and made white and tried" (12:10). Total Christlikeness alone is what will preserve the church of Laodicea during that time of severe conflict and trial. "As the members of Christ's body approach the period of their final conflict they will grow up into him, and will possess symmetrical characters.... God will preserve his people through that time of peril."[39]

The Cleansing of the Sanctuary

The announcement of the cleansing of the sanctuary in Daniel 8:14 points us back to Leviticus 16, the chapter that describes the cleansing of the sanctuary on the day of atonement. It is important to know the cleansing of the sanctuary involves the process of removing the sins that have polluted it. However, before sins can be removed or blotted out from the sanctuary, a work for the congregation needs to be accomplished first. Leviticus 16:30 describes what this work is: "For on that day shall *the priest* shall make an atonement to cleanse you, [so] *that* you may be clean from all your sins [which are] before the Lord" (emphasis in brackets added).

The sins that are before the Lord are the polluting sins that had been brought into the sanctuary through the daily sin offerings throughout the year. They have been deposited in the books that are before the Lord. "Our transgressions are multiplied before the Lord and testify against us" (Isa. 59:12). "Thou hast set our iniquities before thee, our secret sins in the light of thy countenance" (Ps. 90:8). The removal of those sins that are before the Lord signals the cleansing of the sanctuary.

For the cleansing of the sanctuary to be done, the congregation needs to go through the final cleansing first. The cleansing of the worshippers precedes the cleansing of the sanctuary. The following verse emphasizes these themes: "And he shall make an atonement for the holy sanctuary, and he shall make an atonement for the tabernacle

---

[39] White, "The Great Controversy. Between Christ and His Angels and Satan and His Angels," *The Signs of the Times*, November 27, 1879.

of the congregation, and for the altar, and he shall make an atonement for the *priests*, and for all the *people* of the congregation" (Lev. 16:33).

The Final Cleansing of God's People

The final cleansing of the congregation on the day of atonement is vividly portrayed in the vision depicted in Zechariah 3:1–5: Joshua standing before the Angel. This vision is of particular interest to the church of Laodicea because it graphically depicts the scenes that will lead up to her final cleansing, preparatory to the blotting out of sins.

In this vision, Joshua, the high priest, represents God's people on the day of atonement. The filthy garments with which he was clothed represent the uncleanness and sinfulness of the human heart or character. Concerning the sinfulness of human character, the prophet Isaiah wrote, "But we are all as an unclean thing, and all our righteousnesses are as filthy rags" (64:6). Paul counted the righteousness he had obtained through law-keeping as "dung" so he might obtain the righteousness that is only in Christ by faith (see Phil. 3:5–9).

The Angel of the Lord, who represents Jesus, gives the command to "take away the filthy garments from him" and "clothe him with a change of raiment" (See Zech. 3:4). Jesus is the "Messenger of the covenant"; He suddenly comes to His temple to purify the sons of Levi—to "purge them as gold and silver are purified, that they may offer unto the Lord an offering in righteousness" (Mal. 3:3). The dual process of removing the filthy garments and imparting the perfect righteousness of Christ fully in its place represents the final cleansing of the people of God on the antitypical day of atonement. It fulfills the divine mandate found at the end of the chapter: "I will remove the iniquity of the land in one day" (Zech. 3:9).

As mentioned before, Christ's perfect robe of character is given to God's people as a gift—the benefit of the final atonement. This event paves the way for the blotting out of the sins that have polluted the sanctuary, thereby cleansing it.

The perfecting of the characters of the saints in the final atonement also paves the way for another great event: the marriage of the Lamb.

"Let us be glad and rejoice, and give honour to him: for the marriage of the Lamb is come, and his wife hath made herself ready. And to her was granted that she should be arrayed in fine linen, clean and white: for the fine linen is the righteousness of saints" (Rev. 19:7–8).

Hundreds of years before, Isaiah spoke of the same event: "I will greatly rejoice in the LORD, my soul shall be joyful in my God; for he hath clothed me with the garments of salvation, he hath covered me with the robe of righteousness, as a bridegroom decketh himself with ornaments, and as a bride adorneth herself with her jewels" (Isa. 61:10).

The Timing of the Final Cleansing

In the book *Prophets and Kings* is found an amazing explanation of the vision of Joshua and the Angel as it applies to God's people during the "closing scenes of the great day of atonement." It is both the privilege and duty of every thinking Seventh-day Adventist to study Chapter 47 of that book, entitled "Joshua and the Angel," as it directly applies to them. It traces the events leading up to their final purification and the blotting out of sins just before Jesus leaves the Most Holy Place of the heavenly sanctuary.

> Zechariah's vision of Joshua and the Angel applies with peculiar force to the experience of God's people in *the closing scenes of the great day of atonement*. The remnant church will then be brought into great trial and distress. Those who keep the commandments of God and the faith of Jesus will feel the ire of the dragon and his hosts. Satan numbers the world as his subjects; he has gained control even of many professing Christians. But here is a little company who are resisting his supremacy. If he could blot them from the earth, his triumph would be complete. As he influenced the heathen nations to destroy Israel, so in the near future he will stir up the wicked powers of earth to destroy the people of God. *Men will be required to render obedience to human edicts in violation of the divine law.*[40]

---

[40] White, *Prophets and Kings*, p. 587, 588 (emphasis added).

In the quote above, the timing of the final atonement, as far as the living are concerned, is given. It takes place during the "closing scenes of great day of atonement." The closing scenes of the great day of atonement arrives when "men are required to render obedience to human edicts in violation of the divine law." This expression alludes to the proclamation of a national Sunday law the United States. This event signals the onset of the closing scenes of the great antitypical day of atonement. At that time, the "remnant church" will feel the "ire of the dragon and his hosts" and will be brought into "great trial and distress."

The opening scenes of the great antitypical day of atonement came in 1844 at the expiration of the 2,300-day prophecy of Daniel 8:14. During that time, the righteous dead began receiving the "white robes," and their sins removed from the sanctuary (see Rev. 6:9, 10).

The closing scenes of the great day of atonement is for the living. The "remnant church" that "feels the ire of the dragon" and goes through the closing scenarios of the great day of atonement is none other than the church of Laodicea. Proof of this is seen in the fact that the three items she is told to "buy" to remedy her spiritual malady, namely, the eye salve, gold tried in the fire, and white raiment, are all mentioned in *Prophets and Kings*, chapter 47. It is when the mark of the beast is enforced and the third angel warns against receiving it in the forehead or hand (see Rev. 14:9–11) that Laodicea is to experience her final purification from sin so God will be able to point to her and say, "Here are they that keep the commandments of God and the faith of Jesus" (v. 12).

Laodicea Buys the Eye Salve

The next paragraph speaks of the intense persecution that follows the proclamation of a national Sunday Law. In this hour of great trial, the faithful ones in Laodicea will find themselves "pleading for pardon and deliverance through Jesus their Advocate."

> Those who are true to God will be menaced, denounced, proscribed. They will be "betrayed both by parents, and brethren, and

kinsfolks, and friends," even unto death.... Their only hope is in the mercy of God; their only defense will be prayer. As Joshua pleaded before the Angel, so the remnant church, with brokenness of heart and unfaltering faith, will plead for pardon and deliverance through Jesus, their Advocate. *They are fully conscious of the sinfulness of their lives, they see their weakness and unworthiness*; and they are ready to despair.[41]

The dire situation in which the faithful find themselves in will cause them to "afflict the soul" with greater and still greater passion and intensity. It is at this time that Laodicea finally buys the eye salve. Humbled to the dust, she will no longer claim to be "rich with goods and have need of nothing." Laodicea is fully conscious of the sinfulness of her life. She fully sees her weakness and unworthiness and is ready to despair. Laodicea's nakedness of soul, spiritual poverty, and wretchedness are now in full view. Before this humbling experience, Laodicea had no correct understanding of her real state. Regarding her pathetic spiritual condition, Jesus said, "Thou knowest not that thou art miserable, wretched, poor, blind and naked" (Rev. 3:17).

This development is the result of applying the needed eye salve to the spiritual eyes. The acknowledgment of the sinfulness of character to the fullest extent precedes the final cleansing. Trial and great distress will produce the desired effect of bringing Laodicea to the feet of Jesus, acknowledging her misery, nakedness, poverty, and blindness while trusting in His power to pardon and cleanse.

Satan's Role During the Closing Scenes of the Great Day of Atonement

The next paragraph talks about Satan's role during the closing scenes of the great day of atonement. His job is to prevent Laodicea from receiving the final cleansing and the blotting out of their sins.

---

[41] *Ibid.* (emphasis added).

The tempter stands by to accuse them, as he stood by to resist Joshua. He points to *their filthy garments, their defective characters*. He presents their weakness and folly, their sins of ingratitude, their unlikeness to Christ, which has dishonored their Redeemer. He endeavors to affright them with the thought that their case is hopeless, that the stain of their defilement will never be washed away. He hopes so to destroy their faith that they will yield to his temptations, and turn from their allegiance to God.[42]

Satan is described as having a thorough knowledge of the character defects of God's people. He points to the "filthy garments" or their character defects to frighten them with the thought that "their cases are hopeless" and "the stain of their defilement will never be washed away." Through adversity and trial, Satan hopes to destroy the faith of God's people. Through these means, he endeavors to make them abandon their allegiance to God by giving up the Sabbath and receiving the mark of the beast.

In the next paragraph, Jesus, the Divine Advocate, is described as defending His penitent church from Satan's powerful assaults:

> But while the followers of Christ have sinned, they have not given themselves up to be controlled by the satanic agencies. They have repented of their sins and have sought the Lord in humility and contrition, and the divine Advocate pleads in their behalf. He who has been most abused by their ingratitude, who knows their sin and also their penitence, declares: "The Lord rebuke thee, O Satan. I gave My life for these souls. They are graven upon the palms of My hands. They may have *imperfections of character*; they may have failed in their endeavors; but they have repented, and I have forgiven and accepted them."[43]

Jesus holds up the humility, contrition, and repentance of His people and vindicates them against Satan's strong accusations. He

---

[42] *Ibid.* (emphasis added).
[43] *Ibid.*, p. 589 (emphasis added).

rebukes Satan and declares He has accepted and forgiven them, even though they may have "imperfections of character" and "failed in their endeavors."

Laodicea Buys the Gold Tried in the Fire

The fires of persecution are allowed to purify the church of Laodicea. In the crucible of affliction, the dross and earthliness of character are removed, allowing the gold of faith and love to be perfectly revealed. That is what the next paragraph says:

> The assaults of Satan are strong, his delusions are subtle; but the Lord's eye is upon His people. Their affliction is great, the flames of the furnace seem about to consume them; but Jesus will bring them forth as *gold tried in the fire*. Their earthliness will be removed, that through them the image of Christ may be perfectly revealed.[44]

The experience of God's faithful remnant during the "closing scenes of the great day of atonement" is marked by anguish, humility, unutterable sorrow, and penitence for sin. Since they have learned to fix their eyes on "Christ's perfect purity," they become not only "fully conscious of the sinfulness of their lives," but they also "discern so clearly the exceeding sinfulness of sin."

> In the time of the end the people of God will sigh and cry for the abominations done in the land. With tears they will warn the wicked of their danger in trampling upon the divine law, and with unutterable sorrow they will humble themselves before the Lord in penitence. The wicked will mock their sorrow and ridicule their solemn appeals. But the anguish and humiliation of God's people is unmistakable evidence that they are regaining the strength and nobility of character lost in consequence of sin. It is because they are drawing nearer to Christ, because their eyes are fixed on His

---

[44] *Ibid.* (emphasis added).

perfect purity, *that they discern so clearly the exceeding sinfulness of sin.*[45]

Laodicea Buys the White Raiment

The next paragraph explains how Laodicea finally obtains the "white raiment":

> As the people of God afflict their souls before Him, pleading for purity of heart, the command is given, "Take away the filthy garments," and the encouraging words are spoken, "Behold, I have caused thine iniquity to pass from thee, and I will clothe thee with change of raiment." Zechariah 3:4. The spotless robe of Christ's righteousness is placed upon the tried, tempted, faithful children of God. *The despised remnant are clothed in glorious apparel, nevermore to be defiled by the corruptions of the world.* Their names are retained in the Lamb's book of life, enrolled among the faithful of all ages. They have resisted the wiles of the deceiver; they have not been turned from their loyalty by the dragon's roar. *Now they are eternally secure from the tempter's devices.* Their sins are transferred to the originator of sin. A "fair miter" is set upon their heads.[46]

As the faithful ones in Laodicea continue afflicting their souls in the midst of trial and adversity, the command is given: "Take away their filthy garments." The encouraging words are spoken: "Behold, I have caused thy iniquity to pass from thee and I will clothe thee with a change of raiment." "The spotless robe of Christ's character is then placed upon the tried, tempted, faithful children of God." It is at this juncture that Laodicea buys the white raiment. She can now be "cleansed from her sins before the Lord" (Lev. 16:30). Her sins are then blotted out and transferred to the "originator of sin." Her name is "retained in the book of life, enrolled among the faithful of all ages."

---

[45] *Ibid.*, p. 590 (emphasis added).
[46] *Ibid.*, p. 591 (emphasis added).

A Permanent and Final Change

The character change in the final atonement is permanent and final, as seen in the encouraging words from Prophets and Kings, page 591: "The despised remnant are clothed in glorious apparel, *nevermore* to be defiled by the corruptions of the world. Their names are *retained* in the Lamb's book of life, enrolled among the faithful of all ages. They have resisted the wiles of the deceiver; they have not been turned from their loyalty by the dragon's roar. Now they are *eternally* secure from the tempter's devices." These solemn declarations echo the words in Revelation 22:11: "He that is righteous, let him be righteous still: and he that is holy, let him be holy still."

During the final atonement, the final disposition of the characters and destinies of God's people are fixed forever. They will no longer choose to sin. "When the decree goes forth and the stamp is impressed, their *character* will remain pure and spotless for eternity."[47]

The characters of those who fail to receive the benefit of the final atonement and cleansing remain filthy forever. After Jesus leaves the heavenly sanctuary, He no longer sits to refine characters. There is no more priestly work to bear sin and remove blemishes and deformities of character. Therefore, everything that needs to be done for humanity's redemption must all be done before Jesus leaves the heavenly sanctuary.

> When Jesus leaves the sanctuary, then they who are holy and righteous will be holy and righteous still; for all their sins will then be blotted out, and they will be sealed with the seal of the living God. But those that are unjust and filthy will be unjust and filthy still; for then there will be no Priest in the sanctuary to offer their sacrifices, their confessions, and their prayers before the Father's throne. *Therefore, what is done to rescue souls from the coming storm of wrath must be done before Jesus leaves the most holy place of the heavenly sanctuary.*[48]

---

[47] White, *Testimonies for the Church*, vol. 5, p. 216 (emphasis added).
[48] White, *Early Writings*, p. 48 (emphasis added).

Once the characters of God's faithful people are purified and fixed for all eternity, His seal is placed on their foreheads, and they become part of the 144,000. That is what the next paragraph says:

> While Satan has been urging his accusations, holy angels, unseen, have been passing to and fro, placing upon the faithful ones the seal of the living God. These are they that stand upon Mount Zion with the Lamb, having the Father's name written in their foreheads. They sing the new song before the throne, that song which no man can learn save the hundred and forty and four thousand which were redeemed from the earth.[49]

The Great Controversy Settled

Today, the church of Laodicea is privileged to enter by faith into the sanctuary, as did David, and have a clear understanding of how the sin problem will be resolved and the great controversy settled. It is during the "closing scenes of the great day of atonement," just before Jesus leaves the Most Holy Place of the heavenly sanctuary, that both issues will be resolved.

The perfecting of the characters of a faithful remnant allows God to point to a people and at last say, "Here are they that keep the commandments of God and the faith of Jesus" (Rev. 14:12). This development disproves Satan's claim that the law is impossible to keep. It forever settles the question in the great controversy as to who is right, God or Satan.

It is the privilege of every Seventh-day Adventist to be on the right side of the great controversy now and during the

> **"**
> It is the privilege of every Seventh-day Adventist to be on the right side of the great controversy now and during the final movements of earth's history. There is no reason why anyone who understands present truth should miss out on the blessings of the final atonement and be found in the lake of fire reserved for Satan and his angels.
> **"**

---

[49] White, *Prophets and Kings*, p. 591.

final movements of earth's history. There is no reason why anyone who understands present truth should miss out on the blessings of the final atonement and be found in the lake of fire reserved for Satan and his angels.

6

The Christian Experience Promised

Idea in Brief: This chapter examines the Christian experience in light of the promises of the new covenant. The fulfilment of the five promises found therein results in five stages of the Christian experience: conviction, justification, adoption, sanctification, and character perfection.

The Blessed Christian Experience

In this chapter, we shall attempt to look at the Christian experience, also known as "righteousness by faith," in connection with the new covenant. The relationship between the new covenant and the Christian experience is apparent and should be clearly recognized.

> Behold, the days come, saith the LORD, that I will make a new covenant with the house of Israel, and with the house of Judah… But this *shall be* the covenant that I will make with the house of Israel; After those days, saith the LORD, I will put my law in their inward parts, and write it in their hearts; and will be their God, and they shall be my people. And they shall teach no more every man his neighbour, and every man his brother, saying, Know the LORD: for they shall all know me, from the least of them unto the greatest of them, saith the LORD: for I will forgive their iniquity, and I will remember their sin no more. (Jer. 31:31–34)

Paul described the blessedness of the Christian experience in the following words: "Blessed are they whose iniquities are forgiven, and whose sins are covered. Blessed is the man to whom the Lord will not impute sin" (Rom. 4:7, 8). It is through the continuous fulfillment of the promises of the new covenant in the believer's life that makes the blessed Christian experience possible. In other words, the application of these new-covenant promises in the believer's life results in progress in the Christian walk. Were it not so, our spiritual development would be at a standstill. There would be no pardon for sin and no growth in grace.

The "Better Covenant"
Believers today ought to rejoice in the fact that the covenant God establishes with them is not according to the covenant He made with ancient Israel. It is better for several reasons. Unlike the old covenant, which Paul said had faults (see Heb. 8:7, 8), the new covenant has no faults. It is also better because it is "established upon better promises" (v. 6). It is God Himself, not the poor, flawed sinner, who makes the promises. "I will be their God... I will write my laws in their hearts, I will forgive their sins... I will remember their sins no more." It is God Himself who promises to enable weak sinners to conform their lives to the terms of His covenant; it is He who "wills in us and works in us to do according to His good pleasure" (Phil. 2:13). Human promises and resolutions are like "ropes of sand."[50] Our efforts are feeble and inconsistent at best. For the struggling sinner, the new covenant works better!

The new covenant is also better because its benefits are retroactive. In other words, the benefits of the new-covenant promises apply even to those who lived under the old covenant: "And for this cause he is the mediator of the new testament, that by means of death, *for the redemption of the transgressions that were under the first testament*, they which are called might receive the promise of eternal inheritance" (Heb. 9:15, emphasis added).

---

[50] White, *Steps to Christ*, p. 47.

Not only that. The new covenant is better because certain sins that could not be forgiven under the terms of the old covenant are forgiven under the new. "Be it known unto you therefore, men and brethren, that through this man is preached unto you the forgiveness of sins: And by him all that believe are justified from all things, from which ye could not be justified by the law of Moses" (Acts 13:38, 39). Hence, people like David and Bathsheba, who should have been stoned to death under the terms of the old covenant for their sin, found hope of mercy, pardon, and justification under the new covenant.

As Christians living under the new covenant, we have so much for which to be thankful. We live under an umbrella of grace as profuse and pervasive as is the air we breathe. "Where sin abounds, grace doth much more abound" (Rom. 5:20). Paul made a point that Christians living under the new covenant do not live in fear as the Israelites did; for when they came to the foot of Mount Sinai to make a covenant with God, they quaked in their sandals and feared for their lives at the sight of that mountain, which appeared to be on fire. They were seized with terror on account of hearing the voice of God. Even Moses "exceedingly feared and quaked" (see Heb. 12:18–21).

Christians living under the new covenant are "come to mount Sion, and unto the city of the living God, the heavenly Jerusalem, and to an innumerable company of angels, To the general assembly and church of the firstborn, which are written in heaven, and to God the Judge of all, and to the spirits of just men made perfect, And to Jesus the mediator of the new covenant, and to the blood of sprinkling, that speaketh better things than *that of* Abel" (vs. 22–24).

The Christian Experience

As mentioned earlier, the Christian experience (which consists of conviction, conversion, pardon, adoption, justification, acceptance, daily sanctification, and glorification), is nothing but the result of applying the benefits of the new-covenant promises to the believer's experience. From beginning to end, it is based on and backed by five promises contained in the new covenant: 1) "They shall all know me," 2) "I will be their God, and they shall be my people," 3) "I will forgive their sins," 4) "I will put my law in their inward parts and write it in their hearts," and 5) "I will remember their sins no more." Let us analyze each of these promises.

"They shall all know me" (conviction)—In this new-covenant promise, God vows to give lost sinners a saving knowledge of Himself. In fulfillment of this promise, He "commands the light to shine out of darkness"—to "shine in our hearts to give the light of the knowledge of the glory of God in the face of Jesus Christ" (2 Cor. 4:6). The fulfillment of this promise is what jumpstarts the Christian experience.

It is the revelation of God's lovingkindness and goodness that moves the sinner from ignorance to a knowledge that saves. The fulfillment of this promise allows the sinner to transition from darkness to light—from death to life. "And this is life eternal, that they might know thee the only true God, and Jesus Christ, whom thou hast sent" (John 17:3).

Paul's prayer for the believers in the church of Ephesus was that they might increase in the knowledge of God and their understanding become enlightened: "That the God of our Lord Jesus Christ, the Father of glory, may give unto you the spirit of wisdom and revelation in the knowledge of him: The eyes of your understanding being enlightened; that ye may know what is the hope of his calling, and what the riches of the glory of his inheritance in the saints" (Eph. 1:17, 18). This prayer can receive an answer based on the new-covenant promise, "They shall all know me."

The knowledge of God's goodness leads one to repent (see Rom. 2:4). A saving knowledge of God brings conviction of sin on the one hand and the assurance of pardon and grace on the other. Getting to know God brings peace and goodness. "Acquaint now thyself with him, and be at peace: thereby good shall come unto thee" (Job 22:21).

Jesus invites everyone to "Learn of me" so they can "find rest unto their souls" (Matt. 11:28, 29). Having an intimate knowledge of the Lord Jesus awakens faith and repentance and brings rest into the soul. It is the Christian's privilege to obtain an ever-advancing understanding of the work and mission of Jesus as atoning Sacrifice and High Priest, based on the promise, "They shall all know me."

In 2 Corinthians 3:18, Paul said it is by "beholding the glory of the Lord as in a glass" that we become "changed into the same image from glory to glory." The transforming power found in acquiring a saving knowledge of God, as described in that passage, is also expressed in the following statement:

> The experimental knowledge of God and of Jesus Christ whom He has sent, transforms man into the image of God. It gives to man the mastery of himself, bringing every impulse and passion of the lower nature under the control of the higher powers of the mind. It makes its possessor a son of God and an heir of heaven. It brings him into communion with the mind of the Infinite, and opens to him the rich treasures of the universe.[51]

On the flip side, it is the absence of a saving and transforming knowledge of God in Jesus Christ that causes people to walk and grope in moral darkness. It was because the Pharaoh of Egypt did not know the Lord that he contemptuously declared, "Who is the LORD, that I should obey his voice to let Israel go? I know not the LORD, neither will I let Israel go" (Exod. 5:2). The sons of the high priest Eli "knew not the Lord," and their sins "were very grievous before the Lord" (see 1 Sam. 2:12–17). The unconverted are described in Romans 1:28–32 as being given over to reprobate minds and doing a host of foolish and unprofitable things, such as worshipping four-footed creatures, being full of unrighteousness, fornication, wickedness, envy, deceit, murder, and malice because they "will not retain God in their knowledge."

The prophet Habakkuk prophesied of a future time when the earth is to be filled with the knowledge of God's glory as the waters fill the sea (2:14). This prophecy will find fulfillment during the time of the outpouring of the latter rain just before the second coming

---

[51] White, *Christ's Object Lessons*, p. 114.

of Jesus. At that time, God's character will be on full display for a skeptical world to see. They will behold it through a people who will reflect that character in its fullness by unwavering obedience to His commandments (see Rev. 14:12). The firsthand knowledge of the character of God, as demonstrated in the 144,000 perfected saints, will result in the conversion of a great multitude of people described as coming from many "nations, kindreds, people and tongues" (7:9).

"I will be their God, and they shall be my people" (acceptance and adoption)—The next stage in the Christian experience is what the Bible calls "adoption." "Having predestinated us unto the adoption of children by Jesus Christ to himself, according to the good pleasure of his will" (Eph. 1:15). It is the fulfillment of the new-covenant promise, "I will be their God, and they shall be My people." As a result of this beautiful promise, believers not only know God from a distance but are to be drawn close to Him in an intimate, personal relationship. There is untold power in this relationship: "But as many as received him, to them gave them the power to become the sons of God, even to them that believe on his name" (John 1:12). God Himself declares He will be "a Father unto you, and ye shall be my sons and daughters" (2 Cor. 6:18).

Israel received the adoption as God's firstborn (see Rom. 9:4); likewise, the church of Christ today is called "the church of the firstborns" (Heb. 12:23).[52] On account of this new-covenant promise, it is our privilege to address the eternal God in prayer as "Our Father, which art in heaven."

"I will be merciful and forgive their iniquity" (justification)—Pardon or forgiveness for sin is possible because of this gracious new-covenant promise. "If we confess our sins, he is faithful and just to forgive us our sins and to cleanse us from all unrighteousness" (1 John 1:9). "In whom we have redemption through his blood, the forgiveness of sins, according to the riches of his grace" (Eph. 1:7).

---

[52] In the Greek, the word "firstborn" is actually in the plural form. It should read "firstborns."

Moreover, the sinner is not only forgiven but restored to favor with God based on one's faith and repentance. "Being justified by faith, we have peace with God through our Lord Jesus Christ" (Rom. 5:1). "There is therefore now no condemnation to them which are in Christ Jesus, who walk not after the flesh, but after the Spirit" (8:1).

"I will put my laws in their inwards parts and write them in their hearts" (sanctification)—This new-covenant promise is the basis of Christian sanctification or growth in grace, which, as we know, is a daily process. "Our sanctification is the work of the Father, the Son, and the Holy Spirit. *It is the fulfillment of the covenant* God has made with those who bind themselves up with Him, to stand with Him, His Son, and His Spirit in holy fellowship."[53]

When this promise is fulfilled in one's life, obedience is no longer a drudgery but a service of love. "I delight to do thy will, O God, thy law is within my heart" (Ps. 40:8). "Therefore I love thy commandments above gold; yea, above fine gold" (119:127).

Obedience to God's commandments becomes instinctive or second nature. When the law of God is written in the heart, the redeemed Christian will naturally do the precepts contained therein. "For when the Gentiles, which have not the law, do *by nature* the things contained in the law, these, having not the law, are a law unto themselves: Which shew the work of the law written in their hearts, their conscience also bearing witness, and their thoughts the mean while accusing or else excusing one another" (Rom. 2:14, 15, emphasis added). This passage states that when one does *by nature* those things contained in the law, it shows that the law is written within that person's heart. Any obedience short of this is legalism.

> All true obedience comes from the heart. It was heart work with Christ. And if we consent, He will so identify Himself with our thoughts and aims, so blend our hearts and minds into conformity to His will, that *when obeying Him we shall be but carrying out*

---

[53] White, *The Seventh-day Adventist Bible Commentary*, vol. 7, p. 908 (emphasis added).

our own impulses. The will, refined and sanctified, will find its highest delight in doing His service. When we know God as it is our privilege to know Him, our life will be a life of continual obedience.[54]

"I will remember their sins no more" (perfection)—The perfection of the character is the final stage of the Christian experience and is based on the best promise of the new covenant: "I will remember their sins no more." When this promise is fulfilled, sins are blotted out from the books of record, never more to be remembered. "I, even I, am he that blotteth out thy transgressions for mine own sake, and will not remember thy sins" (Isa. 43:25).

The blotting out of sins from the books of heaven is a judicial act of God in fulfillment of His promise, "I will remember their sins no more." Along with this act comes the blotting out of sins from the believer's mind so there is no more remembrance or awareness of sins committed. Paul labeled this incredible experience as the "perfecting of the conscience" (Heb. 9:8).

Paul wrote that the offering of animal sacrifices under the old covenant fell short of accomplishing this objective for the worshippers:

> For the law having a shadow of good things to come, and not the very image of the things, can never with those sacrifices which they offered year by year continually make the comers thereunto perfect. For then would they not have ceased to be offered? Because *that the worshippers once purged should have had no more conscience of sins*. But in those sacrifices there is a remembrance again made of sins every year. (Heb. 10:1–3)

Here, Paul put forth the argument that if the perfection of the conscience could be achieved for the people through the offering of animals, there would be no need to offer them continuously year after year. In other words, once the perfection of the conscience is achieved,

---

[54] White, *The Desire of Ages*, p. 668.

the worshippers would have had no more memory or consciousness of sin.

The object of the new-covenant promise "I will remember their sins no more" is to accomplish for believers what the old covenant animal sacrifices could not. Sin is to be removed from our experience to the point where we not only cease from sin but also possess consciences that no longer accuse us of past sins. This is, no doubt, a most blessed experience! The blotting out of sin means the *complete* fulfillment of the new-covenant promise.

> *Thus will be realized the complete fulfillment of the new-covenant promise*: "I will forgive their iniquity, and I will remember their sin no more." "In those days, and in that time, saith the Lord, the iniquity of Israel shall be sought for, and there shall be none; and the sins of Judah, and they shall not be found."[55]

Conclusion

To reiterate, the fulfillment of the promises of the new covenant is the basis of the entire Christian experience from beginning to end—from conviction, conversion, adoption, and justification to daily sanctification and, finally, the perfection of the mind and character, which is also known as "glorification."

Without the fulfillment of the new-covenant promises in the life of the believer through a work of continuous mediation in the heavenly sanctuary, there would be no such things as salvation by grace through faith, conviction of sin, righteousness by faith, change of status from children

> " To reiterate, the fulfillment of the promises of the new covenant is the basis of the entire Christian experience from beginning to end— from conviction, conversion, adoption, and justification to daily sanctification and, finally, the perfection of the mind and character, which is also known as "glorification." "

---

[55] White, *The Great Controversy*, p. 485 (emphasis added).

of wrath to children of God, repentance, forgiveness, or change of heart. Without the new-covenant promises, there would be no gospel, no "power of God unto salvation," and no "righteousness of God revealed from faith to faith" (Rom. 1:16, 17).

Therefore, the fulfillment of these promises in the Christian's experience through Christ's more excellent ministry as the Mediator of a better covenant is everything to the believer.

7

The Christian Experience Put Into Effect

Idea in Brief: This chapter introduces the sanctuary service as the mechanism by which the new-covenant promises are made real in the believers' experience. As Mediator of the better covenant, Jesus brings gifts and sacrifices, makes atonement for sins, and claims covenant favors on behalf of His people. Without the continuous ministration of Jesus in the sanctuary, the wonderful promises of the new covenant cannot be fulfilled and applied in the Christian experience.

The New Covenant and the Sanctuary

The importance of seeing the connection between the new covenant and the service going forward in the heavenly sanctuary cannot be overemphasized. Paul highlighted the vital relationship between the covenants and their respective sanctuaries: "Then verily the first covenant had *also* ordinances of divine service, and a worldly sanctuary" (Heb. 9:1). This verse teaches that the operation of a sanctuary is needed to make available the provisions of the covenants. The old covenant needed the operation of an earthly sanctuary and the services of human priests to mediate or make available its limited benefits. Likewise, the new covenant depends on the operation of a sanctuary in heaven and the ministration of Jesus to mediate its superior benefits.

Whether one realizes it or not, it is the continuous service going on in the sanctuary in heaven that guarantees the uninterrupted fulfillment and application of the new-covenant promises in believers' lives. Terminate this service, and the benefits of the new covenant cease to become available. The Christian experience is nothing but the end product of Jesus' work as High Priest in the heavenly sanctuary. That work serves as the mechanism by which the blessings of the new covenant are bestowed upon God's obedient children.

Gifts and Sacrifices Needed for Sin

To repeat, the benefits of the new-covenant promises are mediated or dispensed exclusively through the continuous, daily ministration of Jesus Christ as High Priest in the heavenly sanctuary. It is not and cannot be mediated by human priests officiating in earthly temples and cathedrals. As Mediator of the new covenant, Jesus enters into the presence of the Father to claim its promises on behalf of sinners. He only claims what the Father has promised in the new covenant. What the Father has not promised, Jesus does not claim.

As Mediator, Jesus does not approach the Father empty-handed. He does not beseech covenant favors from His Father on behalf of sinful humanity without bringing something to offer for their sins. The law of the priesthood stated that "every high priest taken from among men is ordained for men in things pertaining to God, that he may offer both gifts and sacrifices for sins" (5:1). "For every high priest is ordained to offer gifts and sacrifices: wherefore *it is* of necessity that this man [referring to Jesus] have somewhat also to offer" (8:3).

In compliance with this requirement for priests, which He Himself instituted through Moses, Jesus also brings gifts and sacrifices for sins. He does not bring the blood of bulls and goats, but His own precious blood, which He offered at Calvary for the sins of the world. "Neither by the blood of goats and calves, but by his own blood he entered in once into the holy place, having obtained eternal redemption for us" (9:12). Jesus did not enter into temples made with hands, which are figures of the true, but into heaven itself, as Paul said, "to appear in the presence of God for us" (v. 24).

Bringing gifts and sacrifices for sin is an absolute necessity in the work of atonement and mediation of the covenants. Paul went on to say if Jesus were *living* on earth, He could not have qualified Himself as a priest: "For if he were on earth, he should not be a priest, seeing that there are priests that offer gifts according to the law" (8:4). Paul's argument in this verse is profound. Until Jesus had something to offer, He could not *officially* and *effectively* function as a priest, unlike the priests who had sacrifices to offer in the temple "according to the law." In short, Jesus' priesthood had to wait until He had something to offer for sin.

Establishing the Cross in the Right Place

For this very reason, the atoning death of Jesus was absolutely necessary for Him to have something to offer for sin and mediate the blessings of the new covenant. The death of Jesus not only ratified the new covenant but also validated His priesthood. His sacrificial death legitimized His priesthood and put it into effect. This truth places the death of Jesus in its proper perspective. The death of Jesus on the cross neither minimized His role as High Priest nor made it of no effect. Instead, it validated and activated it. The death of Christ is not everything, as many suppose it to be, as if nothing else mattered for mankind's salvation. Bear in mind, it is the priest who makes atonement for sin, not the sacrifice (see Lev. 4:35; Heb. 2:17).

However, it is just as important to recognize that a priest without a sacrifice is useless. "Without the shedding of blood, is no remission for sin" (Heb. 9:22). Therefore, to achieve humanity's complete redemption from sin, both roles are needed, namely, Christ as atoning Sacrifice, consummated on earth, and High Priest, continuously offering gifts and sacrifices for sin in the heavenly sanctuary at the present time. Both roles are on equal footing as far as humanity's redemption is concerned.

A Continuous Round of Service

The service conducted daily in the earthly sanctuary was continuous by design. The fire that burned on the altar of burnt offerings burned continually (see Lev. 6:12, 13; Deut. 4:24); the candlesticks were to burn continually (see Exod. 27:20; Lev. 24:2–4); the altar of showbread was laden with bread continually (see Lev. 24:5–8; Exod. 25:30; Num. 4:7); Aaron was to wear the plate of gold upon his miter, with the signet "Holiness unto the Lord," to bear the iniquity of holy things continually (see Exod. 28:36–38); the high priest had to bear the twelve names of the children of Israel in the breastplate of judgment (the Urim and Thummim) continually (see Exod. 29, 30); incense had to burn perpetually (see 30:7, 8); finally, the morning and evening sacrifice had to be offered continually (see 29:38–42).

The continuous nature of the service conducted daily in the sanctuary stems from the need to provide continuous cover for the congregation. As the congregation sinned continuously, they came under the law's constant condemnation and curse (see Ezek. 18:4, 20; Rom. 6:23; Gal. 3:10). Hence, the service in the sanctuary that provided cover for Israel was not to be sporadic and intermittent, but rather continuous and enduring.

Likewise, Christ's ministration in the heavenly sanctuary is a continuous round of uninterrupted service, made necessary on account of humanity's constant sinning and need for constant pardon and justification. It is tireless, unending work. Jesus continuously approaches the throne of grace—the throne of His Father—to claim new-covenant favors on behalf of a church in constant need of *forgiving* and *empowering* grace.

> Wherefore he is able also to save them to the uttermost that come unto God by him, seeing he *ever liveth* [ever continues][56] to make intercession for them. (Hebrews 7:25)

> Christ Jesus is represented as *continually* standing at the altar, momentarily offering up the sacrifice for the sins of the world.... the

---

[56] The Greek word *pantote*, which is translated "ever" in Hebrews 7:25, means "at all times," "always," "continually" (*Strong's Exhaustive Concordance of the Bible*, G3842).

atoning sacrifice through a mediator is essential because of the *constant commission of sin.*[57]

The Service of God

Paul described the two services performed in the typical sanctuary throughout the year in the following words: "Now when these things were thus ordained, the priests went always into the first tabernacle, accomplishing the service *of God.* But into the second *went* the high priest alone once every year, not without blood, which he offered for himself, and *for* the errors of the people" (Heb. 9:6, 7).

The service conducted in the sanctuary daily was called "the service of God" [58] in the above passage. In verse 1, that expression is translated as "divine service." Paul wrote that the Jews were entrusted with the adoption, the glory, the covenants, the giving of the law, the promises, and the "service of God" (see Rom. 9:4).

Hence, that expression is a direct reference to the sanctuary service, which is God serving sinners on account of their sins; it is His loving service for lost humanity. "Thou hast made me to serve with thy sins; thou hast wearied me with thine iniquities" (Isa. 43:24). "For even the Son of Man did not come to be served, but to serve, and to give His life as a ransom for many" (Mark 10:45, NIV).

During the "service of God" or the daily service, atonement was made by the priests with the blood of the sin offerings, making it possible for the worshippers to obtain pardon for sins committed in ignorance as well as a limited number of willful sins or trespasses (see Lev. 4:27–31; 5:1–10). Besides this, it was possible to obtain ceremonial cleansing from various forms of physical defilement and impurities.[59] Hence, forgiveness for sin and cleansing from various

---

[57] White, *Selected Messages*, book 1, pp. 343, 344 (emphasis added).
[58] The Greek word λατρεία (*latreia*), translated "the service of God," means "divine ministration" or "divine service."
[59] For instance, purification after childbirth (see Lev. 12:6–8); cleansing of lepers (see 14:1–20); cleansing from various bodily discharges (ch. 15).

impurities were the two major benefits obtained by the worshippers through the daily service.

Therefore, it should come as no surprise that in the new covenant, pardon for sin and cleansing are also offered through the continuous daily ministration of Jesus in the heavenly sanctuary. "If we confess our sins, He is faithful and just to *forgive* us our sins and to *cleanse* us from all unrighteousness" (1 John 1:9, emphasis added). Paul taught this, too: "And such were some of you: but ye are *washed*, but ye are *sanctified*, but ye are *justified* in the name of the Lord Jesus, and by the Spirit of our God" (1 Cor. 6:11, emphasis added).

Mark this vital point well: The daily, continuous ministration of Jesus in the first apartment of the heavenly sanctuary serves as the mechanism by which the first four promises of the new covenant are claimed and applied in the believer's experience. The fulfillment of the fifth and final promise, "I will remember their sins no more," waits until the antitypical day of atonement.

"They shall all know me." Through His ministration in the sanctuary, our Great High Priest claims this promise for individuals daily. This is why, like Paul, we can pray, "That the God of our Lord Jesus Christ, the Father of glory, may give unto you the spirit of wisdom and revelation in the knowledge of him" (Eph. 1:17). We can "be filled with the knowledge of his will in all wisdom and spiritual understanding" (Col. 1:9). Our prayers for divine wisdom and guidance are graciously answered due to the work of Jesus in the heavenly sanctuary.

> Because of the new covenant, membership in His royal family is not restricted to people of Jewish background. For the sake of Jesus and through His powerful high-priestly ministry, God fulfills His promise to be our God and Father. Through Christ's ministry, Jews and Gentiles become God's sons and daughters

"I will be their God, and they shall be My people." Because Jesus "ever liveth to make intercession" for us, we stand in a much more favored relationship with God than we can ever think. "Which in time past were not a people, but are now the people of God: which had not obtained mercy, but now have obtained mercy" (1 Peter 2:10). Because of the new covenant, membership in His royal family is not restricted to people of Jewish background. For the sake of Jesus and through His powerful high-priestly ministry, God fulfills His promise to be our God and Father. Through Christ's ministry, Jews *and* Gentiles become God's sons and daughters (see 2 Cor. 6:18).

> For both he that sanctifieth and they who *are* sanctified are all of one: for which cause he is not ashamed to call them brethren, Saying, I will declare thy name unto my brethren, in the midst of the church will I sing praise unto thee. And again, I will put my trust in him. And again, Behold I and the children which God hath given me. (Heb. 2:11–13)

"I will forgive their iniquity." Forgiveness for sin is only possible because Jesus offers His shed blood and claims the Father's promise in the new covenant, which says, "I will forgive their sins." As long as our Great High Priest officiates at the right hand of God in the heavenly sanctuary, penitent believers can claim the new-covenant promise of pardon for sin. "Who shall lay any thing to the charge of God's elect? It is God that justifieth. Who is he that condemneth? It is Christ that died, yea rather, that is risen again, who is even at the right hand of God, who also maketh intercession for us" (Rom. 8:33, 34).

It is Christ's work of intercession that makes pardon and justification by faith possible. Even repentance is a benefit of that work. "Him hath God exalted with his right hand to be a Prince and a Saviour, for to give repentance to Israel, and forgiveness of sins" (Acts 5:31).

"By the manifestation of His love, by the entreating of His Spirit, He woos men to repentance; for repentance is the gift of God, and whom He pardons He first makes penitent."[60]

---

[60] White, *Selected Messages*, book 1, p. 324.

"**I will write my laws in their hearts.**" In the new covenant, God promises to not only forgive sins but also make the sinner obedient to His commandments. Obedience is evidence that the law is being written in the heart (see Rom. 2:14, 15). This is called "Bible sanctification." Sanctification or growth in grace is the process of being "changed from glory to glory into the same image, even as by the Spirit of the Lord" (2 Cor. 3:18). In the new covenant, it is the Spirit of God who writes His law in our hearts. Without the Holy Spirit's powerful regenerating work, the law of God cannot be enshrined in the heart and mind.

The impartation of the Spirit is itself a direct benefit of Christ's work of intercession as High Priest at the right hand of God. "Therefore being by the right hand of God exalted, and having received of the Father the promise of the Holy Ghost, he hath shed forth this, which ye now see and hear" (Acts 2:33).

In Zechariah's vision of the two olive trees pouring the golden oil out of themselves into the seven-branched golden candlesticks, we see a beautiful picture of how the Holy Spirit is continuously imparted to the church as a benefit of the sanctuary service (see 4:1–6). It is to put into effect the new-covenant promise, "I will write my laws in their hearts" (Jer. 31:33).

The Sanctuary Truth Cannot Be Treated Lightly

It cannot be denied that as a result of the continuous ministration of Jesus in the sanctuary above, believers have not failed to receive the blessings contained in the promises of the new covenant: illumination, adoption, justification, and sanctification. Consequently, it makes no sense to belittle the sanctuary service when it is the only means by which the blessings of the new covenant promises are obtained. To marginalize the sanctuary and think it is insignificant is to shoot oneself in the foot!

If the sanctuary service is the divinely appointed mechanism through which new-covenant promises can be fulfilled and put into effect in the life, then it makes no sense to say, "Everything was finished at the cross," for this mindset gives the impression that whatever Jesus is doing in heaven post-crucifixion has nothing to add to humanity's salvation and is therefore insignificant. Those who say this naturally tend to take Christ's work as High Priest in the heavenly sanctuary for granted. They treat it as inconsequential and having little to do with the work of salvation.

There is a lot more to that work in the sanctuary than what most people think. It is through the sanctuary service that a) the blessings of the new covenant are obtained, b) forgiveness of sin is received, c) sin is expelled from the heart, d) the Holy Spirit is imparted to the believer, and e) gracious answers to prayers are granted. Furthermore, it is through the cleansing of the sanctuary that the wicked kingdoms of this world are to be eventually taken down. Therefore, no one can deny the significance of Christ's mediatorial work in the heavenly sanctuary without putting his or her eternal salvation at risk.

The Best New-covenant Promise Saved for Last

Be aware, though, that not all the new-covenant promises are applied in the believer's experience as benefits of the continuous daily ministration of Jesus in the heavenly sanctuary. The last new covenant promise, "I will remember their sins no more," is neither claimed nor applied. Jesus, the Mediator of the new covenant, does not now appropriate for the believer this beautiful promise, which points to the blotting out of sin from the books of heaven and the memory banks. Hence, it is not now experienced in the believer's life.

No follower of Jesus up to this day can claim his or her conscience has been perfected and he or she is no longer conscious or aware of past sins (see Heb. 10:1, 2). The fact that the memory of sins committed continues to remain intact in one's consciousness also shows that sins still remain in the books of heaven, even though they have been pardoned. We are told past sins wound the conscience and the "scars of a wounded conscience *will ever remain*" even after conversion.[61] Everyone knows from experience how the memory of

---

[61] White, "The Christian Rule in Deal," *The Signs of the Times*, February, 7, 1884 (emphasis added).

sins committed continues to haunt them throughout life, even though they confessed and repented of them and were forgiven.

Worse yet, the sins that are in the books continue to testify against believers, even though they have been pardoned. Isaiah declared, "For our transgressions are multiplied before thee, and our sins testify against us: for our transgressions are with us; and as for our iniquities, we know them" (59:12). The sins that are "multiplied before thee" are the sins kept in the books, which are before God's throne even after they have been pardoned. These transgressions and iniquities are also still with the believers, and incredibly enough, they still know them. This means they are still conscious of those sins and, frankly, still remember them.

In the next chapter, we shall attempt to answer the question, Why sins are not canceled and blotted out from the books of heaven even after they have been forgiven? We shall try to understand why Jesus does not claim for the believers the new-covenant promise, "I will remember their sins no more," as a benefit of His *daily* ministration in the heavenly sanctuary.

8

The Christian Experience Consummated

Idea in Brief: This chapter explains why, after Jesus had ministered for eighteen centuries in the first apartment of the heavenly sanctuary, a second service in the Most Holy Place is still needed. Christ's final ministration in the second apartment of the heavenly sanctuary is necessary to claim the last unfulfilled promise of the new covenant, "I will remember their sins no more."

Serious Questions Needing Serious Answers

In the previous chapter, the following questions were asked and left unanswered: Why are sins not blotted out of the books of heaven even after they have been forgiven? Why wait until the antitypical day of atonement for this to happen? These questions are serious because as long as sins remain in the books, they testify against believers—not to mention these sins also continue defiling the sanctuary. The fact that pardoned sins remain in the books shows justified believers are not entirely and permanently released from the condemnation of the law.

Worse yet, as long as sins remain in the books, they are also retained in the believer's memory banks, leaving scars in the conscience and haunting one's entire life! With that said, why does Jesus wait until the antitypical day of atonement to claim the new-covenant promise, "I will remember their sins no more"? Why are sins not erased from the books of heaven and believers' memory until then?

The Law Is Holy, Just, and Good

To answer the questions above, we need to understand something about the nature of the law and its demands. The law is holy, just, and good (see Rom. 7:12). It calls sin by its right name. The law looks at the entire individual, not just one's behavior. The law penetrates the heart and sees the hidden deformities within it. The law of God takes note of the depravity and deceitfulness of the human heart or character and condemns it: "The heart is deceitful above all things and desperately wicked; who can know it? I the LORD search the heart, I try the reins, even to give every man according to his ways, and according to the fruit of his doings" (Jer. 17:9, 10).

God's holy law sees the defilement that exists behind the facades of human goodness and passes judgment upon it. It sees the corruption within the deepest recesses of the heart. "For out of the heart proceed evil thoughts, murders, adulteries, fornications, thefts, false witness, blasphemies: These are the things which defile a man" (Matt. 15:19, 20).

Not only does the law demand perfect obedience, perfect righteousness; it also detects the slightest deviation from its precepts and calls it sin. As long as the law finds something in the believer's life that is not in harmony with its principles, it cannot release him or her from condemnation, even though the believer may have been pardoned and stands justified and complete in Christ. As long as the law has claims on the believer that are not met, his or her sins cannot be blotted out from the books of heaven. "By the offering of blood, the sinner acknowledged the authority of the law, confessed the guilt of his transgression, and expressed his faith in Him who was to take away the sin of the world; *but he was not entirely released from the condemnation of the law.*"[62]

Believers, though they stand before God justified, righteous, and perfect because of Christ's borrowed, imputed righteousness, are nonetheless accountable to the law and must acknowledge they have no righteousness of their own. Believers do not stand before the law

---

[62] White, *Patriarchs and Prophets*, p. 356 (emphasis added).

of God holy and perfect of themselves. The fact that justified believers need Christ as their Substitute to be accepted and accounted righteous only shows they are deficient and unable to satisfy the demands of the law by themselves.

The Problem with Forgiveness

Thus, the fact that sins continue remaining in the books of record even though they have been pardoned, shows the experience of pardon and justification by faith are not sufficient grounds for sins to be blotted out. They may be remitted, but they are not blotted out. This is not to downplay the significance of the experience of pardon and justification by faith. Receiving forgiveness of sin or being justified by faith is a wonderful experience. Paul called it a "blessed" experience: "Even as David also describeth the blessedness of the man, unto whom God imputeth righteousness without works, Saying, Blessed are they whose iniquities are forgiven, and whose sins are covered. Blessed is the man to whom the Lord will not impute sin" (Rom. 4:6–8).

Being forgiven of sin and accounted righteous by faith guarantees acceptance with God and provides the assurance of present salvation. The Spirit of Prophecy describes the experience of justification by faith in the following, beautiful words:

> If you give yourself to Him, and accept Him as your Saviour, then, sinful as your life may have been, for His sake you are accounted righteous. *Christ's character stands in place of your character, and you are accepted before God just as if you had not sinned.*[63]
>
> *Your imperfection is no longer seen*; for you are clothed with the robe of Christ's perfection.[64]

Wonderful as the experience of justification by faith may sound, there is a serious limitation. The heart remains deformed—the

---

[63] White, *Steps to Christ*, p. 62 (emphasis added).
[64] White, *The Seventh-day Adventist Bible Commentary*, vol. 7, p. 907 (emphasis added).

character, defective. Sinful traits of character remain; they are not yet completely and permanently eradicated. This is seen in the fact that Christ's character needs to stand in place of our character. This only shows our characters are deficient and sinful. In righteousness by faith, one's imperfection is no longer seen only because it is covered with the robe of Christ's perfection. The perfection is *in Christ*, not in the believer; the imperfection is *covered*, not eradicated. This is the experience of justification or righteousness by faith, the benefit of the daily service.

Simul Justus et Peccator

When describing the standing of the forgiven and justified believer, the great reformer Martin Luther used this formula: *simul justus et peccator*, literally meaning "just and sinful" simultaneously. This notion may sound like a contradiction of terms at first glance, but it is absolutely true. Justified believers are accounted just and perfect *in Christ*, but not in themselves. They remain sinful and defective in character, even though they are pronounced by heaven as righteous by faith.

> "When describing the standing of the forgiven and justified believer, the great reformer Martin Luther used this formula: simul justus et peccator, literally meaning "just and sinful" simultaneously. This notion may sound like a contradiction of terms at first glance, but it is absolutely true."

Imperfections and sinfulness of the character, which, unfortunately, are not removed entirely in the experience of forgiveness and justification, are condemned by God's holy law. "Moral perfection is required of all. Never should we lower the standard of righteousness in order to accommodate inherited or cultivated tendencies to wrong-doing. *We need to understand that imperfection of character is sin.*"[65]

---

[65] White, *Christ's Object Lessons*, p. 330 (emphasis added).

Therefore, until the law no longer detects blemishes and defects in the character, it cannot release the pardoned sinner entirely from condemnation. It will continue holding on to the records of sin in the books of heaven to signify it has claims on the pardoned sinner that remain unsatisfied. Sinfulness of character, the root of human sinning, must be uprooted from the heart. Believers' lives must be found to be in harmony with the law before they can be entirely released from condemnation and have their sins blotted out from the books of heaven.

All who have truly repented of sin, and by faith claimed the blood of Christ as their atoning sacrifice, have had pardon entered against their names in the books of heaven; as they have become partakers of the righteousness of Christ, and *their characters are found to be in harmony with the law of God, their sins will be blotted out,* and they themselves will be accounted worthy of eternal life.[66]

The believer must become a partaker of the righteousness of Christ if his or her character is to be found in harmony with the law of God. The righteousness of Christ is bestowed as a gift, received by grace through faith as a benefit of His final ministration in the second apartment of the heavenly sanctuary.

It must be reiterated that the command to take away the filthy garments in the final atonement is not about eradicating the sinful, hereditary *nature*, but rather removing the defective *character*.

The Spirit of Prophecy makes it very clear what constitutes the "filthy garments" that are taken away in the final atonement and replaced with the robe of Christ's perfect righteousness; they refer to the "defective character," not the sinful, dilapidated, fallen, hereditary nature. "The tempter stands by to accuse them, as he stood by to resist Joshua. He points to their filthy garments, their *defective characters*."[67]

---

[66] White, *The Great Controversy*, p. 483 (emphasis added).
[67] White, *Prophets and Kings*, p. 588 (emphasis added).

Character and Nature Differentiated

Some have mistakenly assumed that it is the hereditary nature that is eradicated during the final cleansing and atonement. Part of the confusion and misunderstanding lies in not making the correct distinction between character and nature. Many make the assumption that character and nature are synonyms when they are not. This misunderstanding is part of the problem. Character and nature are not interchangeable. Theological confusion results when the distinction between them is not properly recognized.

Nature is the "equipment" or "wiring" with which we are born. We have no choice in this matter. On the other hand, character is what we produce or make out of the equipment with which we were endowed at birth. It is entirely based on the choices we make. Character is transformable. Nature is unchangeable; it remains sinful and fallen during the entire life. It remains sinful and fallen even after the character is perfected in the final atonement. Jesus does not deal with humanity's sinful nature until His second coming. For this reason, God's people will still be harassed by sinful thoughts and have corrupt desires urged upon them by their sinful natures, even though their characters may have been perfected in the final atonement.

Following Christ's Example of a Sinless Life

Christ's perfection of character consisted of being able to subdue the inner promptings of His fallen, hereditary nature. He "condemned sin in sinful *flesh*" (Rom. 8:3, emphasis added). His flesh was no different from ours. The reason why He could consistently condemn or subjugate the evil promptings of that nature was because He had no character defects. He would have developed a defective character if He had once cherished and yielded to a sinful desire urged on by His fallen, hereditary nature. The presence of character flaws makes one weak and unable to suppress and subdue the sinful clamors of the fallen nature.

The perfection of the character of the saints during the final atonement is what enables them to emulate Christ's example of a sinless life. When their "filthy garments" or defective characters are removed and replaced with Christ's perfect righteousness, they will be able to consistently put under and subdue every evil prompting of their fallen natures. Like Jesus, they will no longer cherish any sinful, unholy thoughts as they used to do or yield to them as they have often done in the past.[68] They will constantly be "casting down imaginations, and every high thing that exalteth itself against the knowledge of God, and bringing into captivity every thought to the obedience of Christ" (2 Cor. 10:5).

To reiterate, the perfection of character during the final atonement cannot be equated with eradicating sinful nature with its corrupt desires and passions. Instead, it is the removal of the defects that mar and weaken the character.

The New-covenant Promise Completely Fulfilled

Just as soon as the defects of believers' characters are removed in the command "take away their filthy garments" and replaced with Christ's perfect character, Jesus will claim the last, unfulfilled promise of the new covenant: "I will remember their sins no more." Then and only then will the new-covenant promises be completely fulfilled:

> Thus will be realized the *complete fulfillment* of the new-covenant promise: "I will forgive their iniquity, and I will remember their sin no more." "In those days, and in that time, saith the Lord, the iniquity of Israel shall be sought for, and there shall be none; and the sins of Judah, and they shall not be found."[69]

The Final Cleansing

The last question to be settled at this point is, When do the people of God become partakers of the righteousness of Christ? In other words, when are their lives going to be found to be in harmony with the Law of God? This is a very important question for those who belong to the church of Laodicea, since it is not until then that their sins will be blotted out of the books of record and the sanctuary cleansed.

---

[68] See White, *The Great Controversy*, p. 623.
[69] White, *The Great Controversy*, p. 485 (emphasis added).

On the day of atonement, the high priest entered into the second apartment of the sanctuary to make a final atonement to cleanse the people from all their sins. This work had to be accomplished before the sanctuary could be cleansed from all the sins that had polluted it. The inspired record says, "For on that day shall the priest make an atonement for you, to cleanse you, that ye may be clean from all your sins before the LORD" (Lev. 16:30).

The expression "all their sins before the Lord" is a direct reference to the sins in the books of record, which are kept before the Lord. The psalmist points out our sins are before the Lord. "Thou hast set our iniquities before thee, our secret sins in the light of *thy countenance*" (90:8, emphasis added). In other words, our "hidden sins" are before His face.

The prophet Isaiah adds, "For our iniquities have been multiplied *before thee*, and our sins have testified against us, for our transgressions are with us, as for our iniquities, we know them" (59:12, emphasis added). Daniel saw these books opened when "the Ancient of days came... thrones were cast down, and the judgment was set" (7:9, 10).

The final atonement made by the high priest on the day of atonement was designed to rid the worshippers of their "filthy garments, their defective characters" [70] so they can become partakers of the righteousness of Christ and their lives may be found in harmony with the law of God. This satisfies the demands of the law and paves the way for sins to be removed from the sanctuary and transferred onto the head of the scapegoat (see Lev. 16:21).

During the closing scenes of the great, antitypical day of atonement, the final purification of the church of Laodicea takes place. "As the people of God afflict their souls before Him, pleading for purity of heart, the command is given, 'Take away their filthy garments... and I will clothe thee with change of raiment.' Zechariah 3:4. The spotless robe of Christ's righteousness is placed upon the tried, tempted, faithful children of God."[71] At this point, God's people

---

[70] White, *Prophets and Kings*, p. 588.
[71] White, *Prophets and Kings*, p. 591.

become partakers of the righteousness of Christ, and their lives are found to be in harmony with His law.

This final cleansing is not offered as a benefit of the daily service in the sanctuary. It is a benefit of the work of Jesus in the second apartment of the heavenly sanctuary. This explains why the blotting out of sin and the cleansing of the sanctuary wait until the day of atonement.

The Cleansing of the Heavenly Sanctuary Now in Progress

The actual work of cleansing the sanctuary in heaven has been in progress since 1844. It commenced when the prophesied 2,300 evening-mornings of Daniel 8:14 terminated during that year.[72] The pattern of heavenly things was purified with animals' blood, but "the heavenly things themselves are to be purified with better sacrifices" (Heb. 9:23). Jesus has gone to the Father with His shed blood to make a full and final atonement and blot out the sins that have polluted the heavenly sanctuary for centuries. He stands before the Father, claiming for His faithful people in every generation the fulfillment of the last new-covenant promise, "I will remember their sins no more." Simultaneously, there is a work of examining the books of record to determine who, through faith in Christ and repentance of sin, are entitled to receive the benefits of His final atonement—that is, the final cleansing or perfecting of the characters and the blotting out of sins forever from the books of heaven and the memory.[73]

The Sins That God Will Remember

When Jesus steps out of the Most Holy Place of the heavenly sanctuary and probation closes, the characters of those who failed to receive the benefit of His final atonement remain filthy forever. Failing to become partakers of the righteousness of Christ, their

---

[72] For a deeper understanding of the meaning of the 2,300-day prophecy of Daniel 8:14, read *The Great Controversy*, pp. 409, 410.

[73] For a more detailed explanation of the subject of the cleansing the sanctuary and concurrent work of investigative judgment, read *The Great Controversy*, pp. 479–491.

lives remain out of harmony with the law. As a result, their sins are not blotted out of the books of record. As the plagues begin falling, their sins come up in remembrance before God. "Babylon came in remembrance before God, to give unto her the cup of the wine of the fierceness of his wrath" (Rev. 16:19). "For her sins have reached unto heaven, and God hath remembered her iniquities" (18:5). The wrath of God, which is poured out without mixture of mercy into the cup of His indignation, is visited on the heads of these individuals who have slighted God's mercy and refused His offer of salvation.

Ye Shall Afflict Your Souls

Since 1844, we have been living in the great, antitypical day of atonement. As we inch closer to its closing scenes, we will need to take the call to "afflict the soul" more and more seriously. The decree will soon be made, compelling the conscience to reverence the false sabbath and "render obedience to human edicts in violation of the divine law."[74] We shall either be cut off from among God's people when that time comes or experience the taking away of the "filthy garments" and become partakers of the righteousness of Christ.

We dare not take lightly the preparatory work that has been placed upon us individually and corporately. We can only do so at the peril of our souls. The times in which we are living call for sobriety and fixedness of purpose. "Gird the loins of your mind" and "Be ye sober and vigilant" are our marching orders today as we steadily draw closer to the time of the grand fulfillment for the living in Laodicea of the new-covenant promise, "I will remember their sins no more."

> We are now living in the great day of atonement. In the typical service, while the high priest was making the atonement for Israel, all were required to afflict their souls by repentance of sin and humiliation before the Lord, lest they be cut off from among the people. In like manner, all who would have their names retained in the book of life should now, in the few remaining days of their

---

[74] White, *Prophets and Kings*, p. 588.

probation, afflict their souls before God by sorrow for sin and true repentance. There must be deep, faithful searching of heart. The light, frivolous spirit indulged by so many professed Christians must be put away. There is earnest warfare before all who would subdue the evil tendencies that strive for the mastery. The work of preparation is an individual work. We are not saved in groups. The purity and devotion of one will not offset the want of these qualities in another.[75]

---

[75] White, *The Great Controversy*, pp. 489, 490.

9

The Cleansing of The Soul Temple Illustrated

Idea in Brief: In this chapter, the dual nature of human sinfulness is discussed and illustrated. The dual nature of sin necessitates a dual solution, which is implemented in the two services performed in the sanctuary: the daily and yearly services. The daily service, being incomplete, does not deal with the sin problem fully and permanently. Hence, a final ministration is needed.

The Dual Cleansing of the Temple in Jerusalem

The Gospels record two instances where Jesus cleansed the temple in Jerusalem from buyers and sellers. The first was at the beginning of His public ministry (see John 2:13–17). At the close of His public labors, Jesus returned to the temple and once again found it teeming with unholy traffic, just like before. Therefore, He cleansed it a second time. "And he went into the temple, and began to cast out them that sold therein, and them that bought; Saying unto them, it is written, My house is the house of prayer: but ye have made it a den of thieves" (Luke 19:45, 46).

The cleansing of the temple in Jerusalem powerfully illustrates Christ's high-priestly work of purifying the soul temple from the defilement of sin.

The courts of the temple at Jerusalem, filled with the tumult of unholy traffic, represented all too truly the temple of the heart, defiled by the presence of sensual passion and unholy thoughts. *In cleansing the temple from the world's buyers and sellers, Jesus announced His mission to cleanse the heart from the defilement of sin*,—from the earthly desires, the selfish lusts, the evil habits, that corrupt the soul.[76]

The Dual Cleansing of the Soul Temple

It is significant to note that just as Jesus cleansed the temple in Jerusalem twice, once at the beginning of His ministry and again at its close, His work of cleansing the soul temple from the pollution of sin is also accomplished in two stages. In the Christian experience, cleansing begins at the new birth and ends in the final purification of the character and the blotting out of sin from memory and the books of heaven. The cleansing that begins at conversion and continues daily is the benefit of Christ's continuous work of intercession in the heavenly sanctuary. The final cleansing of the soul temple is the benefit received from His ministration in the second apartment of the heavenly sanctuary—to cleanse it from the sins that have polluted it.

The Daily Service Cleansing, an Incomplete Work

The primary benefits obtained through the daily service in the sanctuary were *forgiveness* for sin and *cleansing* from various types of bodily impurities. Leviticus 4 depicts how sins committed in ignorance could be forgiven through the sin offerings. Chapters 5 and 6 explain how certain willful sins could be atoned for and forgiven through the trespass offering. Chapters 12–15 discuss various regulations and procedures meant to purify the congregation from many forms of physical defilement.

Likewise, in the new covenant, forgiveness for sin and cleansing from its corrupting influences are the principal benefits of the daily ministration of Jesus in the heavenly sanctuary. The apostle John

---

[76] White, *The Desire of Ages*, p. 161 (emphasis added).

declared, "If we confess our sins, he is faithful and just to *forgive* us our sins, and to *cleanse* us from all unrighteousness" (1 John 1:9, emphasis added).

Before this, he wrote, "But if we walk in the light, as he is in the light, we have fellowship one with another, and the blood of Jesus Christ his Son *cleanseth* us from all sin" (v. 7, emphasis added). As long as sin is repented of and confessed, the believer is assured of the forgiveness of his or her sin and cleansing from its guilt and power.

Paul referred to the cleansing of the soul temple from sin daily as "purging the conscience of dead works." "How much more shall the blood of Christ, who through the eternal Spirit offered himself without spot to God, purge your conscience from dead works to serve the living God?" (Heb. 9:14). Similarly, Peter called this daily cleansing experience the "sanctification of the spirit unto obedience," obtained through the "sprinkling of the blood of Jesus" (1 Peter 1:2).

The drastic, life-changing effects of Christ's daily soul-cleansing work for believers are described in the following passage:

> Know ye not that the unrighteous shall not inherit the kingdom of God? Be not deceived: neither fornicators, nor idolaters, nor adulterers, nor effeminate, nor abusers of themselves with mankind, nor thieves, nor covetous, nor drunkards, nor revilers, nor extortioners, shall inherit the kingdom of God. *And such were some of you: but ye are washed, but ye are sanctified, but ye are justified* in the name of the Lord Jesus, and by the Spirit of our God. (1 Corinthians 6:9–11, emphasis added)

Hence, the Christian experience known as justification and sanctification are seen to be nothing but benefits of Christ's daily ministration in the heavenly sanctuary, aimed at cleansing the soul temple from sin's polluting influence.

However, one could say the cleansing of the soul experienced daily by the Christian is only partial and incomplete. While it, to a large extent, transforms one experientially and gives one a new standing, it does not eradicate the root of the sin problem. Character defects

> *All sincere Christians know from experience that even though the sins they acknowledge and confess daily are forgiven, sinful character traits such as ambition, pride, and selfishness nevertheless remain, to a large extent. In pardon and justification, the sinfulness of character is not wholly and permanently addressed. Because character flaws still exist, the believer has to battle against them through daily dying to self.*

remain intact, for the most part. As a result, one goes through life still prone to sinning, eventually falling into sin and pleading for forgiveness and cleansing all over again. Does this experience sound familiar?

All sincere Christians know from experience that even though the sins they acknowledge and confess daily are forgiven, sinful character traits such as ambition, pride, and selfishness nevertheless remain, to a large extent. In pardon and justification, the sinfulness of character is not *wholly* and *permanently* addressed. Because character flaws still exist, the believer has to battle against them through daily dying to self.

A Classic Case Study of Sanctification

The life of Moses is a classic illustration of the limited reach of sanctification. While in Egypt, Moses slew an Egyptian slave master out of rage and had to flee for his life. While in voluntary exile in Midian, Moses had the privilege of communing with God directly and experiencing the power of transforming grace for forty years. He continued living a sanctified life forty more years in the wilderness on the way to the Promised Land, often communing with God face to face and witnessing firsthand His mighty works. Moses became so emptied of self that he was willing to be blotted out of God's book for the sake of his rebellious people (Exod. 32:32). He received the label of "meekest man on earth" (Num. 12:3).

Since Moses lived in the presence of the Lord for such a long time and attained to such heights of character transformation rarely seen in people, one might think he finally became cleansed of all his character flaws. Not so! Just before he died, he once again yielded to the natural feelings of his corrupt heart when he struck the rock twice in great anger and cried, "Hear now ye rebels; must we fetch you water out of this rock?" (20:10). For this sin, Moses was denied entry into Canaan and allowed to fall under the power of death.

Earlier in their journey to Canaan, when the people worshipped the golden calf, Moses yielded to the natural feelings of his heart when he, in great anger, threw down the tables of stone containing the ten commandments, breaking them in the process. The Lord excused Moses' behavior at that time since his wrath was kindled out of a concern for His honor and glory.[77] Hence, even though Moses lived a sanctified life, his character defects remained with him until he died.

The Dual Nature of Sin

There is more to the problem of sin than meets the eye. Sin is a dual problem, and a dual solution is required to solve it permanently. Jesus Himself taught that sin goes much deeper than just outward acts of lawlessness. He said, "That which cometh out of the man, that defileth the man. For *from within, out of the heart of men*, proceed evil thoughts, adulteries, fornications, murders, thefts, covetousness, wickedness, deceit, lasciviousness, an evil eye, blasphemy, pride, foolishness: All these evil things *come from within*, and defile the man" (Mark 7:20–23, emphasis added).

The long laundry list of sins mentioned by our Lord Jesus here has a source: the evil that resides in the heart. What Jesus calls "evil things coming from within," Paul labeled "sin dwelling in me" (Rom. 7:17, 20). Deep-seated character defects are the reason why the good that Christians want to do, they cannot do, and the evil they do not want to do, they end up doing (v. 15). Converted Christians have good intentions, but character flaws and weaknesses often prevent them from following through with and making good on those intentions.

---

[77] See White, *Early Writings*, p. 163.

The Sin-Iceberg Analogy

The dual nature of human sinfulness is best illustrated using the analogy of an iceberg. A typical iceberg seen floating about in the colder regions of the Atlantic Ocean will have two parts: a relatively tiny portion called the tip of the iceberg, which is above the water line and visible to the naked eye; and a greater mass of solid ice below the water line, which is hidden from view. The lower part of the iceberg poses a greater risk to navigators since it is more massive, hidden from view, and has more capability to inflict severe damage to the hulls of unsuspecting ocean-bound vessels.

The visible tip of the iceberg represents sins *on* us, or sinful behavior. Sins on us can either be sins of *commission,* meaning immoral, unlawful behavior, or sins of *omission*, meaning sins of neglect. Both of these categories of sin are observable. "Whosoever committeth sin transgresseth also the law: for sin is the transgression of the law" (1 John 3:4). Transgressions of the law are sins of commission. Sins of neglect involve the willful nonperformance of known duties. "Therefore to him that knoweth to do good, and doeth it not, to him it is sin" (James 4:17). Here, James is talking about sins of omission.

The greater part of the iceberg beneath the surface and hidden from sight represents sin *in* us, or better still, sin *inside* us. It is a reference to the sinfulness of the heart or character. This is the origin or source of all human sinning. Sin in us makes us morally weak and therefore susceptible to falling into temptation and sinning.

In harmony with the Bible, the Spirit of Prophecy clearly distinguishes between outward sinning and the hidden sinfulness of character: "From the cross to the crown there is earnest work to be done. There is wrestling with *inbred sin*; there is warfare against *outward wrong*."[78]

The Depths of Human Sinfulness Unknown

Though fully known to God, the extent of the human heart's sinfulness is unknown to and hidden from the justified believer. Jesus does not

---

[78] White, "Peace in Christ," *The Review and Herald*, November 29, 1887 (emphasis added).

have to be told what was in humanity, for He knows (see John 2:25). However, people need to be told because they do not know the depths of their hearts' depravity. "The heart is deceitful above all things, and desperately wicked: who can know it?" (Jer. 17:9). Men do not have a correct understanding of what the sinful heart is capable of doing if presented with the right opportunity.

It is during extreme circumstances that the hidden, unknown sinfulness of character is revealed. When in a crisis and under severe pressure, people manifest what is buried in their hearts through desperate actions. Hidden elements in the heart suddenly and unexpectedly fan into life and spring into action. Take the Jews, for instance. When the Babylonian king Nebuchadnezzar besieged Jerusalem in 587 BC and the city's food supply ran out, the inhabitants of the city resorted to cruelty and cannibalism in a desperate effort to survive.

The words of the prophet were literally fulfilled: "And I will cause them to eat the flesh of their sons and the flesh of their daughters, and they shall eat every one the flesh of his friend in the siege and straitness, wherewith their enemies, and they that seek their lives, shall straiten them" (Jer. 19:9). Thousands of years before, Moses declared this very thing would happen because of their unbelief and disregard of God's commands (see Deut. 28:52–55).

Again, when Rome's armies descended on Jerusalem in AD 70 and starved the inhabitants within that city, they resorted to the same desperate measures to survive.[79] The evil lurking within the heart, unknown to its possessors, surfaced when the circumstances were right.

Jesus told Peter in advance that he would deny Him three times. Not knowing how false and deceitful his own heart was, Peter naturally refused to believe the words of His Lord until he came face to face with danger. The night he denied Jesus, Peter realized his love for the Master was not as strong as was his natural desire for self-preservation. The latter overpowered the former when the circumstances were right. "Peter had just declared that he knew not

---

[79] Josephus, *The Jewish War*, book 6, chapter 3, paragraph 4, https://1ref.us/1sf (accessed October 10, 2021).

Jesus, but he now realized with bitter grief how well his Lord knew him, and how accurately *He had read his heart, the falseness of which was unknown even to himself.*"[80]

Another Analogy

Here's yet another analogy: A tube of toothpaste is a great tool to illustrate the sin problem. The paste that resides inside the tube represents sin dwelling in the heart. When no pressure is applied to the tube, no toothpaste comes out; when pressure is applied, it naturally starts flowing out. The more pressure is applied, the more toothpaste comes out. This is how the evil from within is manifested when the conditions are right. The purpose of the final cleansing is to flush the toothpaste out of the tube so nothing will come out, no matter how much pressure is applied during the time of trouble (see Dan. 12:1).

The Final Cleansing Waits Until the Day of Atonement

The purpose of the final cleansing is to rid the soul of the unknown sinfulness of character. However, the complete and permanent cleansing of the soul temple from sin and sinfulness is not provided as a benefit of the daily service; instead, it waits until the day of atonement. This is because Jesus does not make a full and final atonement to cleanse His people entirely and permanently from their defective characters until they come to a full realization of the sinfulness of their lives. Until the bottom of the iceberg, representing the unknown sinfulness of the heart, is fully disclosed and brought to light, the full and final cleansing of the soul temple does not take place.

Partial Admission of Guilt Results in Partial Cleansing

A fundamental principle needs to be introduced here: The Lord deals with sin only to the extent that it is acknowledged and confessed. The history of the Jews shows that non-admission of guilt results in

---

[80] White, *The Desire of Ages*, p. 713 (emphasis added).

non-remission of sin. The proud Pharisees who would neither admit nor confess their sins could not receive pardon for those sins; their souls remained tainted with sin and guilt. "And some of the Pharisees which were with him heard these words, and said unto him, Are we blind also? Jesus said unto them, If ye were blind, ye should have no sin: but now ye say, We see; therefore your sin remaineth" (John 9:40, 41).

On the other hand, *"If we confess our sins*, then He is faithful and just to forgive us our sins and to cleanse us from all unrighteousness" (1 John 1:9, emphasis added). Forgiveness and cleansing are offered to those who show repentance towards God and faith towards our Lord Jesus Christ.

Partial admission of guilt results in partial remission of sin. The cleansing of the soul temple obtained through the daily ministration in the sanctuary is, at best, partial and incomplete because guilt is partially acknowledged and confessed. The worshippers who went into the sanctuary with sin offerings confessed their sins only to the degree that they understood their guilt. They came confessing only what came to their knowledge. "If his sin, which he hath sinned, *come to his knowledge*: then he shall bring his offering, a kid of the goats, a female without blemish, for his sin which he hath sinned" (Lev. 4:27, 28, emphasis added).

The iceberg analogy tells us there is more to sin than what is known and, therefore, more to guilt than what is confessed on a daily basis.

Laodicea's Unknown Sin Problem

This brings us down to the church of Laodicea, God's church for the last days. The Faithful and True Witness confronts her with the words, "Thou sayest, I am rich, and increased with goods, and have need of nothing; and *knowest not* that thou art wretched, and miserable, and poor, and blind, and naked" (Rev. 3:17, emphasis added). Laodiceans, like Peter, do not now understand the true condition of their hearts. Believing their condition is more favorable than what it really is, they currently have no correct estimate of the sinfulness of their lives; they

> *The call to the church of Laodicea to be "zealous therefore and repent" is no less than the Day of Atonement call to "afflict the soul." This call is for her to keep searching her heart to gain a greater understanding of her unknown sinfulness of character.*

have no accurate assessment of their spiritual poverty, nakedness of soul, misery, and lack of spiritual discernment.

The call to the church of Laodicea to be "zealous therefore and repent" is no less than the day of atonement call to "afflict the soul." This call is for her to keep searching her heart to gain a greater understanding of her unknown sinfulness of character.

"Thou *knowest not* that thou art miserable, wretched, naked, poor and blind... As many as I love, I rebuke and chasten. Be zealous therefore and repent."

Laodicea's problem lies beneath the surface and is, therefore, harder to bring to light. The church of Laodicea is faced with the formidable challenge of bringing to the consciousness the bottom part of the iceberg: her unknown, indwelling sinfulness of character. Laodicea needs to apply the "eye salve" to discern her true state, which is unknown to her as yet. "Who can understand his errors? Cleanse thou me from secret [hidden] faults" (Ps. 19:12). As challenging and painful as it is, this is a process Laodicea must go through before she can "buy the white raiment" and be fully and permanently cleansed.

The churches before Laodicea, representing previous generations of Christian believers, were neither rebuked nor asked to repent of something they did not know. They were asked to repent of things that were known to be sinful. The church of Ephesus, for instance, was asked to repent because she had "left her first love." Marital infidelity, a known sin, is presupposed. Likewise, the church of Pergamos was asked to repent of "eating things sacrificed to idols" and practicing fornication, all of which are also known sins. The church of Thyatira was to repent of fornication, idolatry, and adultery. The church of Sardis was called to repent of the known sin of hypocrisy—professing Christ's name while being spiritually dead.

The representative sins these churches previous to Laodicea were asked to repent of were known sins, represented by the tip of the iceberg in our analogy. Laodicea, the last church, on the other hand, is asked to repent of something much bigger and deeper: the unknown sinfulness of the human heart. Is there hope that one day, Laodicea will finally measure up with the Lord's command to "be zealous therefore and repent" of a deep-seated problem?

Laodicea's Time of Greatest Eschatological Opportunity

We are told it is during "the closing scenes of the great day of atonement" when Laodicea will finally come to grips with her unknown sinful condition. In the midst of the refining fires of persecution brought about by the Sunday law crisis, the believers, for the first time, become "fully conscious of the sinfulness of their lives."[81] The bottom of the iceberg is fully disclosed as the eye salve is applied. Laodicea sees her unworthiness and weakness to the point of despairing.

Totally broken at this point, Laodicea is described as afflicting her soul and "pleading for purity of heart."[82] Jesus then makes His final atonement and cleanses her soul temple fully and permanently. Full admission of guilt results in complete cleansing. Her filthy garments, the defective character, are taken away and replaced with the robe of Christ's perfect character. She is "nevermore to be defiled by the corruptions of the world." She is "eternally secure from the tempter's devices."[83] This is a picture of the final cleansing of Laodicea's innermost soul temple.

The "Errors of the People"

Paul described the cleansing process on the day of atonement: "But into the second went the high priest alone once every year, not without blood, which he offered for himself and for the *errors* of the people" (Heb. 9:7, emphasis added). According to Paul, the purpose of the final

---

[81] Ellen G. White, *Prophets and Kings*, p. 588.
[82] *Ibid.*, p. 591.
[83] *Ibid.*

cleansing on the day of atonement was to cleanse the people of their "errors." What did he mean by "errors"? Some modern Bible versions (e.g., NIV) translate "errors" in this passage as "sins committed in ignorance." This makes very little sense because sins committed in ignorance were already dealt with during the daily service (see Lev. 4:27, 28). Why deal with them again on the day of atonement?

The word "error" Paul used here is not the typical Greek word used elsewhere in the New Testament for "mistakes" or "errors" in judgment. The usual Greek word for "error" in the New Testament is *planao,* which simply means "to be led astray," "misled," or "deceived."[84] To the Sadducees who denied the reality of the resurrection, Jesus said, "Ye do err [deceived], not knowing the scriptures, nor the power of God" (Matt. 22:29). When discussing the true nature of sin, James said, "Do not err [or be misled], my beloved brethren" (1:16). God was grieved with the Israelites in the wilderness because they always "erred" [went astray] in their hearts (see Heb. 3:10).

The Greek word for "errors" used by Paul in Hebrews 9:7 in connection with the work of cleansing on the day of atonement comes from the root word *agnoeo,* which literally means "not to know," "to be ignorant," or "something ignored for lack of information."[85] Paul used this word here to refer to the hidden or unknown sinfulness of the natural heart, which is ignored for the most part, for lack of knowledge. It refers to the unrecognized sinful traits of character, such as selfishness, pride, ambition, envy, and others, all of which predispose one to commit sinful acts. The prophet Zechariah referred to it as the "filthy garments" of iniquity, which is taken away and replaced by a "change of raiment" in the final atonement (3:4). In Romans 7, Paul referred to this as "sin dwelling within me." It is the submerged, hidden mass of ice in our iceberg analogy.

---

[84] *Strong's Exhaustive Concordance of the Bible,* G4105; see also Hebrews 3:10; James 5:19.
[85] Greek ἀγνοέω (*agnoéō,* [ag-no-eh'-o]); from G1 (as a negative particle) and G3539; not to know (through lack of information or intelligence); by implication, to ignore (through disinclination):—(be) ignorant(-ly), not know, not understand, unknown. *Strong's Exhaustive Concordance of the Bible,* G50.

The purpose of the antitypical day of atonement cleansing is to rid the true worshippers of this deeply-rooted, subconscious problem once and for all, paving the way for the perfecting of the character. This work, in turn, also clears the way for the records of pardoned sins to be blotted out from the books of heaven. This is the experience Laodicea will go through in the final cleansing.

A Complete Savior

In cleansing the soul temple entirely from sin, Jesus is revealed as a complete Savior. What He has begun in the heart, He is able to finish (see Phil. 1:6). Therefore, when taken to its natural conclusion, the sanctuary service shows us victory over sin and the sinfulness of character is possible. The sanctuary service teaches us we can be "more than conquerors through Him that loves us" (Rom. 8:37). "More than conquerors"! This is to be the blessed experience of those who overcome in the church of Laodicea—the final generation.

What is impossible with humanity is possible through the sanctuary. After all, perfection is received as a benefit of the sanctuary service, received solely by grace through faith in the all-powerful ministration of Jesus in the heavenly sanctuary. The Christian experience God requires from those who will go through the rigors, tests, and trials of the time when the great controversy is coming to a close, He Himself provides.

10

The Day of Atonements

Idea in Brief: This chapter discusses the pivotal place of the Day of Atonement in redemptive history. Its importance, especially for those living in the time of the end, is underscored, notwithstanding there is almost nothing said about it in the New Testament canon.

The Enigma of the Day of Atonement

The question is asked, "If the Day of Atonement is so important, then why is there practically nothing said about it in the New Testament?" In other words, why are the New Testament writers virtually silent about this supposedly crucial doctrine of the church? Why is it that there are practically no explicit mentions in the New Testament of it ever being kept? This observation is somewhat surprising, given the mandate that keeping the Day of Atonement was to be an everlasting statute. "And this shall be an everlasting statute unto you, to make an atonement for the children of Israel for all their sins once a year. And he did as the LORD commanded Moses" (Lev. 16:34).

There is evidence in secular literature that the Day of Atonement was kept during the time of Christ. The biblical scholar Alfred Edersheim has written a book entitled *The Temple: Its Ministry and Services*,[86] in which he takes a fascinating look at the temple services

---

[86] Alfred Edersheim, *The Temple—Its Ministry and Services*, an online copy of which may be found at https://1ref.us/1s7 (accessed November 4, 2021).

in Jerusalem during the first century. Additionally, it is a well-known fact that modern-day Jews observe *Yom Kippur* as a matter of tradition.

However, these observations do not change the fact that the New Testament canon is itself silent on the Day of Atonement, doctrinally and historically. It has nothing to say about its doctrinal relevance for the church, especially for the end times. Neither does it contain sufficient evidence to warrant the supposition that the Day of Atonement was ever kept in New Testament times.

There are plenty of biblical references showing that other national feasts, such as the Passover and the Feast of Tabernacles, were kept. The observance of the Passover, Pentecost, and the Feast of Tabernacles are duly noted in both the Old and New Testaments. The Passover was celebrated after the second year of deliverance from Egypt (see Num. 9:1–5). It was observed again after the crossing of the Jordan River; its celebration also coincided with the cessation of the raining of manna (see Josh. 5:10–12).

Hezekiah, King of Judah, called for a celebration of the Passover after the Assyrians overthrew the northern kingdom. This act resulted in a national revival and destruction of idols throughout the land (see 2 Chron 30:1–5; 31:1). Passover was celebrated in the days of King Josiah (see 2 Kings 23:22). Jesus Himself kept the Passover and even the Feast of Tabernacles (see John 7:2). As for the Day of Atonement, there is no record in Scripture showing that Jesus' disciples and the early church ever observed it.

Some scholars think the fast mentioned in Acts 27:9 may be an allusion to the Jewish Day of Atonement. However, the word "fast" was merely used here to date Paul's travel. Nothing theological is attached to its use in the passage.

Others believe the word "day" in Hebrews 10:25 may be a reference to the Day of Atonement. "Not forsaking the assembling of ourselves together, as the manner of some is; but exhorting one another: and so much the more, as ye see the *day* approaching." Might not this day also refer to the coming of Christ? Even if that word was used in the passage to refer to the Day of Atonement, it is only used in a homiletical sense. It is used in connection with an appeal for faithfulness in attending church gatherings.

Perhaps the New Testament passage that most directly alludes to the Day of Atonement and carries with it some substance of theological value is Hebrews 9:23: "*It was* therefore necessary that the patterns of things in the heavens should be purified with these; but the heavenly things themselves with better sacrifices than these." Here, however, all that Paul was doing was merely differentiating between the cleansing of the typical sanctuary and that of the heavenly. He is not necessarily expounding on the theological meaning of the cleansing of the sanctuary on the Day of Atonement, especially as it applies to God's church in the time of the end.

We must therefore ask ourselves, 'Why is there silence in the New Testament with regards to the theology of the Day of Atonement and its projection into the future?' If the Day of Atonement is of such tremendous theological significance, especially for those living in the time of the end, should not the New Testament speak volumes about it? Why, then, is there virtual silence on the subject of the Day of Atonement and the cleansing of the heavenly sanctuary?

The Place of the Day of Atonement in Israel's Seven National Feasts

First of all, to understand the importance of the Day of Atonement to the church, its place as one of Israel's seven national feasts needs to be grasped and appreciated. These feasts are listed in Leviticus 23 and are as follows: Passover, Feast of Unleavened Bread, Feast of Firstfruits, Feast of Weeks (or Pentecost), Feast of Trumpets, Day of Atonement, and Feast of Tabernacles.

The Day of Atonement, which fell on the tenth day of the seventh month (the Jewish month of *Tishri*), stood out among the seven as not only being oddly unique but also highly significant:

- It was the only feast where there is mention of atonement being made on behalf of the congregation:

    Also on the tenth day of this seventh month there shall be a day of atonement: it shall be an holy convocation unto you; and ye shall afflict your souls, and offer an offering made by fire unto the LORD. And ye shall do no work in that same day: for it is a day of atonement, to make an atonement for you before the LORD your God.... For on that day shall the priest make an atonement for you that you may be clean from all your sins before the Lord. (Lev. 16:27, 28, 30)

- It was the only feast that carried a degree of solemnity so great that anyone who treated it lightly and ignored its imperatives was placed under severe threat of death. "For whatsoever soul *it be* that shall not be afflicted in that same day, he shall be cut off from among his people. And whatsoever soul *it be* that doeth any work in that same day, the same soul will I destroy from among his people" (23:29, 30).

- The Day of Atonement was a day of fasting and self-denial, while the other feasts were days of feasting and celebration.

- An entire chapter was written to explain, in great detail, the rituals performed on that day to cleanse the sanctuary and congregation (see ch. 16).

- All seven national feasts were considered ceremonial sabbaths in which work was prohibited. All the feasts, however, except the Day of Atonement, only prohibited "servile work" or heavy manual labor usually assigned to the slaves and servants.[87] On the Day of Atonement, "no work," "no manner of work," or "any

---

[87] Regarding the Passover, it is written: "In the first day ye shall have an holy convocation: ye shall *do no servile work* therein" (Lev. 23:7, emphasis added). Servile work was also prohibited on the Day of Pentecost. "And ye shall proclaim on the selfsame day, that it may be an holy convocation unto you: ye shall *do no servile work* therein: it shall be a statute for ever in all your dwellings throughout your generations" (v. 21, emphasis added). Regarding the Feast of Trumpets, "Ye shall *do no servile work* therein: but ye shall offer an offering made by fire unto the LORD" (v. 25, emphasis added). Regarding the Feast of Tabernacles, "On the first day shall be an holy convocation: ye shall *do no servile work* therein. Seven days ye shall offer an offering made by fire unto the LORD: on the eighth day shall be an holy convocation unto you; and ye shall offer an offering made by fire unto the LORD: it is a solemn assembly; and ye shall *do no servile work* therein" (vs. 35, 36, emphasis added). On the Day of Atonement, however, no manner of work was to be done.

work" was to be done. It carried the same work prohibition as did the Seventh-day Sabbath. "Six days shall work be done: but the seventh day is the sabbath of rest, an holy convocation; ye shall do no work therein: it is the sabbath of the LORD in all your dwellings" (23:3).

- It is therefore evident that the yearly Day of Atonement sabbath was placed on the same level of importance as is the weekly moral Sabbath.

The Day of Atonement Compared with the Daily Service

The service on the day of atonement carries greater significance when compared to the daily service. During the daily service, the common priests' ministration was restricted to the courtyard and the first apartment of the sanctuary. On the day of atonement, however, the officiating high priest went as far as the second apartment of the sanctuary and made a final atonement, which resulted in the cleansing of the entire camp from sin and uncleanness, namely the priests, congregation and two apartments of the sanctuary (see 16:30, 33).

The atonement made by the common priests daily was merely *partial*,[88] resulting in the forgiveness of confessed sin and its transfer into the sanctuary, thus defiling it in the process. On the day of atonement, the atonement made for sin was *full* and *final*, resulting in the complete and permanent cleansing of the congregation, priests, and the sanctuary from all the sins that had polluted it, transferring them on to the head of the scapegoat (See Lev. 16:21).

The Day of Atonements

Interestingly enough, the word "atonement," as used in connection with the day of atonement, is in the plural form in the original Hebrew. "Also on the tenth day of this seventh month there shall be

---

[88] "Important truths concerning the atonement were taught the people by this yearly service. In the sin offerings presented during the year, a substitute had been accepted in the sinner's stead; but *the blood of the victim had not made full atonement* for the sin. It had only provided a means by which the sin was transferred to the sanctuary" (White, *Patriarchs and Prophets*, pp. 355, 356, emphasis added).

a day of *atonement[s]*: it shall be an holy convocation unto you; and ye shall afflict your souls, and offer an offering made by fire unto the LORD. And ye shall do no work in that same day: for it is a day of *atonement[s]*, to make an atonement for you before the LORD your God" (Lev. 23:27, 28, emphasis added). In this passage, the plural form *kippurim* ("atonements") is used instead of the singular word *kipper* ("atonement").

In Exodus 30:10, the word "atonement" is expressed in the plural form, even in the English translation: "And Aaron shall make an atonement upon the horns of it once in a year with the blood of the sin offering of *atonements*: once in the year shall he make atonement upon it throughout your generations: it is most holy unto the LORD" (emphasis added). The altar of incense in the first apartment of the sanctuary was to be cleansed once a year "with the blood of the sin offering of atonements."

Why then use the plural form of the word "atonement" (*kippurim*) when referring to the day of atonement? An apparent reason may be found in the fact that on that day, the high priest made several atonements. In Leviticus 16:33, Aaron shall:

1. "make an atonement for the holy sanctuary" (The most holy place)

2. "make an atonement for the tabernacle of the congregation" (holy place)

3. "make an atonement for the priests"

4. "and for all the people of the congregation"

Here, we see why the plural form of the word "atonement" is used. Multiple atonements were made on that day. But there is more.

In Hebrew, the plural form of a word is often used to denote a larger *quantity* or better *quality* than if the word had been expressed in the singular form. For instance, when speaking of an individual member of the Godhead, the word *El* is used, as in *El Shaddai* ("The Almighty God," see Exod. 6:3). On the cross, Jesus addressed His Father in this manner: "And about the ninth hour Jesus cried with a loud voice, saying, *Eli, Eli, lama sabachthani? that is to say, My God, my God, why hast thou forsaken me?*" (Matt. 27:46, emphasis added). The singular form of "God" (*El*) is again used because the prayer was addressed to a single member of the Godhead: the heavenly Father.

The plural form of "God," *Elohim*, is often used to denote the Godhead's totality. For example, "And God [*Elohim*] said, Let *us* make man in our image, after *our* likeness" (Gen. 1:26, emphasis added). The entire Godhead was involved in the work of creation. Therefore, the plural form of "God" was used in the passage.

The singular form of the word "holy" in Hebrew is *qodesh*, which is used to refer to the holy place or first apartment of the sanctuary. The plural form of that same word is *qodeshim*, which is used when speaking of the second apartment of the sanctuary. "And thou shalt hang up the vail under the taches, that thou mayest bring in thither within the vail the ark of the testimony: and the vail shall divide unto you between the holy place [*qodesh*] and the most holy [*qodeshim*]" (Exod. 26:33). It is also used for "most holy things" (Lev. 2:3, 10). In the Greek, "hagia" (holies) which is the plural form of "hagios" (holy), is used in Heb. 9:12 and 24 to refer to the entire sanctuary with its two apartments.

Finally, the plural form of the word "atonement," *kippurim*, is used to differentiate it from the partial atonement (*kippur*) made daily by the priest. During the great antitypical day of atonement, the final atonement Jesus makes is full and complete—of the highest quality and greatest degree possible. It results in the fixing of the characters of God's people, the eradication of the records of their sins from the books of heaven, the permanent cleansing of the heavenly sanctuary from sin, the final downfall of the oppressive kingdoms of this world, and the great controversy being brought to an end!

Why the Silence on the Subject of the Day of Atonement?

We must now delve into the meaning of the silence in the New Testament when it comes to the theology and observance of the Day of Atonement. One might be inclined to think the subject would loom prominently in the biblical landscape, since it is such an important topic. One might even suppose the New Testament writers would naturally be inclined to expound upon it to a very substantial degree, since it points to the glory-filled, closing work of the gospel on earth in the last days. On the contrary, the New Testament authors are admittedly very uncommunicative when it comes to the subject. Outside the Old Testament mention of the cleansing of the sanctuary on the day of atonement (see Lev. 16; Dan. 8:14), projections of it in the New Testament are extremely rare and lacking theological substance.

> *We must now delve into the meaning of the silence in the New Testament when it comes to the theology and observance of the Day of Atonement. One might be inclined to think the subject would loom prominently in the biblical landscape, since it is such an important topic.*

One significant consideration needs to be taken into account at this point. As a matter of principle, light is given on an "on-demand" basis. In other words, light is given only to those who need it, when they need it. Truths that do not pertain to individuals or groups of individuals are not imparted to them; light is not revealed when it is not necessary.

To illustrate, as Jesus was walking with some of His disciples on the shores of the Sea of Tiberias after He had risen from the dead, Peter had the occasion to inquire as to what John's future was going to be. "Peter seeing him saith to Jesus, Lord, and what *shall* this man *do*?" Jesus replied by saying, "If I will that he tarry till I come, what *is that* to thee? follow thou me" (John 21:21, 22). Peter was denied light on something that did not pertain to him.

Again, when asked by His disciples as to when He would restore the kingdom of Israel, an event that would take place far into the future, "Jesus said unto them, It is not for you to know the times or the seasons, which the Father hath put in his own power" (Acts 1:6, 7). This fact helps us understand why the New Testament writers did not and could not write much at all about the Day of Atonement during their time.

The truths relating to the cleansing of the sanctuary on the antitypical day of atonement in the time of the end would find no significance or application to the people living either in the time of Jesus and the apostles or the many eras beforehand. Therefore, in His infinite wisdom, God saw it fit to seal up the truth until then. "But thou, O Daniel, shut up the words, and seal the book, even to the time of the end: many shall run to and fro, and knowledge shall be increased" (Dan. 12:4).

Daniel himself wanted to know the meaning of these truths but was denied. In 12:7, the angel Gabriel explained that after God's people are persecuted for centuries, everything would be finished. "And I heard the man clothed in linen, which was upon the waters of the river, when he held up his right hand and his left hand unto heaven, and sware by him that liveth for ever that it shall be for a time, times, and an half; and when he shall have accomplished to scatter the power of the holy people, all these things shall be finished." The prophetic timeline "time, times, and an half" translates to 1,260 literal years using the day-year principle and reaches to the time of the end. [89]

In the next verse, Daniel expressed a desire to know about the events that would transpire after this long period of time is fulfilled: "And I heard, but I understood not: then said I, O my Lord, what shall be the end of these things?" The CEV says, "How will it all end?" The ESV says, "What shall be the outcome of these things?" The ISV renders the verse as follows: "I heard, but I didn't understand. So I asked, 'Sir, what happens next?'" Daniel wanted to personally know what would happen after the period designated as "time, times and half a time" is fulfilled.

---

[89] This prophetic timeline, "time, times, and a half," is known as the Dark Ages. It stretched from AD 538 to 1798, for a total of 1,260 long years. During this period, as history attests, God's church endured horrendous persecution at the hands of Roman ecclesiastical powers. See Numbers 14:34 and Ezekiel 4:4-6 for precedents of the day-year equivalency.

To this, the angel Gabriel merely responded by saying, "Go thy way, Daniel: for the words are closed up and sealed till the time of the end" (v. 9). Rather than satisfying Daniel's curiosity and explaining the events that would transpire after the Dark Ages, the angel merely reminded him that light on these events had been sealed up even to the time of the end. Hence, not even the prophet Daniel was to know about the nature of the momentous events that would transpire in the time of the end: the cleansing of the sanctuary, the day of atonement, the investigative judgment, etc. No one was to understand the truths concerning the closing work of Jesus in the Most Holy Place of the heavenly sanctuary until it is unsealed during the time of the end.

In the book of Hebrews, written around AD 65, Paul described the first apartment of the sanctuary this way: "For there was a tabernacle made; the first, wherein was the candlestick and the table, and the shewbread; which is called the sanctuary" (9:2). He described the service conducted in that apartment daily by saying, "Now when these things were thus ordained, the priests went always into the first tabernacle, accomplishing the service of God" (v. 6). Regarding the work in the second apartment of the sanctuary, this is what he had to say:

> And after the second veil, the tabernacle which is called the Holiest of all; Which had the golden censer, and the ark of the covenant overlaid round about with gold, wherein [was] the golden pot that had manna, and Aaron's rod that budded, and the tables of the covenant; And over it the cherubims of glory shadowing the mercyseat; *of which we cannot now speak particularly*. (Heb. 9:3–5, emphasis added)

When it came to the work that was to be accomplished in the second apartment of the heavenly sanctuary, an event still future in Paul's time, he could not *now* (during his time) speak about it. The NIV translation says it more clearly: "But we cannot discuss these things in detail now." Understandably so, for the cleansing of the sanctuary on the antitypical day of atonement was still sealed up in Paul's time. It would remain sealed up until the time of the end, as the angel told Daniel. Even Paul, the great apostle had nothing particular to say about the final ministration of Christ in the second apartment of the heavenly sanctuary.

This understanding explains why the New Testament writers were silent on the topic of the Day of Atonement. Jesus spoke nothing about it, and neither did His disciples after Him. Along with Daniel, the New Testament writers were "left in the dark" when it came to the critical knowledge and understanding of the final ministration of Jesus in the heavenly sanctuary. This knowledge has been reserved for those who would live in the last days.

The Light on the End-time Truths Unsealed

This is where the Seventh-day Adventist Church comes in. This church has become the recipient of the bright, glorious, unsealed light of the cleansing of the sanctuary on the antitypical day of atonement! The Seventh-day Adventist church today possesses the light that had been kept secret for many centuries. We dare not take this truth for granted. There is no reason for us to remain in the dark when it comes to understanding this truth, for light on the subject is now shining brightly.

After the 2,300-day prophecy of Daniel 8:14 expired in 1844, this once-sealed portion of Daniel's prophecy has been unsealed. Paul's words regarding the closing ministration of Jesus in the Most Holy Place of the heavenly sanctuary, "of which we cannot now speak particularly" (Heb. 9:5), no longer hold. It is the privilege of every serious student of the Bible today to fully grasp the truth about the final ministration of Jesus in the heavenly sanctuary. "Many will run to and fro [in their Bibles], and knowledge [about the sanctuary] shall be increased" (Dan. 12:4). There is no more reason for the truth about the cleansing of the sanctuary on the day of atonement to remain sealed up in our understanding, since God has permitted the light on that subject to shine out of darkness.

Cherishing the Light for Our Day

Just as it was the privilege of the Jews to understand those prophecies that pertained to *their* time,[90] it is our privilege today to understand the prophecies that pertain to *our* time: the cleansing of the sanctuary, the investigative judgment, the three angels' messages, and other related truths. There is no excuse for anyone to be ignorant of these truths, as they have been fully unsealed since 1844. Neglecting to study these topics is willful ignorance!

The Jews in the time of Jesus suffered eternal loss because of their willful neglect to receive the truths that pertained to their time. We dare not repeat the same mistakes they made. We cannot afford to be ignorant or silent with respect to the cleansing of the sanctuary and other truths, for heaven looks upon it as a betrayal of sacred trusts.

> The Lord has made his people the repository of sacred truth. Upon every individual who has had the light of present truth devolves the duty of developing that truth on a higher scale than it has hitherto been done. But should we be in trust of sacred, advanced truth, and yet be satisfied to work in narrow, selfish lines? The Lord will hold us accountable for the influence we might have exerted but did not, because we have not earnestly tried to understand our accountability in this world. We shall either glorify or dishonor God.[91]

---

[90] See White, *The Desire of Ages*, p. 204.
[91] White, "Ye are the Light of the World," *The Home Missionary*, July 1, 1897.

11

Investigating the Investigative Judgment

Idea in Brief: This chapter examines historic Adventism's core teaching of the investigative judgment in light of some of the major objections being leveled against it. It gives arguments from Scripture to show that those objections are misplaced and without basis.

A Problematic Teaching

Along with the sanctuary doctrine, the investigative judgment has received much flak from within and without Adventism. Prominent church figures, pastors, and members alike have concluded they can no longer honestly sustain their position on that core belief of the church.

Just before he died in 1916, Ellet J. Waggoner, who rose to fame at the 1888 General Conference Session in Minneapolis, Minnesota, wrote that he could no longer subscribe to the idea of an investigative judgment and remain a believer in Christ.[92] To him, the thought

> Along with the sanctuary doctrine, the investigative judgment has received much flak from within and without Adventism. Prominent church figures, pastors, and members alike have concluded they can no longer honestly sustain their position on that core belief of the church.

---

[92] See Waggoner, *Confession of Faith*. Online copy available at https://1ref.us/1s8 (accessed November 4, 2021).

that God investigates the lives of those who believe in Christ is objectionable and irreconcilable with his concept of righteousness by faith. The list of detractors from Adventism's distinctive teaching of the investigative judgment continues to grow.

Needless to say, the church stands or falls depending on whether or not her teaching of an investigative judgment can withstand scrutiny and... well... investigation.

Why Adventists Believe in the Investigative Judgment

Historic Adventists teach that at the termination of 2,300 prophetic years in 1844, the Ancient of days (God the Father) and the Son of man (Jesus) moved to the second apartment of the heavenly sanctuary to begin a work of investigative judgment (see Dan. 8:14; 7:9–13). They teach that an investigation of the books of record is conducted in conjunction with the cleansing of the heavenly sanctuary from the sins that have polluted it. Seventh-day Adventists believe this work of examining the books of record and people's lives determines their eternal destiny.[93] They also believe the announcement "Fear God and give glory to Him for the hour of judgment is come," contained in the first angel's message of Revelation 14, is an announcement that the investigative judgment prophesied in Daniel 7:9–10 has been convened.

How important is the doctrine of the investigative judgment to Seventh-day Adventists? It is a core belief of the church. It is a central pillar in their theology. Take this doctrine away, and Adventism loses its reason for being. The denomination becomes the proverbial salt that has lost its savor. In all honesty, one cannot call himself or herself a Seventh-day Adventist and not subscribe to the teachings of an investigative judgment and the sanctuary.

Adventists hold that the subject of the investigative judgment, along with the sanctuary, is a faith and salvation issue and therefore needs to be clearly understood:

---

[93] See White, *The Great Controversy*, pp. 479, 482, 490; *Sons and Daughters of God*, p. 355.

The subject of the sanctuary and the investigative judgment should be clearly understood by the people of God. All need a knowledge for themselves of the position and work of their great High Priest. *Otherwise, it will be impossible for them to exercise the faith which is essential at this time or to occupy the position which God designs them to fill. Every individual has a soul to save or to lose.* Each has a case pending at the bar of God. Each must meet the great Judge face to face. [94]

Objections to the Investigative Judgment

Unfortunately, as already mentioned, this teaching of a pre-advent judgment, instead of being accepted and appreciated, is under vigorous attack by the Christian world at large and many within Adventism itself. Here are some of the objections being leveled against the teaching of the investigative judgment:

> **OBJECTION #1:** The Adventist teaching of the investigative judgment is only a fabrication of Ellen White. It was introduced to explain away the great disappointment of 1844.[95] It is not taught in the Bible.

> **OBJECTION #2:** The expression "investigative judgment" is not even found anywhere in the Bible. Therefore, it is unbiblical.

> **Objection #3:** Only the wicked are judged, but not God's people; they are exempt from this judgment. Therefore, it is not correct to teach that Christian believers go through an investigative judgment.

---

[94] White, *The Great Controversy*, p. 488 (emphasis added).
[95] In his September 1957 *Eternity* editorial, Donald Barnhouse, a prominent Evangelical speaker and publisher, labeled Adventism's teaching of an investigative judgment "the most colossal, psychological, face-saving phenomenon in religious history." In that same article, he further wrote, "We personally do not believe that there is even a suspicion of a verse in Scripture to sustain such a peculiar position, and we further believe that any effort to establish it is stale, flat and unprofitable."

Objection #4: Objectors insist the Adventist doctrine of the investigative judgment robs the Christian of peace and the assurance of present salvation. Therefore, the Adventist teaching of an investigative judgment undermines the gospel and should be rejected.

Answer to Objection #1:

Indeed, it cannot be denied that Ellen White wrote much on the subject of the investigative judgment. What follows is just a small sampling of what she had written on the subject:

> In 1844 our great High Priest entered the most holy place of the heavenly sanctuary, to begin the work of the investigative judgment. The cases of the righteous dead have been passing in review before God. When that work shall be completed, judgment is to be pronounced upon the living.[96]
>
> When we become children of God, our names are written in the Lamb's book of life, and they remain there until the time of the Investigative Judgment. Then the name of every individual will be called, and his record examined, by Him who declares, 'I know thy works.'[97]

The Origin of the Doctrine of the Investigative Judgment

While it is true that Ellen White wrote much about the investigative judgment, so did many prominent Adventists who were contemporary with her. Their writings on the subject are found in numerous books and articles in various denominational papers. Foremost of these were O. R. L. Crosier, Uriah Smith, J. N. Andrews, Joseph Bates, J. H. Waggoner, James White, and others.

A study of the historical development of Seventh-day Adventist theology reveals the investigative judgment doctrine did not originate with Ellen White. The concept of a pre-advent judgment

---

[96] White, *Selected Messages*, book 1, p. 125.
[97] White, *The Seventh-day Adventist Bible Commentary*, vol. 7, p. 987. See also *Christ's Object Lessons*, p. 310; *The Great Controversy*, pp. 421, 422, 425.

was introduced to the Millerite believers by Methodist theologian Josiah Litch as early as 1840.[98] It was based on Daniel 7, the Day of Atonement in Leviticus 16, and the marriage parables in Matthew 22 and 25. After the great disappointment of 1844, the Sunday-keeping Millerites continued to promote Litch's concept of a pre-advent judgment. These were published in the Millerite papers. Ellen White had no contribution here whatsoever.

By the mid-to-late 1840s, the idea of an investigative judgment was soon abandoned by the non-Sabbatarian Millerites. However, the Sabbatarian Adventists retained it and developed it further with the sanctuary and the atonement. Joseph Bates then became the principal writer on the matter of the investigative judgment from 1846 to 1850.[99] At this time, J. N. Loughborough and Uriah Smith systematically developed the Adventist doctrine of the investigative judgment.[100]

In 1857, James White embraced the teaching and was the first among the pioneers of the Seventh-day Adventist Church to use the expression "investigative judgment."[101] He also wrote the most extensive article on the subject during that year.[102] During this time, White saw the connection between the investigative judgment and the message to the church of Laodicea. He saw it as a much-needed appeal for repentance and spiritual preparedness on the part of God's people living in the time of judgment.[103]

Over the years, pioneers of the Seventh-day Adventist Church have developed the doctrine of the investigative judgment further, not by deriving material from the writings of Ellen White, but by using a large pool of biblical data from both the Old and New Testaments.

- **Daniel 7:9–13**—The investigative judgment in heaven is convened; both the Ancient of days and the Son of man come to

---

[98] See Holbrook, ed., *The Seventy Weeks, Leviticus, and the Nature of Prophecy*, p. 119.
[99] *Ibid.*, p. 120.
[100] See Schwarz *Light Bearers*, p. 164.
[101] See Appendix, Exhibit A: James White, "The Judgment," *The Review and Herald*, January 29, 1857, pp. 100, 101.
[102] See Holbrook, ed., *Doctrine of the Sanctuary: A Historical Survey*, p. 89.
[103] *Ibid.*

the place of judgment: the Most Holy Place. The context pinpoints this judgment as occurring after the 1,260 years of activity by the little horn power but before the second advent.

- **Daniel 8:14**—This passage provides the timing of the commencement of the investigative judgment: 1844.

- **Daniel 12:1–2; Revelation 20:6**—Those whose names are found in the book of life are delivered and resurrected to receive eternal life at the second coming of Jesus. The investigative judgment determines whose names are either found in the book of life or not.

- **Leviticus 16 and 23**—Those who do not afflict their souls on the day of atonement are cut off; the work of cutting off presupposes a work of examination—a work of judgment.

- **Malachi 3**—the purging of the sons of Levi in the temple parallels the events of Leviticus 16 and Daniel 7 and 8.

- **Acts 3:19**—This sheds light on the blotting out of sins by the heavenly High Priest before His return to the earth; this work of blotting out sins presupposes a work of examining the records to see whose sins will be blotted out and whose sins will not be blotted out before the second coming of Jesus.

- **Matthew 22 and 25**—The examination of the guests in the parable of the wedding garment (22) portrays a work of investigation and judgment to determine who has a part in the marriage supper. Likewise, the parable of the ten virgins (25) implies a work of investigation to determine who will or will not have a part in the marriage supper of the Lamb.

- **Revelation 14:6–13**—The projection into the future of the judgment scenario described in Daniel 7 is found in the first angel's proclamation of the judgment hour. "The hour of his judgment is come." People's destinies are determined in the judgment based on their responses to these messages.

- **1 Peter 4:17**—The work of investigative judgment begins at the house of God.

- **Ezekiel 9:6**—This verse assumes a work of investigation to determine who receives the mark of deliverance on the forehead before the slaughter, which begins at God's sanctuary.

- **Revelation 7:1–3**—The sealing work presupposes a work of judgment to determine who receives the seal of God on the foreheads and who does not.

- **Revelation 22:11**—The investigative judgment ends with this solemn verdict for each case, from which there is no appeal. "He that is holy let him be holy still, and he that is filthy let him be filthy still."

- **Matthew 24:13; 1 John 5:12**—These passages have to do with the doctrine of perseverance. The investigative judgment determines who has endured until the end. Believers who have the Son have life right now, but their ultimate salvation is determined if they endure until the end.

- **Spring and Autumn typology**—Spring ceremonies (Passover, Firstfruits, Pentecost) were fulfilled in connection with the first advent of Jesus. In contrast, the autumn ceremonies (Feast of Trumpets, Day of Atonement, Feast of Tabernacles) apply to events associated with the second coming of Jesus. This observation places the timing of the investigative judgment during the antitypical day of atonement as an end-time event.

Recovery of Long-hidden Truths

When the history of the development of Adventist beliefs is brought into consideration, one realizes prophecy was being fulfilled. The establishment of Adventism's unique system of truth is nothing short of the fulfillment of Daniel 12:4, when truths pertaining to the time of the end are unsealed: "Many shall run to and fro and knowledge will be increased." The investigative judgment falls within the category of these unsealed truths and therefore demands a thorough investigation.

The rapid discovery of light on the sanctuary, investigative judgment, Sabbath, and other related truths after 1844 corroborates divine working within Adventism to bring about the recovery of truths that have been long hidden.

> This recovery involved the truth of the one-for-all Act of Atonement on the cross and subsequent mediatorial Priesthood of Christ in the heavenly sanctuary, together with the eternal moral law and its enshrined Sabbath. And along with that was the awesome transaction we have come to call the 'Investigative Judgment'—and thence on to the final events.
>
> Such a revival of these specific truths, just at this time, came not through the foresight and planning of man. Rather, the appointed hour had come in the plan and provision of God for the discovery—or, more accurately, the recovery—and establishment of these neglected but latent truths.
>
> The hour on the prophetic clock had struck. And so, with the coming of the hour, men obviously called of God were impelled to search out and proclaim the special truths now due to the world—truths that were fundamental to the emergence and development of God's distinctive Church and Message for the last days. It was an epochal hour.[104]

It is the privilege of the church to be the repository of these once-sealed-up, sacred truths. Rather than making apologies for this unpopular doctrine, the church needs to restore it to the forefront of its theology, where it belongs! They are enjoined to "earnestly contend for the faith that was once delivered to the saints" (Jude 3).

Answer to Objection #2

Objectors discredit the teaching of the Investigative Judgment based on the observation that the term itself is found nowhere in Scripture. The truth is, just because "investigative judgment" is not found in the

---

[104] Froom. *The Movement of Destiny*, p. 78.

Investigating the Investigative Judgment

Bible does not mean it is unbiblical. This technical objection falls apart when it is realized that certain core teachings of Christianity are accepted as legitimate, even though the expressions used to identify them are not necessarily found in the Bible.

For instance, the word "trinity" is not found in the Bible, yet most Christians do not question the teaching of the triune nature of the Godhead, based on passages like Matthew 28:19: "Go ye therefore, and teach all nations, baptizing them in the name of the Father, and of the Son, and the Holy Ghost."

The expression "close of probation" is not found in the Bible, either. Still, Christians have no problem embracing the concept of the closing of humanity's probation, based on such texts as Daniel 12:1, Revelation 11:17–18, and 15:1. The closing of humanity's probation is implied in the shutting of the door to the marriage chamber in the parable of the ten virgins: "And while they went to buy, the bridegroom came; and they that were ready went in with him to the marriage: and the door was shut" (Matt. 25:10).

Neither "substitution" nor "substitute" are found anywhere in the Bible. However, Christians believe Christ is their Substitute, based on texts like 1 Peter 3:18: "For Christ also hath once suffered for sins, the just for the unjust, that he might bring us to God, being put to death in the flesh, but quickened by the Spirit" (see also Rom. 5:6; Heb. 2:9). Substitution is what gives life to the gospel, and without it, salvation is not possible. Therefore, the teaching of an "investigative judgment" should not be rejected simply because the expression is not found in the Bible.

The expression "investigative judgment" may not be found in Scripture, but the *concept* is entirely biblical. Hundreds of years ago, Daniel was given a prophetic view of this judgment taking place in heaven:

> I beheld till the thrones were cast down, and the Ancient of days did sit, whose garment [was] white as snow, and the hair of his head like the pure wool: his throne [was like] the fiery flame, [and] his wheels [as] burning fire. A fiery stream issued and came forth

from before him: thousand thousands ministered unto him, and ten thousand times ten thousand stood before him: the *judgment was set*, and the *books were opened*. (Daniel 7:9, 10, emphasis added)

The Ancient of days is God the Father. "Before the mountains were brought forth, or ever Thou hadst formed the earth and the world, even from everlasting to everlasting, Thou art God" (Ps. 90:2). The expression "the judgment was set" shows the scenario being depicted is a work of judgment in progress. The expression "the books were opened" presupposes a work of investigation and examination of the books of record. Therefore, the use of the term "investigative judgment" is appropriate.

Furthermore, this work of judgment taking place in heaven occurs just before Jesus returns to establish His kingdom on earth. This is why it is also referred to as the "pre-advent judgment." It is an end-time event, as seen in the fact that it occurs at the tail end of a long chronology of events from Daniel's time until the second coming of Christ. These events include:

1. The establishment of the Babylonian kingdom (v. 4—represented by the lion)

2. The establishment of the kingdoms of the Medes and the Persians (v. 5—represented by the bear)

3. The establishment of the Greek empire (v. 6—represented by the leopard)

4. The rise of imperial Rome (v. 7—represented by the non-descript beast with ten horns)

5. The formation of papal power from the ruins of pagan Rome (v. 8—represented by the little horn)

6. The convening of the investigative judgment (v. 9, 10— "thrones cast down… the judgment was set, and the books were opened")

7. The establishment of Christ's kingdom of glory at His second coming (v. 14).

The projection of this end-time, pre-advent, investigative judgment prophecy into the future is found in Revelation 14:7: "Fear God and give glory to Him for the hour of his judgment is come." What comes next is the harvest of the earth at the coming of Jesus (see vs. 14–20). If the judgment-hour proclamation of Revelation 14 is not the fulfillment of the judgment prophecy of Daniel 7:9–10, then that prophecy has neither a literal fulfillment in the Old Testament nor a prophetic fulfillment in the future. This would make it a prophecy that was never intended to be fulfilled, which goes entirely against God's modus operandi (see Amos 3:7; Hab. 2:2–4).

Answer to Objection #3:

This objection contemplates the idea of an investigative judgment, but only for the wicked and the lost. The saints are supposedly "exempt" from this investigative judgment according to this objection. Their cases need no examination, supposedly, because of their faith in Christ. Desmond Ford has maintained that the judgment scenario described in Daniel 7:9–14 is not the investigative judgment of the saints, as Adventists have traditionally interpreted it, but rather the judgment of the little horn power—according to him, Antiochus Epiphanes.[105]

Walter Martin, a prominent evangelical author and apologist in the 1960s and 1970s, and a vehement opponent of the Adventist teaching of the investigative judgment, wrote the following:

> Since our Lord knows the disposition of cases allegedly being reviewed in heaven, what need is there of an Investigative Judgment? We believe that the Scriptures decidedly do not warrant such a doctrine.[106]
>
> The Greek deals a devastating blow to the Seventh-day Adventist concept of Investigative Judgment: "He that hears my word and believes on Him that sent me has everlasting life

---

[105] See *Daniel 8:14, The Day of Atonement, and the Investigative Judgment*, p. 29.
[106] *The Truth About Seventh-day Adventism*, p. 182.

and shall not come under judgment but has passed from death to life." Christians therefore, need not anticipate any Investigative Judgment for their sins.[107]

The Rationale for the Investigative Judgment

The investigative judgment is not for the Lord's benefit. "The Lord knoweth them that are His" (2 Tim. 2:19). It is for the onlooking universe. It is to remove any doubts as to why any given individual is decreed to be either saved or lost. Satan had insinuated doubts into the minds of the angels, and human beings for that matter, accusing God of injustice and unfairness in dealing with His creatures. Therefore, an investigative judgment is convened; the books of heaven are opened to set the record straight. In the end, this judgment will reveal that Satan's claims about the character of God have been false all along.

> And they sing the song of Moses the servant of God, and the song of the Lamb, saying, Great and marvellous *are* thy works, Lord God Almighty; just and true *are* thy ways, thou King of saints. Who shall not fear thee, O Lord, and glorify thy name? for *thou* only *art* holy: for all nations shall come and worship before thee; for thy judgments are made manifest. (Rev. 15:3, 4)

The investigative judgment is not to discover truth but rather to reveal it. This work of examination will reveal the rebellion Satan began in heaven, with all its bitter consequences over time, was inexcusable. In the investigative judgment, the 144,000 perfected saints are called in to demonstrate there is no excuse for sinning. Then, the wicked will know how offensive sin is to God as the plagues start falling on their shelterless heads (see vs. 5–7).

Examining the Greek Text

Walter Martin concluded, from the Greek text of John 5:24, there is no pre-advent, investigative judgment for believers in Christ.

---

[107] *Ibid.*, p. 178.

"Verily, verily, I say unto you, He that heareth my word, and believeth on him that sent me, hath everlasting life, and shall not come into *condemnation*; but is passed from death unto life" (emphasis added). The word "condemnation" in the passage comes from the Greek word *krisis*. The same Greek word is used in Revelation 14:7: "the hour of His judgment [*krisis*] is come."

Martin assumed the proclamation of the judgment-hour message in Revelation 14:7 does not concern the saints because they do not come into judgment but are passed from death to life, according to John 5:24. It is somewhat premature to come to that conclusion when there are other passages where *krisis* is not translated as "judgment" but rather as "condemnation":

> And this is the condemnation [*krisis*], that light is come into the world, and men loved darkness rather than light because their deeds were evil. (John 3:19).
>
> But above all things, my brethren, swear not, neither by heaven, neither by the earth, neither by any other oath: but let your yea be yea; and your nay, nay; lest ye fall into condemnation [*krisis*]. (James 5:12)

Getting deeper into our analysis of the Greek of the passage in question, John 5:24, the verb phrase "shall not come under condemnation" is not in the future tense but rather the present indicative tense. It is more accurately translated as "*is not come* under condemnation." In other words, the saints are not under condemnation at the present time. This tells us John 5:24 is not speaking of judgment in the future, eschatological sense, but instead of the Christian's current standing. The tense of the verb in the phrase that follows is also in the perfect tense, not future: "but *is passed* from death unto life."

Hence, in the Greek of John 5:24, the tenses of both expressions in question show the passage is not addressing a future, latter-day judgment of the saints, but rather their present status in Christ. It is concerned with affirming what believers in Christ already possess in their hands at present: justification and life. It is not concerned about their standing during a future judgment.

It seems Walter Martin tried to build an argument from one Greek word (*krisis*) without considering the whole meaning of the passage or finding out whether it is speaking of the Christian's current standing before God or has in mind the future, eschatological aspect of the judgment. We, therefore, need to respectfully disagree with his opinion that "the Greek [of John 5:24] deals a devastating blow to the Seventh-day Adventist concept of Investigative Judgment."[108]

John 5:24 is not talking about the "hour of judgment" that started in 1844, which was still future in John's time. It is saying the believer who stands justified in Christ and is perfect in Him is not condemned at present. This is the case because Jesus sits at the right hand of God and intercedes for that believer. "Who is he that condemneth? It is Christ that died, yea rather, that is risen again, who is even at the right hand of God, who also maketh intercession for us" (Rom. 8:34).

John 5:24 perfectly agrees with what Paul stated regarding the Christian's current standing: "There is therefore *now* no condemnation to them which are in Christ Jesus who walk not after the flesh but after the Spirit" (Rom. 8:1).

In the words of Ellen White, "If you give yourself to Him, and accept Him as your Saviour, then, sinful as your life may have been, for His sake you are accounted

> If Dr. Martin still insists there is no future judgment of the saints, then he is in plain disagreement with Scripture, which declares that everyone, both good and bad, will pass through a future judgment, which is convened before Jesus comes, just as Seventh-day Adventists teach

---

[108] "Is not come into condemnation" is "καὶ εἰς κρίσιν οὐκ ἔρχεται" in the Greek. The verb "ἔρχεται" (*erchetai*), which means "to come into," is in the present tense, indicative mood, passive voice.
"But has passed from death unto life" is "ἀλλὰ μεταβέβηκεν ἐκ τοῦ θανάτου εἰς τὴν ζωήν." The verb μεταβέβηκεν (*metabebeken*) is in the perfect tense, indicative mood, active voice.

Investigating the Investigative Judgment

righteous. Christ's character stands in place of your character, and you are accepted before God just as if you had not sinned."[109]

If Dr. Martin still insists there is no future judgment of the saints, then he is in plain disagreement with Scripture, which declares that everyone, both good and bad, will pass through a future judgment, which is convened before Jesus comes, just as Seventh-day Adventists teach:

- "I said in mine heart, God shall judge the righteous and the wicked: for there is a time there [future] for every purpose and for every work" (Eccles. 3:17).

- "But we are sure that the judgment of God is according to truth against them which commit such things. And thinkest thou this, O man, that judgest them which do such things, and doest the same, that thou shalt escape the judgment of God?" (Rom. 2:2, 3).

- "For as many as have sinned without law shall also perish without law: and as many as have sinned in the law shall be judged by the law" (v. 12).

- "God forbid: yea, let God be true, but every man a liar; as it is written, That thou mightest be justified in thy sayings, and mightest overcome when thou art judged" (3:4).

- "For *we* shall all stand before the judgment seat of Christ [a future event]" (14:10, emphasis added).

- "For I know nothing by myself; yet am I not hereby justified: but he that judgeth me is the Lord" (1 Cor. 4:4).

- "But when *we* are judged, we are chastened of the Lord, that we should not be condemned with the world" (11:32).

- "For *we* must all appear before the judgment seat of Christ; that every one may receive the things [done] in [his] body, according

---

[109] *Steps to Christ*, p. 62.

to that he hath done, whether [it be] good or bad" (2 Cor. 5:10, emphasis added).

- "The Lord shall judge his people [not just the wicked]" (Heb. 10:30).

- "So speak ye, and so do, as they that shall be judged by the law of liberty" (James 2:12).

- "Judgment begins at the house of God" (1 Peter 4:17).

When the larger body of Scripture is taken into account, it becomes evident that it argues strongly for a future judgment for the saints, not just the wicked.

Answer to Objection #4:

Perhaps the most serious objection to the Seventh-day Adventist teaching of the investigative judgment is the idea that it robs the Christian of peace and the assurance of present salvation. The next chapter is devoted to addressing this objection.

12

Justifying the Investigative Judgment

Idea in Brief: In this chapter, the investigative judgment is examined in view of its crucial role in the plan of redemption. Satan challenges the ultimate salvation of every believer in the courts of heaven, and the investigative judgment is convened to silence the accuser of the brethren once and for all.

A Most Serious Objection

Many well-meaning Christians shun the idea of an investigative judgment, thinking it is something that robs them of their peace in Christ and the assurance of present salvation. It is "the enemy of righteousness by faith," they say. In the minds of many, the investigative judgment makes no sense if one has been justified and accounted righteous by faith.

"If we confess our sins, he is faithful and just to forgive us our sins and to cleanse us from all unrighteousness" (1 John 1:9). If our sins have already been forgiven, it makes no sense to keep records of them in the books of heaven to be investigated later.

"Being justified by faith, we have peace with God through our Lord Jesus Christ" (Rom. 5:1). Why should believers be subjected to an investigative judgment if they already have peace with God through their Lord Jesus Christ? Why put them on trial when they have been justified by faith, meaning they have already been pronounced just and innocent by faith in Christ?

Paul also stated that believers have been reconciled to God by the death of His Son (see v. 10). If they have already been reconciled to God, then why subject them to an investigate judgment? Doesn't this make the gospel and the teaching of an investigative judgment a contradiction of terms?

John also stated that those who have the Son already have life (see 1 John 5:12). If that is the case, then the idea of an investigative judgment being conducted sometime in the future to determine whether believers have eternal life or not, is pointless.

Paul additionally taught that those who are in Christ now are no longer under condemnation (see Rom. 8:1). If that is true, then it makes no sense to subject them to a process of investigation to determine if they are condemned or not.

In short, if the saints have peace with God already, been reconciled with Him, and possess eternal life, for that matter, what is the point of having them face a future judgment to investigate their cases? Why keep a record of their sins to be investigated later if these have already been pardoned? Thus, Seventh-day Adventists who adhere to the teaching of an investigative judgment are seen as complicating the gospel and negating the plan of salvation unnecessarily.

This is a serious objection!

The Investigative Judgment and the Great Controversy

First of all, it must be understood that the Adventist doctrine of the investigative judgment is an adjunct to a larger theme called the great controversy. This term refers to the war between God and Satan that originated in heaven and has been in progress on earth since time began (see Rev. 12:7–9). The investigative judgment can be understood and appreciated better if seen through the lens of this great, all-embracing theme. Understood in the light of the grander scheme of the cosmic battle between good and evil, the concept of an investigative judgment makes a lot more sense, as will now be seen. The great controversy explains why there is a need for an end-time investigative judgment.

Satan's Agenda

As the great controversy continues to unfold, Satan is unhappy with those who make efforts to leave his camp of rebels. He treats them as deserters in his army and marks them as ripe for destruction. He targets those who leave his service to serve God and follow Jesus. He continually harasses them because they expose his claim that the law of God cannot be kept as a lie. He does not want anyone to receive the benefit of Christ's final atonement. He never wants to see the day when God will be able to point to a people and say, "Here are they that keep the commandments of God and the have the testimony of Jesus," for that would mean the end of his career and existence.

For this reason, Satan makes the lives of men and women who seek deliverance from his control miserable to dissuade them from abandoning his ranks. "Yea, and all that will live godly in Christ Jesus shall suffer persecution" (2 Tim. 3:12).

Jesus gave Peter a startling revelation of Satan's plot to destroy him. Poor Peter had no knowledge that this scenario was going on behind the scenes. "And the Lord said, Simon, Simon, behold, Satan hath desired *to have* you, that he may *sift* you as wheat: But I have prayed for thee, that thy faith fail not: and when thou art converted, strengthen thy brethren" (Luke 22:31, 32).

Here, Jesus lifts the curtain so Peter—and we, for that matter—can get a glimpse of the reality of the great controversy, which is happening in the unseen world. Unobserved, Satan constantly strategizes and schemes to bring about the destruction of God's faithful, commandment-keeping people. He tempts them, causes them to fall, then pleads for their souls so he can destroy them. Satan's modus operandi is to deceive or drive people to transgress the law of God, then destroy and devour them. "Be sober, be vigilant; because your adversary the devil, as a roaring lion, walketh about, seeking whom he may devour" (1 Peter 5:8).

Satan Challenges the Ultimate Salvation of Every Man

Satan thinks he has legitimate claims over every redeemed sinner on this planet, which, incidentally, he also claims as his very own. He disputes Christ's right to wrest souls from under his dominion and control. Satan claims dominion not only over the living but also the dead. The Bible tells us Satan contended for the body of Moses when Jesus attempted to resurrect him from the grave. "Yet Michael the archangel, when contending with the devil he disputed about the body of Moses, durst not bring against him a railing accusation, but said, The Lord rebuke thee" (Jude 9). In Satan's mind, Moses belonged to him because, like countless others, he fell under his temptations and sinned.

And if causing people to sin and incur guilt is not good enough, Satan finds occasion to denounce them before God of the wrongs he has tempted them to commit so they will not find favor with Him. He is called the "accuser of the brethren who accuses them day and night before God" (Rev. 12:10). His accusations are not limited to the misdeeds and follies he has instigated the brethren to commit; he even presents their good deeds in a bad light. In the story of Job, we see how Satan wrongfully accuses the righteous of serving God merely for selfish motives.

> And the LORD said unto Satan, Hast thou considered my servant Job, that there is none like him in the earth, a perfect and an upright man, one that feareth God, and escheweth evil? Then Satan answered the LORD, and said, Doth Job fear God for nought? Hast not thou made an hedge about him, and about his house, and about all that he hath on every side? thou hast blessed the work of his hands, and his substance is increased in the land. But put forth thine hand now, and touch all that he hath, and he will curse thee to thy face. (Job 1:8–12)

The prophet Zechariah's vision of Joshua and the angel is a graphic portrayal of Satan's work of accusing the saints before God as part of his efforts to challenge their eternal salvation.

> And he shewed me Joshua the high priest standing before the angel of the LORD, and Satan standing at his right hand to resist him.

And the LORD said unto Satan, The LORD rebuke thee, O Satan; even the LORD that hath chosen Jerusalem rebuke thee: is not this a brand plucked out of the fire? Now Joshua was clothed with filthy garments, and stood before the angel. (Zechariah 3:1–4)

We will turn to inspired writings for a moment to understand more clearly what Satan's work of accusation involves:

The tempter stands by to accuse them, as he stood by to resist Joshua. *He points to their filthy garments, their defective characters.* He presents their weakness and folly, their sins of ingratitude, their unlikeness to Christ, which has dishonored their Redeemer. He endeavors to affright them with the thought that their case is hopeless, that the stain of their defilement will never be washed away. He hopes so to destroy their faith that they will yield to his temptations, and turn from their allegiance to God.

Satan has an accurate knowledge of *the sins* that he has tempted God's people to commit, and he urges his accusations against them, declaring, that by their sins they have forfeited divine protection, and claiming that he has the right to destroy them. He pronounces them just as deserving as himself of exclusion from the favor of God. "Are these," he says, "the people who are to take my place in heaven, and the place of the angels who united with me? They profess to obey the law of God; but have they kept its precepts? Have they not been lovers of self more than lovers of God? Have they not placed their own interests above His service? Have they not loved the things of the world? Look at the sins that have marked their lives. Behold their selfishness, their malice, their hatred of one another. Will God banish me and my angels from His presence, and yet reward those who have been guilty of the same sins? Thou canst not do this, O Lord, in justice. Justice demands that sentence be pronounced against them."[110]

---

[110] White, *Prophets and Kings*, pp. 588, 589 (emphasis added).

Satan's accusations against the saints revolve around two areas: 1) the sins he had tempted God's people to commit, of which he has an accurate record, and 2) their defective characters. "He points to their filthy garments, their defective characters...." Based on the sins he had tempted them to commit and their imperfections of character, Satan disputes their salvation and claims them as his prey. He pronounces them just as deserving as he is of exclusion from God's favor.

The Redemptive Aspect of the Investigative Judgment

The investigative judgment, therefore, reduced to its simplest terms, is no less than the process of examining these two areas of human existence by the Father Himself in light of Satan's accusations. Its purpose is to ascertain the validity of the charges Satan makes against the saints. Considering the challenges posed by Satan, the heavenly Father is obligated to investigate: 1) the records of the lives of His people, as well as their 2) characters. The Father's work of investigation into the records of men's lives is so crucial the Bible presents two scenarios to portray it. In Daniel 7:9–10, the Ancient of Days, who is no less than the heavenly Father Himself, opens the books containing the record of men's words and actions. In Matthew 22:1–14, the Father, who is the King that gave a marriage for His Son in the parable, examines the robes of character worn by those present at the marriage feast. These two Bible scenarios point to the same event—that of the heavenly Father presiding over a work of investigation into the lives and characters of men prior to the return of Jesus.

The investigation of the records in the books of heaven is necessary because Satan challenges every person's ultimate salvation. As will be explained more fully in the next chapter, the primary purpose of the investigative judgment is not just to examine the lives and characters of the saints, but to defend them against Satan's strong accusations. Whether one realizes it or not, the investigative judgment is part of the redemptive process. It is Christ's response to the challenge made by Satan against the salvation He has wrought for His people on earth. It is to silence the accuser of the brethren by showing that his arguments against believers in Christ have no real basis. "The Lord rebuke, O Satan, even the Lord who hath chosen Jerusalem, rebuke thee."

> *The primary purpose of the investigative judgment is to defend the saints against Satan's strong accusations. Whether one realizes it or not, the investigative judgment is part of the redemptive process. It is Christ's response to Satan's challenge. It is to silence the accuser of the brethren by showing that his arguments against believers in Christ have no real basis.*

For this reason, the angels faithfully record not only the sins and misdeeds of humans but also their good deeds. "Then they that feared the LORD spake often one to another: and the LORD hearkened, and heard it, and a book of remembrance was written before him for them that feared the LORD, and that thought upon his name" (Mal. 3:16). In the book of God's remembrance, every deed of righteousness is immortalized. Every temptation resisted, every evil overcome, every word of tender pity expressed, is faithfully chronicled. Every act of sacrifice, every suffering and sorrow endured for Christ's sake, is recorded.

In this book, their acts of faith and repentance are recorded, as well. Even their tears of repentance are chronicled in the books. "Thou tellest my wanderings: put thou my tears into thy bottle: are they not in thy book? When I cry unto thee, then shall mine enemies turn back: this I know; for God is for me" (Ps. 58:8–9).

The book of life contains the service record of all who have entered into God's service. It contains the names of those who have overcome the wicked one through faith in Christ (see 1 John 2:13). Jesus bade His disciples, "Rejoice, because your names are written in heaven" (Luke 10:20). Paul spoke of his faithful fellow workers, "whose names are in the book of life" (Phil. 4:3).

Jesus, the Advocate of His people, is seen going into the presence of His Father to engage in His last act of ministration before He cleanses the sanctuary: to determine who, through faith and repentance, deserve to have their names retained in the book of life.

> I saw in the night visions, and, behold, one like the Son of man came with the clouds of heaven and came to the Ancient of days, and they brought him near before him. And there was given him dominion, and glory, and a kingdom, that all people, nations, and languages, should serve him: his dominion is an everlasting dominion, which shall not pass away, and his kingdom that which shall not be destroyed. (Daniel 7:13, 14)

When the investigative judgment is convened, Jesus, as the Son of man, takes up the cases of the saints and presents powerful arguments in their defense against Satan's accusations. He shows their good deeds, faith, and repentance to counter Satan's arguments and secure their salvation.

There is nothing to fear in the investigative judgment because Jesus, the Friend of sinners, defends His people from Satan's accusations. "Who shall lay any thing to the charge of God's elect? It is God that justifieth. Who is he that condemneth? It is Christ that died, yea rather, that is risen again, who is even at the right hand of God, who also maketh intercession for us" (Rom. 8:33, 34).

> But while the followers of Christ have sinned, they have not given themselves up to be controlled by the satanic agencies. They have repented of their sins and have sought the Lord in humility and contrition, and the divine Advocate pleads in their behalf. He who has been most abused by their ingratitude, who knows their sin and also their penitence, declares: "The Lord rebuke thee, O Satan. I gave My life for these souls. They are graven upon the palms of My hands. They may have imperfections of character; they may have failed in their endeavors; *but they have repented, and I have forgiven and accepted them.*"[111]

---

[111] White, *Prophets and Kings*, p. 589 (emphasis added).

Barking Up the Wrong Tree

It must be clearly pointed out and stressed that it is Satan, not the Father, who is challenging the eternal salvation of every man in the courts of heaven. If the Father Himself were questioning the saints' ultimate salvation, then the objections being leveled against an investigative judgment might contain some weight. For why should God subject the saints to an investigation if He Himself had already justified them, forgiven their sins, and reconciled them to Himself through faith in Christ? The objections being made against the investigative judgment are therefore misplaced. The objectors are barking up the wrong tree! They need to hurl their objections at Satan, not God!

It is Satan, not the Father, who is finding reasons in the investigative judgment to exclude the saints from the kingdom. "Fear not, little flock; for it is your Father's good pleasure to give you the kingdom" (Luke 12:32). How does this judgment scenario rob the genuine Christian of his or her peace in Christ and assurance of present salvation?

The Saints Vindicated in the Judgment

As a result of Christ's powerful defense of the saints, the outcome of the investigative judgment will be favorable to them. "Until the Ancient of days came, and judgment was given in favor of the saints of the Most High; and the time came that the saints possessed the kingdom" (Dan. 7:22, NKJV). The verdict handed down by the Ancient of days, the presiding Judge, favors the saints. The saints are acquitted, and Satan's charges are dropped. The investigative judgment silences the accuser of the brethren and guarantees their place in the kingdom of heaven.

For this reason, the investigative judgement is such good news to the church! It is not something about which believers need to murmur or complain. It is not something that needs to cause genuine Christians fear or uneasiness. How can anyone think of the investigative judgment as something that robs the Christian of the assurance of present salvation when, in fact, it does the very opposite?

When properly understood, the investigative judgment does not deny Christians of the assurance of *present salvation* but establishes it beyond doubt and uncertainty. Not only that, it gives them assurance of *future salvation* when their names come up in the judgment. Do we have absolute faith in our blessed Redeemer? That is the question.

God Vindicated in the Investigative Judgment
The investigation of the records in the books of heaven before the onlooking universe also vindicates God's character. This work clearly explains why God and His Son must allow some to be saved and some lost.

> And they sing the song of Moses the servant of God, and the song of the Lamb, saying, "Great and marvelous are thy works, Lord God Almighty; just and true are thy ways, thou King of saints. Who shall not fear thee, O Lord, and glorify thy name? for thou only art holy: for all nations shall come and worship before thee; for thy judgments are made manifest." (Rev. 15:3, 4).
>
> I have sworn by myself, the word is gone out of my mouth *in* righteousness, and shall not return, That unto me every knee shall bow, every tongue shall swear. (Isa. 45:23)

The Investigative Judgment and the Everlasting Gospel
We will never fully understand why the investigative judgment is proclaimed as part of the everlasting gospel of Revelation 14 until we see its redemptive significance. The proclamation "Fear God and give glory to Him for the hour of His judgment is come" should be a cause for rejoicing. The accuser of the brethren is about to be silenced forever in that work of judgment, and our salvation is about to be sealed for all eternity. Why should this prospect cause alarm and dismay? The proclamation of a judgment hour should only worry the wicked, not the saints of God. Could it be that faith and repentance are lacking among God's elect today, which is why there is apprehension and lack of confidence to face the judgment?

Justifying the Investigative Judgment

To deny the investigative judgment is to destroy the completeness of the gospel. Humanity's redemption, which is started on earth, is not completed until the accuser is silenced forever in the courts of heaven. The saints' salvation is not guaranteed until all of Satan's charges against them are disproved and dropped.

Let us remember that Satan disputes every believer's salvation just as he disputed for the body of Moses. Let us remember that more problematic than falling into sin is the prospect of facing a powerful accuser who knows every sin we have committed and is determined to challenge our salvation before heaven's highest tribunal. Let us also remember that Jesus does not only have the power to save His people from the instigator and slave master of sin on earth, but also from the accuser of the brethren in the judgment halls of heaven.

In the investigative judgment, Jesus is the repentant sinner's only hope of justification. "Does Satan plead loudly against our souls, accusing of sin, and claiming us as his prey, the blood of Christ pleads with greater power."[112]

Therefore, to accept the gospel while denying the necessity of an investigative judgment is to reject the completeness of Christ's saving work. It is time to disentangle ourselves from the misconceptions and myths that have been woven around the teaching of the investigative judgment. It is time to embrace it gladly for what it is: as part and parcel of the astounding good news of the everlasting gospel! Paul would have us remember that the investigative judgment is part of the proclamation of the gospel: "In the day when God shall judge the secrets of men by Jesus Christ according to my gospel" (Rom. 2:16).

---

[112] White, *Thoughts from the Mount of Blessing*, p. 8.

13

Facing the Investigative Judgment

Idea in Brief: This chapter gives the rationale for the investigative judgment and examines it in light of the distinct and separate roles the Father and Son play during that momentous event. It explains why it is extremely important to make that distinction when studying the subject of the judgment. Being able to see that distinction removes all apprehension and fear of the judgment.

A Challenging Subject

Studying the subject of the investigative judgment can be a daunting experience, especially in light of its complicated nature. To many, trying to understand this subject is like going through a complex maze. Perhaps, the best way to understand the investigative judgment meaningfully is to look at it in light of the distinctive roles the Father and Son play during that event. Many end up embracing a confusing, ambiguous view of the investigative judgment because they cannot distinguish clearly between what the Father does and what the Son does in the judgment. The lines of distinction are blurred, and as a result, confusion sets in. Being able to tell those two roles apart can make the difference between obtaining peace and assurance in the judgment on the one hand and being overwhelmed with panic and fear of the judgment on the other.

The Father's Role in the Investigative Judgment

The Bible teaches us that God the Father has appointed a day in which to judge the world (see Acts 17:31). As was explained in the previous chapter, the purpose of this investigation is mainly to ascertain the validity of Satan's accusations against the saints—accusations that revolve around two areas, namely 1) the sins that they have committed, and 2) their imperfect, un-Christlike characters. Its purpose is also to make known those who serve God and those who serve Him not. "And they shall be mine, saith the LORD of hosts, in that day when I make up my jewels; and I will spare them, as a man spareth his own son that serveth him. Then shall ye return, and discern between the righteous and the wicked, between him that serveth God and him that serveth him not" (Mal. 3:17, 18). Discerning between the righteous and the wicked presupposes a work of investigation.

In the investigative or trial phase of the judgment, all the world's inhabitants are called upon to account for their words and actions (see Matt. 12:36). The great masses of the world are summoned before the heavenly tribunal to face the records of their lives. The apostle Peter declared both the dead and the living are to give an account to Him who is ready to judge all (see 1 Peter 4:5). "Let us hear the conclusion of the whole matter: Fear God, and keep his commandments: for this is the whole duty of man. For God shall bring every work into judgment, with every secret thing, whether it be good, or whether it be evil" (Eccles. 12:13,14). What this work of investigation by God the Father involves is explained more fully in the statement below:

> Every man's work passes in review before God and is registered for faithfulness or unfaithfulness. Opposite each name in the books of heaven is entered with terrible exactness every wrong word, every selfish act, every unfulfilled duty, and every secret sin, with every artful dissembling. Heaven-sent warnings or reproofs neglected, wasted moments, unimproved opportunities, the influence exerted for good or for evil, with its far-reaching results, all are chronicled by the recording angel.[113]

---

[113] White, *The Great Controversy*, p. 482.

The Judgment Prophecy of Daniel 7:9-10

Two scenarios in the Bible portray the role of the Father in the investigative judgment. The first scenario is a prophecy and the other is a parable. In Daniel 7:9–10, the prophet was given a graphic portrayal of the fearful and solemn day when the books of record are to be investigated and examined by heaven's great tribunal. In this judgment scenario, the books of record are opened for investigation by the "Ancient of days," the heavenly Father. "Before the mountains were brought forth, or ever Thou hadst formed the earth and the world, even from everlasting to everlasting, Thou art God" (Ps. 90:2).

The fact that the focus of this scenario is the opening of the books of heaven by the Father shows it is He who presides in this great heavenly tribunal. He convenes the investigative judgment and summons thousands and thousands of angelic beings to begin the work of examining the lives and characters of all who live on the earth to determine their eternal destiny.

The fulfillment of Daniel's judgment prophecy is found in the end-time declaration, "Fear God, and give glory to him for the hour of his judgment is come" (Rev. 14:7). It is the duty of the church to proclaim this solemn announcement to the world so its inhabitants may be warned. Like watchmen on the walls of Zion, those who understand the times in which they live are to give the trumpet a certain sound. Should the church be found unfaithful in her duty to forewarn the world in this matter, the blood of souls will be on her hands.

This *investigative* phase of the judgment must not be confused with *the executive* phase of the judgment, which occurs at Christ's second coming. Regarding this latter phase of the judgment, Jude declared, "Behold, the Lord cometh with ten thousands of his saints, To *execute* judgment upon all, and to convince all that are ungodly among them of all their ungodly deeds which they have ungodly committed, and of all their hard [speeches] which ungodly sinners have spoken against him" (vs. 14, 15, emphasis added).

The harvest scenario portrayed in Revelation 14:14–20, which follows right after the announcement of the coming of the judgment hour, is symbolic of Christ's work to execute the heavenly court's verdict at the close of the work of investigation. In this scenario, Jesus is portrayed symbolically as coming back to earth with a trumpet and a sickle in His hand to harvest two classes of fully ripened grapes. One class is reaped, and the other trampled in the winepress of God's wrath. When Jesus comes, He does not sit to examine the work of every human being, as that has been accomplished beforehand. Instead, He brings His reward with Him to give to every person according to his or her works (see 22:12). Christ's work of separating the sheep from the goats at His second coming portrays the same climactic event (see Matt. 25:31–33).

The Judgment Parable of Matthew 22

In the judgment parable of the man without a wedding garment found in Matthew 22:1–14, the king examines the guests in attendance. The parable points to the same judgment scenario in Daniel 7 but looks at it from a different angle. It is given to shed more light on the role of the Father in the investigative judgment. The king who gives a marriage feast for his son in the parable and the Ancient of days in Daniel 7 both represent the heavenly Father. In this parable, however, the focus of the father's investigation shifts from the books of record to the *garments* worn by the guests at the wedding. In the parable, the father, not the son, is seen examining the attire worn by the guests to the wedding.

The guests who go into the wedding represent those who have accepted the gospel invitation, Jews and Gentiles alike. The examination of the guests just before the marriage represents a work of investigation by the king (i.e., the heavenly Father) to see if the lives and characters of those who have accepted the gospel conform to his son's image. The garment approved in the parable represents the character that each must possess to be fit for the marriage supper of the Lamb—for heaven. It represents Christ's perfect character, which every person must have as a candidate for the kingdom.

In the parable, only those who have accepted the wedding invitation are examined to see if they are wearing the wedding garment. In the pre-advent investigative judgment, only the cases of those who have accepted the gospel through faith in Christ are closely examined to determine their eligibility for the kingdom. The cases of those who outrightly refuse to believe in Jesus need no examination at that time since their unbelief will result in their automatic condemnation and rejection. Jesus Himself said, "He that believeth on him is not condemned: but he that believeth not is condemned already, because he hath not believed in the name of the only begotten Son of God" (John 3:18). The cases of such are opened for examination by the heavenly host and the redeemed during the Millennium (see Rev 20:11–15).

The cases of those who receive automatic condemnation in the investigative judgment are not opened for examination until the Millennium, before the assembled hosts of the redeemed and the unfallen worlds (see 1 Cor. 6:2, 3; Rev. 20:11, 13). For 1,000 years, the cases of the lost are to be reviewed. At that time, the books of record are again opened to show why the rejecters of God's grace are excluded from heaven.

> And I saw a great white throne, and him that sat on it, from whose face the earth and the heaven fled away; and there was found no place for them. And I saw the dead, small and great, stand before God; and the books were opened: and another book was opened, which is the book of life: and the dead were judged out of those things which were written in the books, according to their works. (Revelation 20:11, 12)

To reiterate, the son in the parable, who represents Jesus, is not the one doing the work of investigation; instead, it is the king (equivalent to the Ancient of days of Daniel 7:9–10) who is seen examining the attire of the guests.

> The guests at the marriage feast were inspected by the king. Only those were accepted who had obeyed his requirements and put on the wedding garment. So it is with the guests at the gospel feast. *All must pass the scrutiny of the great King*, and only those are received who have put on the robe of Christ's righteousness.[114]

---

[114] White, *Christ's Object Lessons*, p. 312 (emphasis added).

Two Areas of Investigation

It is important to understand why two scenarios are given to portray God the Father's role in the investigative judgment. These two judgment scenarios are complementary. They help us know what areas of our lives will come up for review by the heavenly Father, "the Judge of all the earth." The judgment prophecy of Daniel 7:9–10 teaches us that the Father will be examining the *books*, which contain the records of everything we have said and done in our lives. The judgment parable of Matthew 22:1–14, on the other hand, teaches us that the heavenly Father will also be examining the *characters* we develop throughout the course of our lives.

In Daniel 7:9–10, the Ancient of days examines the books to see if those who profess faith in Christ have clean slates, meaning there are no sins recorded in the books that are unconfessed and unforgiven.

> As the books of record are opened in the judgment, the lives of all who have believed on Jesus come in review before God.... When any have sins remaining upon the books of record, unrepented of and unforgiven, their names will be blotted out of the book of life, and the record of their good deeds will be erased from the book of God's remembrance.[115]

In parallel with the parable of the wedding garment, the Father shifts His investigation to the character to see if those who profess to have faith in His Son reflect His image fully. To reflect the image of Jesus fully means having attained "unto a perfect man, unto the measure of the stature of the fulness of Christ" and to "grow up into him in all things, which is the head, even Christ" (Eph. 4:13–15). It is being "conformed to the image of His Son" (Rom. 8:29). It means having no more spots, wrinkles, or any such thing—no more defects or flaws marring the character, such as pride, ambition, selfishness, covetousness, and love of the world.

---

[115] White, *The Great Controversy*, p. 483.

Previous to the wedding, the king comes in to see the guests, to see if all are attired in the wedding garment, the *spotless robe of character* washed and made white in the blood of the Lamb.... This work of *examination of character*, of determining who are prepared for the kingdom of God, is that of the Investigative Judgment, the closing of work in the sanctuary above.[116]

Hence, these two scenarios teach us that the Father will require two things to be approved in the judgment: 1) perfect records in the books and 2) perfect righteousness in character. Not to have these when our cases come up for review is to face rejection. Not to have these two requirements will show that Satan's accusations against us have been true all along!

Many professed Christians, ignorant of the unchanging nature of the standards of the judgment, think they can tamper with them at will. In effect, many attempt to lower them, if not entirely disregard them, to please their carnal hearts. They do this at the peril of their souls.

Dealing with the Dilemma of the Investigative Judgment

How do we deal with the dilemma of the investigative judgment? Humanly speaking, there is no way for anyone to satisfy the Father's requirements in the judgment. Do we then cower in fear? Do we clench our fists in protest against it? Do we try to get around it through one excuse or another? Do we attempt to minimize the claims of the Father in the judgment? or do we face the judgment boldly and with confidence? Whether we realize it or not, we place ourselves in one

> *Many professed Christians, ignorant of the unchanging nature of the standards of the judgment, think they can tamper with them at will. In effect, many attempt to lower them, if not entirely disregard them, to please their carnal hearts. They do this at the peril of their souls.*

---

[116] *Ibid.*, p. 428 (emphasis added).

of five different states of mind with respect to the dilemma of the investigative judgment.

State of Despair
Far too many Seventh-day Adventists are in a state of despair and discouragement over the idea of facing a future investigative judgment. They look at the record of their lives and their characters and say, "Oh no! There's no way I can stand before God in the Judgment! I'm gone! I'm lost!" They quietly worry themselves to death over the matter, not knowing what to do to calm their fears. Many try their best, thinking God will take their best effort and overlook their faults in the judgment. They carry about their business daily, knowing they are not doing enough to meet God's approval in the judgment. Therefore, they are filled with anxiety over the matter every day of their lives.

State of Denial
Some are in a state of denial when it comes to the investigative judgment. They think they possess the ability to excuse themselves from it just by convincing themselves the judgment is only meant for the wicked. They believe faith in Christ somehow exempts them from the judgment, but this is only in their thinking. It is not necessarily what God thinks. Indeed, the idea of being excluded from the judgment sounds very appealing to the carnal nature, but it gives one a false sense of security.

The idea that only the wicked are judged is far from what the Bible teaches on the subject. Paul declared, "All shall appear before the judgment seat of Christ" (2 Cor. 5:10). Solomon the preacher said, "I said in mine heart, God shall judge the *righteous* and the *wicked*: for there is a time there for every purpose and for every work" (Eccles 3:17, emphasis added). "Judgment begins at the house of God" (1 Peter 4:17).

State of Defiance
In the spirit of sheer defiance, some boldly say the concept of an investigative judgment is spiritually unhealthy and should be scrapped altogether. They say the gospel is simple: just "believe in the

Lord Jesus, and you will be saved! Why, then, complicate the gospel with notions of an investigative judgment? Away with it!" Many, with clenched fists, reject the investigative judgment as spiritually counterproductive and anti-gospel because it supposedly robs them of their present assurance of salvation.

State of Delusion

Sadly, there is a very large camp of deluded church members who misunderstand that what is important in the judgment is not *performance*, but one's faith in Christ as personal Savior. This calms their anxious souls by assuming as long as they have faith and repentance, they have nothing about which to worry because Jesus will make up for their lack and defend them when their cases come up before the Ancient of days in the judgment.

This idea sounds pleasant to the ears but is nothing but a subtle and insidious attempt to lower the standard of the judgment to make it more agreeable with the frailties of the fallen, fleshly nature. It is exceedingly dangerous since it leaves one with the impression that the Father does not require perfection of the character in the judgment, only "faith" in Christ. It leaves the wrong impression that one can possess a defective character and still be approved in the judgment as long as he or she "believes" in Christ.

It is true that as long as we believe in Christ *now*, He makes up for our lack and covers us with His *imputed* righteousness. "There is *now* no condemnation to those who are in Christ Jesus." (Rom. 8:1, emphasis added). Today, "we have peace with God through our Lord Jesus Christ" (5:1). However, this status will not suffice when our cases come up for investigation in the judgment. We only need to look back at the judgment parable of Matthew 22 to see that the man who did not possess Christ's perfect robe of character was rejected by the king and cast into outer darkness.

The idea that in the judgment, the Father looks for faith in Christ only, irrespective of performance, is incompatible with the following scripture: "And if ye call on the Father, who without respect of persons judgeth according to every man's work, pass the time of your sojourning here in fear" (1 Peter 1:17). People are judged according to their works recorded in the books (see Rev. 20:12, 13). "We are to be justified by faith, and judged by our works."[117]

Those who are deluded into thinking they can stand before the heavenly Father wearing only their own garments of defective characters will then realize they needed to be squared and polished in preparation for examination, but it will be too late. It is important to note the son in the parable, who represents Jesus, did nothing to defend the man who was not wearing the wedding garment when his attire was examined by king. He did nothing to interpose on his behalf when the Father issued the command to bind him hand and foot and cast him into outer darkness.

State of Deference

To be in a state of deference as far as the investigative judgment goes is to be in a state of humble and respectful submission. Those who have this mindset do not have the presumptuous attitude to question the divine wisdom and rationale for the judgment. They meet the dilemma head-on, believing God is worthy of their trust even when their lives are weighed on the scale. They are fully confident that whatever God requires in the judgment, He Himself is willing and able to provide.

Therefore, they have the boldness and confidence to meet the investigative judgment squarely in the face. They know that in the investigative judgment, God is for them and not against them. "If God is for us, who can be against us?" (Rom. 8:31). They know that in the judgment, the Father is not looking for something to keep them out of heaven. "Fear not, little flock; for it is your Father's good pleasure to give you the kingdom" (Luke 12:32).

The Role of Jesus in the Investigative Judgment

Up to now, only the Father's role in the investigative judgment has been brought to light. As the Ancient of days, He examines the books,

---

[117] White, "Our Duty and Responsibility," *The General Conference Bulletin*, October 1, 1896.

looking for perfect records. As did the king who prepared the marriage for his son in the parable, He examines the robes looking for perfect characters. Humanly speaking, facing the Father in the judgment is a fearful and hopeless dilemma. Who is sufficient for these things? The odds of anyone surviving His meticulous examination are practically nil. Where does Jesus come into the picture?

It is essential to know what Jesus, our compassionate and merciful High Priest, does *not* do in the investigative judgment. Jesus does not *exempt* anyone from His Father's investigation; neither does He *minimize* the Father's requirements in the judgment. Even though He knows believers have no righteousness of their own to meet the Father's requirements in the judgment, He does not *cover* their deficiencies with His merits or substitute His own righteousness for their unrighteousness to the point of absolution from responsibility. Instead, what the Father requires in the judgment, Jesus provides.

A Two-fold Work

The work of Jesus in the investigative judgment is primarily two-fold. He first prepares His people for examination by making them partakers of His perfect righteousness and blotting their sins so their records will be clean and perfect. Then, He presents them before the throne of judgment as faultless. "Now unto Him that is able to keep you from falling, and to *present* you faultless before the presence of his glory with exceeding joy" (Jude 24). "That he might *present* it to himself a glorious church, not having spot, or wrinkle, or any such thing; but that it should be holy and without blemish" (Eph. 5:27, emphasis added). This, in a nutshell, is Christ's role in the investigative judgment.

As already explained in the previous chapters, it is the final atonement Jesus makes before He leaves the sanctuary that prepares the church to stand trial before the heavenly tribunal presided by the Ancient of days.

A Four-fold Rendition of Christ's Role in the Judgment

There are four Bible scenarios that portray Christ's closing work in the sanctuary above to prepare the church for investigation and judgment. These four scenarios are descriptions of the same event: that is, Jesus moving to the second apartment of the heavenly sanctuary in 1844 to enter into the concluding phase of His high-priestly work.

These four scenarios are listed as follows:

1. Christ as the Son of man coming to the Ancient of days to receive a kingdom, brought to view in Daniel 7:13

2. Christ as High Priest going into the Most Holy Place of the heavenly sanctuary to cleanse it, brought to view in Daniel 8:14

3. Christ as the Messenger of the covenant coming suddenly to His temple to purify the sons of Levi, brought to view in Malachi 3:1–3

4. Christ as the Bridegroom going into the marriage chamber with the five wise virgins, brought to view in Matthew 25:1–13[118]

Let us examine these four scenarios in greater detail, bearing in mind that each scenario focuses on a particular aspect of Christ's final ministry in the heavenly sanctuary to purify His church in preparation for investigation and judgment. Let us also bear in mind that along with the privilege of understanding that work comes the duty of cooperating with Him in that work. This is how we demonstrate our faith in what He is accomplishing to prepare us to receive the benefits of His final ministration in the sanctuary above.

SCENARIO 1: The Son of Man Comes to the Ancient of Days

Here, Jesus, as the Son of man, is described as coming to the Ancient of days to receive a kingdom (see Dan. 7:13–14). The coming of Christ described here is not to earth the second time, but to the

---

[118] Ellen White spoke of these four contemporaneous events in the following words: "The coming of Christ as our high priest to the most holy place, for the cleansing of the sanctuary, brought to view in Daniel 8:14; the coming of the Son of man to the Ancient of Days, as presented in Daniel 7:13; and the coming of the Lord to His temple, foretold by Malachi, are descriptions of the same event; and this is also represented by the coming of the bridegroom to the marriage, described by Christ in the parable of the ten virgins, of Matthew 25" (*The Great Controversy*, p. 426).

Ancient of days in the Most Holy Place to receive the throne of His father, David, His kingdom, and dominion.

Christ's coming to the Ancient of days in Daniel 7:13–14 to receive a kingdom necessitates and presupposes a prior work of investigation of the books of record by Jesus Himself to determine who will compose the kingdom. He cannot receive a kingdom without first ascertaining who will be part of it through a work of investigation. Eligibility for membership in the kingdom of glory for Jews and Gentiles alike is contingent upon two things: "repentance towards God and faith towards our Lord Jesus Christ" (Acts 20:21). This scenario, therefore, focuses on Christ's prior work of examining the books to see who, through faith and repentance, are to be entitled to the benefits of His final atonement and have a part in the kingdom. Christ's last acts of ministration in the heavenly sanctuary to prepare a people to stand before the Ancient of days consists of performing a work of investigative judgment and making a final atonement for all who are shown to be entitled to its benefits.[119]

Remember, Jesus will not be looking for "perfect records" in the books. He knows we do not have them. It is the Father who will be looking for them when He examines those books. Jesus will be looking for faith and repentance. The question is, When Jesus investigates our cases, will He find ample evidence showing we have been exercising repentance towards God and genuine faith towards our Lord and Savior? Is our remorse and sorrow for sin deep enough for Him to blot them out and give us a clean slate?

It is also essential to know the timing of this work. Jesus examines the books of record *before* the Ancient of days does. When the Father examines the books of records, the sins of Christ's faithful followers will no longer be found, as He will have blotted them out earlier. "In those days, and in that time, saith the LORD, the iniquity of Israel shall be sought for, and there shall be none; and the sins of Judah, and they shall not be found: for I will pardon them whom I reserve" (Jer. 50:20).

---

[119] White, *The Great Controversy*, p. 421.

SCENARIO 2: The Messenger of the Covenant Comes to His Temple

This scenario, found in Malachi 3:1–4, shows Jesus, the Messenger of the covenant, suddenly coming to His temple to purify the sons of Levi. As part of the purification process, He comes to the temple of the *heart* to investigate the character. "Know ye not that ye are the temple of God, and that the Spirit of God dwelleth in you?" (1 Cor. 3:16). Jesus probes the character to expose hidden defects that they may be acknowledged, confessed, pardoned, and blotted out. He said, "The churches shall know that I am he that searcheth [examines or investigates][120] hearts and reins" (Rev. 2:23).

> The Lord comes to His temple to find those who are *sincere*. He measures the worshippers. He knows those who are *true-hearted* and *self-sacrificing*. "Who may abide the day of His coming; and who shall stand when He appeareth?" *Who will stand in the day of investigation? This does not mean the time when the books are opened. It is a preparatory work.* "For He is like a refiner's fire and like fuller's soap." To those who have felt unconcerned, the Spirit comes as a reprover, and shows them that they need to do something to cleanse the temple.[121]

In this work of investigating the character, Jesus does not look for perfection. He does not examine the heart to look for something He knows His people do not possess. It is the Father who will be looking for perfection when He examines the characters of people in the judgment. Instead, Jesus investigates the characters of His professed followers to see if they are sincere, true-hearted and self-sacrificing.

To those who do not possess these precious character traits, Jesus comes to them as a reprover, hoping they will repent and do something about their lack of these positive spiritual graces. The Messenger of

---

[120] From the Greek word ἐρευνάω (*ereunaō*), meaning "to seek, inquire, investigate." *Strong's Exhaustive Concordance of the Bible*, G2045.
[121] White, "An Appeal for Help," *Australasian Union Conference Record*, July 28, 1899 (emphasis added).

the covenant knocks at the doors of the hearts of those who are in the church of Laodicea and says, "As many as I love, I rebuke and chasten. Be zealous therefore and repent" (Rev. 3:19).

A Preparatory Work

Christ's work in the temple of the heart to purify the sons of Levi calls for a thorough work of probing and testing the character to reveal deep-seated flaws and defects. This process of exposing the hidden plague spots of character reaches a climax when God's people become "fully conscious of the sinfulness of their lives" and understand "the exceeding sinfulness of sin." When the church reaches this condition, she is ready for the final atonement and cleansing.

> As the people of God afflict their souls, pleading for purity of heart, the command is given, "Take away their filthy garments and give them a change of raiment…" The spotless robe of Christ's righteousness is placed upon the tried, tempted, faithful children of God. The despised remnant are clothed in glorious apparel, nevermore to be defiled by the corruptions of the world.[122]

In the previous scenario (Daniel 7:13–14), Jesus was shown examining the books of record to determine who, through faith and repentance, are to be entitled to the benefits of His final atonement and have a part in the His kingdom. He assesses whose sins will be blotted out and whose sins will not. This time, the focus of Christ's investigation shifts from the books of record to

> **"**
> *Bear in mind that Christ's work in the temple to purify the sons of Levi calls for a thorough work of probing and testing the character to reveal deep-seated flaws and defects. This process of exposing the hidden plague spots of character is needed so the people of God can come to the point where they become "fully conscious of the sinfulness of their lives" and understand "the exceeding sinfulness of sin."*
> **"**

---

[122] White, *Prophets and Kings*, p. 591.

the examination of the temple of the heart—the character. The focus of this scenario is Christ's work of determining whose garments of character will be purified and made white and whose will remain filthy forever. It is a work preparatory to when the Ancient of days examines the lives and characters of men in the judgment.

SCENARIO 3: The Bridegroom Comes to the Marriage

In the parable of the ten virgins, five virgins are called "wise" because they were "ready." They were ready because they had extra oil and followed the Bridegroom into the marriage chamber through the darkness of midnight. On the other hand, the foolish virgins could not make it in time for the marriage because they had no oil left in their lamps and were left in perfect darkness.

The continuation of this parable is found in the marriage scenario of Revelation 19. The class of believers represented by the five wise virgins who made it to the marriage chamber because they were ready are given the wedding garment needed for the marriage. This wedding garment symbolizes the perfect character required to be approved by the Father in the judgment. "Let us be glad and rejoice, and give honour to him: for the marriage of the Lamb is come, and *his wife hath made herself ready.* And to her was granted that she should be arrayed in fine linen, clean and white: for the fine linen is the righteousness of saints" (vs. 7, 8, emphasis added).

The focus of this scenario is the giving of Christ's perfect righteousness to those who are found ready to receive it. Hence, what the Father requires in the judgment, Jesus provides. Only those who are found wearing the wedding garment are called to the marriage supper of the Lamb. "And he saith unto me, Write, Blessed are they which are called unto the marriage supper of the Lamb. And he saith unto me, These are the true sayings of God" (v. 9).

We make ourselves "ready" by studying the work of Jesus in the second apartment of the sanctuary. Thus, we are able to follow Him there by faith and receive the benefit of His final atonement. This knowledge is represented by the extra "oil" in the parable, which lightens the way to the marriage chamber—the Most Holy Place of the heavenly sanctuary. It is this truth that enlightens our understanding of Christ's closing work in the sanctuary above. Those who accept this truth are represented as going with Him into the marriage chamber.

> In the parable it was those that had oil in their vessels with their lamps that went in to the marriage. Those who, with a knowledge of the truth from the Scriptures, had also the Spirit and grace of God, and who, in the night of their bitter trial, had patiently waited, searching the Bible for clearer light—these saw the truth concerning the sanctuary in heaven and *the Saviour's change in ministration*, and by faith they followed Him in His work in the sanctuary above. *And all who through the testimony of the Scriptures accept the same truths, following Christ by faith as He enters in before God to perform the last work of mediation, and at its close to receive His kingdom—all these are represented as going in to the marriage.*[123]

On the other hand, the foolish virgins are those who willfully lack the knowledge regarding Christ's closing work in the second apartment of the heavenly sanctuary and thus fail to enter there by faith. Jesus makes no atonement to cleanse their hearts of their defilement. Neither does He impart to them the perfect righteousness they need to be approved in the judgment. The characters of this class of professed believers remain "filthy forever," and they are found wanting in the judgment.

The parable of the ten virgins is an appeal to the church to "go ye out and meet the Bridegroom." In short, it is an appeal to follow Jesus, by faith, into the marriage chamber, the second apartment of the heavenly sanctuary, that to her might be granted the array of "fine linen, clean and white," which is "the righteousness of the saints." This is how the church is to be made partakers of the perfect righteousness of Christ.

---

[123] White, *The Great Controversy*, pp. 427, 428 (emphasis added).

SCENARIO 4: The Cleansing of the Heavenly Sanctuary

This last scenario focuses on Christ's ending work as High Priest to cleanse the heavenly sanctuary before He leaves it. "And he said unto me, Unto two thousand three hundred day then shall the sanctuary be cleansed" (see Dan. 8:14). The final cleansing of the heavenly sanctuary is done by the removal or blotting out of the sins that have defiled it for many centuries.

Regarding this event, Moses wrote, "For on that day [the day of atonement], shall the priest make an atonement for you to cleanse you, so that you may be clean from all your sins before the Lord" (Lev. 16:30). As was already explained in previous chapters, it is only after the people of God have been fully cleansed of their filthy garments of character and become partakers of the perfect righteousness of Christ that their sins, which are in the books before the Lord, are purged or blotted out. This final act of removing the sins of the righteous from the sanctuary and transferring them to the head of the scapegoat is what cleanses the sanctuary (16:20–22).

The focus of this scenario is the removal or blotting out of the sins of God's people from the books of record, which not only cleanses the sanctuary but also gives them the perfect records they need to stand before the Ancient of days.

It is now clear that Christ's preparatory work of investigative judgment, portrayed in a four-fold fashion, is what prepares His people to stand trial. Hence, the verdict of the investigation will be favorable to them. "Until the Ancient of days came, and a judgment was made in favor of the saints of the Most High, and the time came for the saints to possess the kingdom" (Dan. 7:22).

The Father Presides, but Jesus Decides

Notice that while it is the Father who *presides* in the investigative judgment and conducts the final examination of the books and characters, it is Jesus who *decides* who is or isn't prepared to stand trial. "For the Father judgeth no man, but hath committed all judgment unto the Son.... And hath given him authority to execute judgment also, because he is the Son of man" (John 5:22, 27).

Our Lord and Savior Jesus Christ decides whether or not one receives the benefits of His final atonement; He decides whose characters are perfected and whose characters remain filthy forever; He decides whose sins are blotted out and whose sins are not; He decides whose names are retained in the Lamb's Book of Life and whose names are removed. Jesus Himself declared, "All power is given unto me in heaven and in earth" (Matt. 28:18).

The Father does not question the Son's decisions concerning the disposition of each man's destiny during the investigative judgment. Whoever the Son accepts, He also accepts. In the parable, the Father commands the servants to bind the hands and feet of those who Jesus had rejected and consequently did not have on the wedding garment. The Father commands that they be cast out into outer darkness where there is weeping and gnashing of teeth.

The Attire the Saints Wear in the Judgment

Before their names come up for investigation by the Ancient of days, sincere believers on earth have the privilege of presenting their cases to their merciful and compassionate High Priest who ever lives to make intercession for them. They must go to Jesus just as they are: wearing only the filthy garments of sin and self-righteousness and carrying with them the records of their broken lives. Jesus will accept them if they come to Him with faith and true repentance for sin. He will reject those who come to Him wearing their own garments of self-righteousness.

After Jesus makes His final atonement, He will present them to His Father, no longer wearing the filthy garments of defective character, but wearing the beautiful fine linen, clean and white (see Rev. 3:18; 19:6–8). By virtue of His shed and sprinkled blood, He will also remove the stains of their sins from the books of record and their memory so they do not have to carry the heavy baggage of their past lives throughout eternity.

Satan Silenced Forever in the Investigative Judgment

The perfecting of the saints in the final atonement and the blotting out of the records of their sins silences Satan forever. Since the filthy garments previously worn by the saints have been taken away, he can no longer point to these to accuse them of imperfections of character. And since their sins have been blotted out from the books of record, as well, nevermore to be remembered, Satan has no sins of which to accuse the saints, either. "And the LORD said unto Satan, The LORD rebuke thee, O Satan; even the LORD that hath chosen Jerusalem rebuke thee: *is* not this a brand plucked out of the fire?" (Zech. 3:2).

14

Ye Shall Afflict Your Souls

Idea in Brief: This chapter explains the meaning of the call on the day of atonement to afflict the soul. It is an appeal not only to examine oneself and repent of one's deep-seated sinfulness of life, but also to identify with the sins of others, confessing them as if they were his own. The chapter also explores the parallel between the call to afflict the soul and the call for the church of Laodicea to be zealous and repent.

A Most Serious Call

Without a doubt, the church of Laodicea's greatest and most urgent need today is to seriously consider the call in Revelation 3:19 to "be zealous therefore and repent." As the church that is about to go through the trying experiences of the closing scenes of the great, antitypical day of atonement, her greatest challenge is found in being able to see the connection between that call made to her by the Faithful and True Witness and the repeated calls on the day of atonement to "afflict the soul."

The call to afflict the soul is mandated twice in Leviticus 16, underscoring its tremendous importance.

> And [this] shall be a statute for ever unto you: [that] in the seventh month, on the tenth [day] of the month, *ye shall afflict your souls*, and do no work at all, [whether it be] one of your own country, or

a stranger that sojourneth among you: For on that day shall [the priest] make an atonement for you, to cleanse you, [that] ye may be clean from all your sins before the LORD. It [shall be] a sabbath of rest unto you, and *ye shall afflict your souls*, by a statute for ever. (Lev. 16:29–31)

The command to afflict the soul on the day of atonement is mentioned three more times in Leviticus 23:27–31, this time with mention of severe consequences if not heeded. "For whatsoever soul it be that shall not be afflicted in that same day, he shall be cut off from among his people." The Lord makes no idle threats. Laodicea needs to understand that this threat to her eternal salvation is no less than that of being spewed out of Jesus' mouth.

Laodicea's Most Pressing Duty

"Afflicting the soul" is Laodicea's most pressing duty at present. Ever since the beginning of the great, antitypical day of atonement in 1844, that call has been in effect, and the nearer she gets to those closing scenes, the more urgent that imperative will become. As with Scripture, the Spirit of Prophecy plainly articulates the urgency of taking the call to afflict the soul to heart by those who are living under the very shadow of the final atonement:

> The church must arise. They do not half heed the message to the Laodicean church. There are those in the church who love this world better than they love Jesus. They love their treasures here better than they love heaven or eternal life, and with their earthly treasure they will perish. The True Witness now speaks to a lukewarm church. Be zealous and repent; but they scarcely hear or heed the message. *A few are afflicting their souls*. A few are heeding the counsel of the True Witness. Unless the church speedily arouses they will go into darkness, be ensnared and overcome by the enemy.
>
> *I saw that the church now must afflict their souls*. They must labor, they must agonize or go down. I saw it was best to leave

the churches to work for themselves now, that they may feel their weakness while there is a chance for them to zealously repent and buy gold, white raiment, and eye salve, the treasures they must possess if they would have eternal life.[124]

What Is Afflicting the Soul?

The day of atonement, which fell on the tenth day of the seventh month, was preceded by ten days of blowing the trumpet (see Lev. 23:24). The blowing of the trumpet was a signal that the day of judgment and final cleansing was approaching. The Jews understood the solemnity of those days. They knew that failure to engage in the work of afflicting the soul during those days of preparation meant facing the prospect of eternal loss on that fateful day. For the Jews, those ten days were days of deep searching of heart and repentance. Sins were confessed, and differences between members of the family and the congregation were settled.

The high priest had to prepare for the day of atonement especially. Seven days before that day arrived, he, who was to officiate in the ceremonies of that day, left the comfort of his home and resided within the precincts of the sanctuary. He spent his time studying the Scriptures, praying, fasting, and examining himself. He also spent much of his time with the assisting priests, meticulously rehearsing every step of the ceremonies to be conducted on that solemn day to ensure there were no errors in procedure that might result in fatal consequences for himself.[125]

When the day finally came, the high priest humbled himself by exchanging his glorious high priestly garments for the linen garments of a common priest (see 16:4). Meanwhile, the congregation waited outside the sanctuary and joined him in prayer, confession, fasting, and deep searching of heart as the rites and ceremonies for the cleansing

---

[124] White, "Lack of Appreciation of the Ministry," Manuscript 1, 1857. Paragraphs 2 and 8 (emphasis added).
[125] Much of what we understand today about how the Jews observed the Day of Atonement in the first century comes from a book written by Alfred Edersheim, *The Temple and Its Ministry and Services at the Time of Jesus Christ*, first published in 1874.

of the sanctuary were being carried out. Aside from repentance of sin, the Jews demonstrated their affliction of soul by acts of self-denial and fasting.

> The whole ceremony was designed to impress the Israelites with the holiness of God and His abhorrence of sin; and, further, to show them that they could not come in contact with sin without becoming polluted. Every man was required to afflict his soul while this work of atonement was going forward. All business was to be laid aside, and the whole congregation of Israel were to spend the day in solemn humiliation before God, with prayer, fasting, and deep searching of heart.[126]

Soul Affliction, an Intensive Work

There is more to the command to afflict the soul than many realize. This call encompasses more than just the act of repenting of specific sins. Soul affliction involves a work of examining self intently, "abasing self, being bowed down and being in despair" because of one's sinfulness of life.[127]

This kind of repentance is more intense and challenging than repenting of sins of a specific nature. After all, sinfulness of character is a deep, subconscious problem. It is not easy to repent of something hidden and not adequately understood. "The heart is deceitful above all things and desperately wicked; who can know it?" (Jer. 17:9). How does one obtain a correct estimate of the extent of the sinfulness of his or her life? How does one understand the magnitude of the selfishness of the human heart? Who can understand the depths of the depravity of the innermost soul? Who can understand one's errors—one's secret or hidden and therefore unrecognized faults? (see Ps. 19:12).

While Jesus understands the full extent of Laodicea's wretchedness, misery, poverty, nakedness of soul, and blindness, she herself does not. "Thou knowest not" is His sad indictment of her spiritual malady.

---

[126] White, *The Great Controversy*, pp. 419, 420.
[127] *Strong's Exhaustive Concordance of the Bible,* H6031.

Laodicea does not fully understand her true state. No wonder she is not up to the challenge of complying with the divine command to "be zealous therefore and repent"!

John the Baptist preached repentance in his day, saying, "Repent, for the kingdom of God is at hand" (Matt. 3:2). Jesus Himself preached repentance in those days, repeating the words of John (see 4:17). There have always been calls in the churches of former times to repent, but those calls are not like the call to repent and afflict the soul on the day of atonement. No generation of believers in the past has ever been asked to repent as deeply as Laodicea is.

Laodicea is to exhibit a level of repentance not seen in former days. It is not a coincidence that she is asked to procure the special ointment called "eyesalve." The application of that special, spiritual anointing is needed to help her understand the exceeding sinfulness of sin as well as the depravity of her life and character. No other generation will become as fully aware of the sinfulness of life as will the remnant church. "They are *fully* conscious of the sinfulness of their lives, they see their weakness and unworthiness; and they are ready to despair."[128]

As the members of the church of Laodicea go through the trial of their faith in the final crisis, they will draw nearer to Christ, fix their eyes on His perfect purity, and be enabled to "discern so clearly the exceeding sinfulness of sin."[129] Thus, through the work of afflicting the soul, the submerged part of the iceberg of sin, so long hidden and unrecognized, will be finally exposed, brought to light, acknowledged to the full extent, and confessed. Laodicea will then afflict the soul and plead for purity of heart. No longer will she say, "I am increased with goods and have need of nothing."

Seeking the Lord in humility and contrition of soul is our duty and work even now. As we approach the closing scenes of the great, antitypical day of atonement, we are to accept reproof so we might, by God's grace, overcome our faults and sins.

---

[128] White, *Prophets and Kings*, p. 588 (emphasis added).
[129] *Ibid.*, p. 590.

Through affliction God reveals to us the plague spots in our characters, that by His grace we may overcome our faults. Unknown chapters in regard to ourselves are opened to us, and the test comes, whether we will accept the reproof and the counsel of God. When brought into trial, we are not to fret and complain. We should not rebel, or worry ourselves out of the hand of Christ. We are to humble the soul before God.[130]

Soul Affliction, an Inclusive Work

Soul affliction is not limited to the act of mourning for one's sinfulness of life and character, as challenging as that is. It includes being in anguish on account of the sins of others. To afflict your soul means to put yourself in the shoes of others and confess their sins as if they were your own. The prophet Daniel's affliction of soul in chapter 9 went beyond merely confessing his own personal sins. His lamentations and prayer for forgiveness were not only for his own sins but also for the sins of his people.

Daniel's lengthy confession revealed he had identified himself with his people and taken ownership of their sins:

> I set my face unto the Lord God, to seek by prayer, supplications, with fasting and sackcloth and ashes and made my confession, "We have sinned and have committed iniquity and have done wickedly and have rebelled… neither have we hearkened unto the servants thy prophets which spake in thy name… We have sinned against thee… We have rebelled against him… neither have we obeyed the voice of the Lord our God to walk in His laws… All Israel have transgressed thy law… We have sinned against him… We obeyed not His voice… We have sinned, we have done wickedly." (Daniel 9:1–15)

This work is included in the call to afflict the soul, be zealous, and repent.

---

[130] White, *The Desire of Ages*, p. 301.

Daniel's affliction of soul serves as a model for those who are seeking to understand truths pertaining to the time of the end. Only when Daniel afflicted his soul in the manner described did the angel Gabriel come to give him the understanding of the meaning of the 2,300-day prophecy (see 8:14).

> And whiles I was speaking, and praying, and confessing my sin and the sin of my people Israel, and presenting my supplication before the LORD my God for the holy mountain of my God; Yea, whiles I was speaking in prayer, even the man Gabriel, whom I had seen in the vision at the beginning, being caused to fly swiftly, touched me about the time of the evening oblation. (Daniel 9:20–23)

Likewise, when God's people today learn to do what the prophet did, confessing their sins and the sins of others, messengers from heaven will be sent to give them the understanding of the truths they need to stand in the last days.

Today, God's faithful children are called upon to sigh and cry for the abominations being done in the church as part of their effort to afflict the soul:

> Mark this point with care: Those who receive the pure mark of truth, wrought in them by the power of the Holy Ghost, represented by a mark by the man in linen, are those "that sigh and that cry for all the abominations that be done" *in the church*. Their love for purity and the honor and glory of God is such, and they have *so clear a view of the exceeding sinfulness of sin*, that they are represented as being in agony, even sighing and crying.[131]

Those who are to receive the seal of God on their foreheads will manifest their love for souls by being grieved because of the wrongs of others: "Especially in the closing work for the church, in the sealing time of the one hundred and forty-four thousand who are to stand

---

[131] White, *Testimonies for the Church*, vol. 3, pp. 266, 267 (emphasis added).

without fault before the throne of God, will they feel most deeply the wrongs of God's professed people."[132]

The statement below serves as a warning to those who do not afflict their souls by mourning for the sins of others: "The class who do not feel grieved over their own spiritual declension, nor mourn over the sins of others, will be left without the seal of God."[133]

As part of the work of afflicting the soul, the members of the church of Laodicea are being called upon to follow Christ's example of interceding on behalf of those who are unable to repent of their own sins. Hanging on the cross, Jesus cried, "Father, forgive them for they know not what they do" (Luke 23:34). Likewise, the remnant church is to plead for the souls of others.

It is easy to see that once the members of the church of Laodicea begin engaging in this work, healing and reconciliation will take place in their homes and the places where they congregate to worship. They will relive the upper-room experience, and revival and reformation will be the quick and sure result!

Soul Affliction, an Individual Work

The work of preparing for the final atonement through soul affliction is a matter that is left with the individual members of the body of Christ. They are commanded individually to engage in this work within their family and church circles:

> In this great Day of Atonement, our work is that of heartsearching, of self-abasement, and confession of sin, *each* humbling his own soul before God, and seeking pardon for *himself individually*. Anciently *every one* that did not on the Day of Atonement afflict his soul, was cut off from the people. God would have us work out our own salvation with fear and trembling. If *each* will search and see what sins are lurking in his own heart to shut out Jesus, he will find such a work to do that he will be ready to esteem others better

---

[132] *Ibid.*
[133] White, *Testimonies for the Church*, vol. 5, p. 211.

than himself. He will no longer seek to pluck the mote out of his brother's eye while a beam is in his own eye.[134]

Zechariah 12 contains a model of how the work of afflicting the soul is to be conducted in the church if total cleansing from sin is desired. The work is to be systematically carried out from the top down to the bottom of the hierarchical structure. The entire land mourns, from the house of David and his family, to the priests and their families, and finally down to the common people and their families.

> And I will pour upon the house of David, and upon the inhabitants of Jerusalem, the spirit of grace and supplications: and they shall look upon me whom they have pierced, and they shall mourn for him, as one mourneth for *his* only *son*, and shall be in bitterness for him, as one that is in bitterness for *his* firstborn. In that day shall there be a great mourning in Jerusalem, as the mourning of Hadadrimmon in the valley of Megiddon. And the land shall mourn, every family apart; the family of the house of David apart, and their wives apart; the family of the house of Nathan apart, and their wives apart; The family of the house of Levi apart, and their wives apart; the family of Shimei apart, and their wives apart; All the families that remain, every family apart, and their wives apart. (Zech. 12:10–14)

The sure result of this great work is seen in the verse that immediately follows: "In that day there shall be a fountain opened to the house of David and to the inhabitants of Jerusalem for sin and for uncleanness" (13:1).

Soul Affliction, Laodicea's Most Important Work

The work of afflicting the soul is Laodicea's most urgent and needful work today. While the church is not to neglect the work of sharing

---

[134] White, *Historical Sketches of the Foreign Missions of the Seventh-day Adventists*, p. 213 (emphasis added).

> **What does it matter if we evangelize the entire globe and add millions of names to the church books, yet end up being spewed out of Jesus' mouth because we failed to heed the call to be zealous and repent?**

the gospel—while she needs to persevere in conducting evangelistic meetings and reaching out to the community—her greatest and most urgent task lies within her own backyard. She is yet to afflict her soul; she is yet to heed the call to "be zealous therefore and repent." Her greatest task continues to remain undone!

It remains to be seen whether we as a church will finally take this work seriously enough to give it top priority or continue putting it off for less urgent tasks, as we have often done. What does it matter if we evangelize the entire globe and add millions of names to the church books, yet end up being spewed out of Jesus' mouth because we failed to heed the call to be zealous and repent?

The humble, devoted followers of Christ at this time will be distinguished, not so much for their outside labors and accomplishments, but for their deep soul affliction:

> In the time when His wrath shall go forth in judgments, these humble, devoted followers of Christ will be distinguished from the rest of the world by their *soul anguish*, which is expressed in *lamentation* and *weeping*, *reproofs* and *warnings*. While others try to throw a cloak over the existing evil, and excuse the great wickedness everywhere prevalent, those who have a zeal for God's honor and a love for souls will not hold their peace to obtain favor of any. Their righteous souls are *vexed* day by day with the unholy works and conversation of the unrighteous. They are powerless to stop the rushing torrent of iniquity, and hence they are *filled with grief and alarm*. They *mourn* before God to see religion despised in the very homes of those who have had great light. They *lament* and *afflict* their souls because pride, avarice, selfishness, and deception of almost every kind are in the church. The Spirit of

God, which prompts to reproof, is trampled underfoot, while the servants of Satan triumph. God is dishonored, the truth made of none effect.[135]

---

[135] White, *Testimonies for the Church*, vol. 5, pp. 210. 211 (emphasis added).

15

Fear God, Give Glory to Him, and Worship Him

Idea in Brief: In this chapter, the three angels' messages are examined in connection with the work of cleansing going forward in the heavenly sanctuary. Amazingly, these messages put into effect seven stages of purification from sin when accepted and demonstrated in the life.

The Theme of Greatest Importance

There is an urgent need to bring the three angels' messages of Revelation 14 back to the forefront of Adventist theology to counter the growing efforts within the church to relegate them to the doctrinal trash heap. Their true meaning needs to be discerned; and their importance, recognized. Otherwise, they will be discarded and thrown into the garbage bin like stale food!

The importance of the three angels' messages is set forth in the statement below:

> The theme of greatest importance is the third angel's message, embracing the messages of the first and second angels. *All should understand the truths contained in these messages and demonstrate them in daily life, for this is essential to salvation.* We shall have to study earnestly, prayerfully, in order to understand these

grand truths; and our power to learn and comprehend will be taxed to the utmost.[136]

A Life-and-Death Message

There are two fearful events mentioned in the three angels' messages of Revelation 14 that make the "earnest and prayerful study" of these messages more urgent and compelling than ever. One event is happening right now in heaven, and the other is soon to take place here on earth:

> **Fearful Event #1:** "The hour of his judgment is come" (14:7)—a reference to the investigative judgment that is going on right now in heaven, in which the cases of the dead are being examined. No one knows how soon this work will move on to the cases of the living.

> **Fearful Event #2:** "If any man receives the mark in his hand or in his forehead..." (v. 9)—a reference to the Sunday Law crisis, an event that will happen sometime in the near future and engulf the whole earth, testing every one of its inhabitants (see vs. 16, 17).

To put it point blank, not understanding the three angels' messages will result in not demonstrating them practically in the daily life and thus forfeiting eternal salvation. It also means not being able to stand in the judgment of the living or survive when the mark of the beast is enforced. These messages are, therefore, not to be taken lightly or discarded. They are life-and-death messages!

Sanctuary Connection

The three angels' messages are, in fact, vitally linked to the sanctuary. When received and demonstrated in the life, they are the very means by which forgiveness for sin and cleansing, the primary

---

[136] White, *Evangelism*, p. 196 (emphasis added).

benefits of the sanctuary service, are obtained. This is the reason why these messages are essential to salvation. These messages are to be embraced as truth for their redemptive significance. It is also equally true that those who tend to marginalize the sanctuary service end up seeing no light in the three angels' messages and, therefore, treating them lightly.

The close connection between the sanctuary and the three angels' messages is plainly stated below:

> While the investigative judgment is going forward in heaven, while the sins of penitent believers are being removed from the sanctuary, there is to be a special work of purification, of putting away of sin, among God's people upon earth. *This work is more clearly presented in the messages of Revelation 14.*[137]

To paraphrase, while the cases of believers who have died are being investigated and their sins are being removed from the sanctuary above, the living, whose cases are to come up next, should undergo "a special work of purification, or of putting away of sins" to prepare themselves for that event. This work of purification from sin is outlined in the three angels' messages of Revelation 14. Hence, the three angels' messages need to be seen as the means by which forgiveness and cleansing from sin may be experienced in the life. Also, since this special work of cleansing from sin is *more clearly* presented in these messages, there is no reason why anyone should have an uncertain and ambiguous understanding of these messages.

Seven Stages of Purification from Sin

The three angels' messages of Revelation 14 outline seven stages of purification from sin. The first three are found in the first angel's message; the fourth is found in the second angel's message; and the last three are found in the third angel's message. These stages of purification from sin are not immediately seen because they are

---

[137] White, *The Great Controversy*, p. 425 (emphasis added).

couched in symbolic expressions. It is not without reason that the Spirit of Prophecy says, "our power to learn and comprehend will be taxed to the utmost" when studying the three angels' messages.

The commands to "fear God," "give glory Him," and "worship Him" in the first angel's message (see vs. 6, 7) comprise the first three of these seven purifying stages. They are to be "understood and demonstrated in the life daily, for it is essential to salvation."

Stage 1: "Fear God" (Conviction)

Scripture explains what the call to fear God means when seen in connection with a work of purification or cleansing from sin. Purification from sin begins when that call is accepted and demonstrated in the life:

> And one of the malefactors which were hanged railed on him, saying, If thou be Christ, save thyself and us. But the other answering rebuked him, saying, Dost not thou *fear God*, seeing thou art in the same *condemnation*?" And we indeed justly; for we receive the due reward of our deeds: but this man hath done nothing amiss. (Luke 23:39–41, emphasis added)

Here, to fear God is to acknowledge one's guilt and condemnation on account of sin. It is to be convicted of wrong-doing. Conviction of wrong-doing is the first step in the cleansing or purifying process. This conviction is wrought in the heart by the Holy Ghost. Describing the work of the Comforter, Jesus said, "And when he is come, he will convict the world of sin, and of righteousness, and of judgment" (John 16:8, NKJV).

When one allows the Spirit of God to convict of sin, the cleansing work begins. There can be no purification from sin if guilt is not acknowledged in the first place. Conviction of wrong-doing must not be ignored or suppressed if cleansing from sin is desired. To the proud Pharisees who would not admit their sins, Jesus said, "If ye were blind, ye should have no sin: but now ye say, We see; therefore your sin remaineth" (9:41).

Where there is no fear of God, conviction of sin or sinfulness is not felt. Hence, sin is not purged from the soul, and iniquity has free reign. In Romans 3:11–18, Paul described a host of lawless deeds done by the unconverted in the world. They do so because "there is no fear of God before their eyes" (v. 18).

Stage 2: "Give glory to Him" (Confession)

The second stage in the cleansing process is the confession of sin. The command to give glory to God is a call to confess the sins brought to light in the previous stage. In other words, to give glory to God in the context of soul-cleansing is to confess the sin promptly after conviction has set in.[138]

We find a good illustration of this truth in the story of Achan. Joshua, the military commander of the armies of Israel, urged Achan "to give glory to the Lord God of Israel" by confessing the sin he had done, resulting in the defeat of Israel's armies at the battle of Ai. Unfortunately for Achan, his confession came a little too late. "And Joshua said unto Achan, My son, give, I pray thee, glory to the LORD God of Israel, and make confession unto him; and tell me now what thou hast done; hide it not from me" (Josh. 7:19).

Therefore, giving God glory is to be understood as not hiding the sin but laying it out in the open through repentance and confession. Forgiveness for sin and cleansing from its defilement are offered when one acknowledges it, confesses it, and repents of it. "If we confess our sins, God is faithful and just to forgive us our sins and to cleanse us from all unrighteousness" (1 John 1:9). Genuine repentance and confession of sin need to be demonstrated daily in the life if pardon, justification, and cleansing from sin are to take place.

---

[138] The call to give glory to God has a more demanding application than merely to repent when applied to those who already know the truth and are part of the church of Christ. Paul urged the believers in the church of Corinth to give glory to God in whatever they do, particularly in the area of eating and drinking (see 1 Cor. 10:31). However, the call to give glory to Him in the first angel's message is addressed to the unbelieving Gentile world (i.e., "languages, nations, tongues and people"). Requiring those who are hearing the everlasting gospel being preached to them for the *first time* to practice strict health reform is hardly the proper approach.

On the flip side, not giving God the glory is doing the very opposite. Sin is not forsaken and confessed. This truth is demonstrated in the experience of those who are made to suffer the effects of the seven last plagues after probation closes: "And the fourth angel poured out his vial upon the sun; and power was given unto him to scorch men with fire. And men were scorched with great heat, and blasphemed the name of God, which hath power over these plagues: *and they repented not to give him glory*" (Rev. 16:8, 9).

Stage 3: "Worship Him" (Conversion)

The third stage in the purifying process is indicated by the call to worship God. There is more to the worship of God than going to church every Sabbath. To worship Him is to forsake sin. It is to be converted and have a changed life. After Jesus forgave Mary Magdalene of her sin, He commanded her to "go and sin no more" (John 8:11). It is a call to live a holy life by putting away sin. "Give unto the LORD the glory due unto his name; worship the LORD in the beauty of holiness" (Ps. 29:2). It is a call to turn away from disobedience and live a life of obedience. "Without obedience to His commandments, no worship can be pleasing to God."[139]

> "There is more to the worship of God than going to church every Sabbath. To worship Him is to forsake sin. It is to be converted and have a changed life."

To recap, the first angel's message is an invitation to experience spiritual cleansing through the process of conviction, confession, and conversion. Expressed in theological jargon, the first angel's message is an invitation to experience justification and sanctification daily. Since these great spiritual truths are couched in symbolic language, they are not discerned immediately. To paraphrase the first angel's message, "Be convicted of your sins and confess them, for the hour of His judgment is come, and be ye converted…"

---

[139] White, *The Great Controversy*, p. 436.

Those who accepted the proclamation of the first angel's message by the Millerites during the Advent movement of the 1840s demonstrated these three stages of purification in their experience.

> Everywhere the searching testimony was heard, warning sinners, both worldlings and church members, to flee from the wrath to come.... The simple, direct testimony of the Scriptures, set home by the power of the Holy Spirit, brought a weight of *conviction* which few were able wholly to resist. Professors of religion were roused from their false security. They saw their backslidings, their worldliness and unbelief, their pride and selfishness. Many sought the Lord with *repentance* and humiliation. The affections that had so long clung to earthly things they now fixed upon heaven. The Spirit of God rested upon them, and with hearts softened and subdued they joined to sound the cry: "Fear God, and give glory to Him; for the hour of His judgment is come."
>
> ...The hearts of parents were turned to their children, and the hearts of children to their parents. The barriers of pride and reserve were swept away. Heartfelt *confessions* were made, and the members of the household labored for the salvation of those who were nearest and dearest. Often was heard the sound of earnest intercession. Everywhere were souls in deep anguish pleading with God. Many wrestled all night in prayer for the assurance that their own sins were pardoned, or for the *conversion* of their relatives or neighbors.[140]

Stage 4: "Come out of Her My People" (Coming out of Babylon)

The fourth stage in the purification process is found in the call to come out of Babylon because she is fallen. The fall of Babylon is first announced in the second angel's message of Revelation 14 and repeated in 18:2–3. "And he cried mightily with a strong voice, saying, Babylon the great is fallen, is fallen, and is become the

---

[140] *Ibid.*, p. 369 (emphasis added).

habitation of devils and the hold of every foul spirit and a cage of every unclean and hateful bird. For all nations have drunk of the wrath of the wine of her fornication and the kings of the earth have committed fornication with her and the merchants of the earth are waxed rich through the abundance of her delicacies."

The proclamation of the fall of Babylon includes an emphatic command to God's honest children in the world and fallen churches to "come out of her that ye be not partakers of her sins and receive not of her plagues" (Verse 4).

Because of her false teachings and corrupt practices, spiritual Babylon has become "the habitation of devils and the hold of every foul spirit and a cage of every unclean and hateful bird." Hence, separating from her communion is necessary to avoid becoming a partaker of her sins by association and influence.

Therefore, to be purified from sin, it is not enough to experience pardon and justification. It is also necessary to separate from everything foul and unclean. This command is in line with Paul's admonition to believers at the church of Corinth to "not be unequally yoked with unbelievers," "come out from among them and be separate," and "touch not the unclean thing" (2 Cor. 6:14, 17). God's people are to maintain their spiritual purity at all times. "Depart ye, depart ye, go ye out from thence, touch no unclean thing; go ye out of the midst of her; be ye clean, that bear the vessels of the LORD" (Isa. 52:11).

> A blessing or a curse is now before the people of God—a blessing if they come out from the world and are separate, and walk in the path of humble obedience; and a curse if they unite with the idolatrous, who trample upon the high claims of heaven.[141]

In 1844, those who accepted the Millerite preaching of the second angel's message demonstrated that message in their lives by coming

---

[141] White, *Testimonies for the Church*, vol. 1, p. 609.

Fear God, Give Glory to Him, and Worship Him

out of the churches, which fell for rejecting the Advent message. Those churches, we are told, have become more corrupt over time.[142]

In the summer of 1844, about fifty thousand withdrew from the churches.[143]

Stage 5: Sabbath Reform (Conformity to the Moral Law)

We have now come to the third angel's message. This message begins with a warning against receiving the mark of the beast, in the hand or on the forehead, and ends with the solemn declaration, "Here is the patience of the saints. Here are they that keep the commandments of God and the faith of Jesus" (Rev. 14:9–12). In the call to "keep the commandments of God and the faith of Jesus" are found the last three stages in the purification process. They are to be demonstrated in the life, for they are essential to salvation.

God's commandments need to be considered on two parallel but separate fronts: the *moral law*, also known as the Ten Commandments, and the *physical laws*, or the laws and principles that govern the health of the human organism. Together, these two sets of laws make up the commandments of God. The moral and physical laws are two sides of the same coin. They are on equal footing. Therefore, violating one is violating the other, and to demonstrate the third angel's message in the life is to keep both sets of laws.

The proclamation of the third angel's message with a loud voice during the mark-of-the-beast crisis, an event that is still future, urges people to keep the law of God, especially the fourth commandment, as it is the part of the moral law that is especially controverted.

> The Sabbath will be the great test of loyalty, for it is the point of truth especially controverted. When the final test shall be brought to bear upon men, then the line of distinction will be

---

[142] White, *Early Writings*, p. 273.
[143] White, *The Great Controversy*, p. 376. In Ezra 2:64–65, we are told about 50,000 left Babylon and returned to Jerusalem to help rebuild the temple under the leadership of Zerubbabel. History repeats itself!

drawn between those who serve God and those who serve Him not. While the observance of the false sabbath in compliance with the law of the state, contrary to the fourth commandment, will be an avowal of allegiance to a power that is in opposition to God, the keeping of the true Sabbath, in obedience to God's law, is an evidence of loyalty to the Creator. While one class, by accepting the sign of submission to earthly powers, receive the mark of the beast, the other choosing the token of allegiance to divine authority, receive the seal of God.[144]

Conformity to the moral law, especially the part that calls for all to rest on the seventh day, is the fifth stage in the purifying process. In 1847, the Lord gave Ellen White a vision stressing the importance of keeping the seventh-day Sabbath, as it is the sign of our being sanctified through the power of Christ (see Ezek. 20:20).[145] It is something that can be achieved if we fully understand and live out the first and second angels' messages.

Stage 6: Health Reform (Conformity to the Physical Laws)

Conformity to the natural laws (i.e., health laws) is the sixth stage in the purifying process.

> Transgression of physical law is transgression of the moral law; for God is as truly the author of physical laws as He is the author of the moral law. His law is written with His own finger upon every nerve, every muscle, every faculty, which has been entrusted

---

[144] *Ibid.*, p. 605.

[145] "Then, on the first Sabbath in April 1847, seven months after they began to keep and teach the Seventh-day Sabbath, the Lord gave a vision to Mrs. White at Topsham, Maine, in which the importance of the Sabbath was stressed. She saw the tables of the law in the ark in the heavenly sanctuary, and a halo of light about the fourth commandment. See pages 32-35 for the account of this vision. The position previously taken from the study of the word of God was confirmed. The vision also helped to broaden the believer's concept of Sabbath observance. In this revelation, Mrs. White was carried down to the close of time and saw the Sabbath as the great testing truth on which men decide whether to serve God or to serve an apostate power" (*Early Writings*, p. xxi).

to man. And every misuse of any part of our organism is a violation of that law.[146]

Because faithful adherence to the health laws is needed to be purified from sin, it is part of the work of the third angel to make plain the natural laws and urge obedience to them: "*Men and women cannot violate natural law by indulging depraved appetite and lustful passions, without violating the law of God.... To make natural law plain, and to urge obedience to it, is a work that accompanies the third angel's message.*"[147] Thus, the health reform work is rightfully called the "right arm of the third angel." It is also called the "entering wedge."[148]

In addition to reverencing the Sabbath, Seventh-day Adventists commit themselves to adhering to the health and temperance principles laid down in the Bible and Spirit of Prophecy. By this, they show they are demonstrating the third angel's message in their daily lives.

Stage 7: "The Faith of Jesus" (Crucifixion)

One final stage in the purification process remains: "the faith of Jesus." Just what is the faith of Jesus, and how is it to be demonstrated in the daily life as essential to salvation? We turn to the apostle Paul for the answers to these questions. He tied the faith of Jesus with the experience of righteousness by faith: "Knowing that a man is not justified by the works of the law, but by *the faith of Jesus* Christ, even we have believed in Jesus Christ, that we might be justified by the *faith of Christ*, and not by the works of the law: for by the works of the law shall no flesh be justified" (Gal. 2:16).

Four verses later, Paul explained what it means to demonstrate righteousness by faith, or "the faith of Jesus," by experience: "I am crucified with Christ: nevertheless I live; yet not I, but Christ liveth in me: and the life which I now live in the flesh I live by *the faith of the*

---

[146] White, *Christ's Object Lessons*, p. 347.
[147] White, *Christian Temperance and Bible Hygiene*, p. 9 (emphasis added).
[148] White, *Testimonies for the Church*, vol. 6, p. 327.

Son of God [or the faith of Jesus], who loved me, and gave himself for me" (v. 20).

"The faith of Jesus" is described as the experience of being dead and alive at the same time. "I am crucified with Christ" means I am dead (to self). "Nevertheless I live" means I am still alive (in Christ). "But the life I now live in the flesh, I live by the faith of the Son of God" means the life I now live is no longer the old, fleshly, selfish life I used to live, for that life has been crucified and no longer exists. Christ's life of faith and obedience now animates and permeates my entire being. This is what it means to live by the faith of Jesus.

Jesus illustrated this lofty principle of character development in the following words: "Verily, verily, I say unto you, Except a corn of wheat fall into the ground and die, it abideth alone: but if it die, it bringeth forth much fruit" (John 12:24). It is easy to see it is only through living by the faith of Jesus that the genuine fruits of the Spirit can be produced in the Christian life: "love, joy, peace, longsuffering, gentleness, goodness, faith, meekness, temperance: against such there is no law" (Gal. 5:22, 23).

To live by the faith of Jesus is to be dead to self and live *like* Jesus lived. Self no longer appears. The life of Jesus exemplified total death to self by a life of self-denial. He voluntarily laid down His power as the Son of God and fully exercised faith in His Father's strength alone to resist Satan's temptations and maintain His purity of character in His adopted human nature. "Jesus emptied Himself, and in all that He did, self did not appear. He subordinated all things to the will of His Father."[149]

Jesus challenges His disciples: "If any man will come after me, let him deny himself, and take up his cross daily, and follow me" (Luke 9:23). Paul followed Christ's example by saying, "I die daily" (1 Cor. 15:31). To live by the faith of Jesus means self is no longer to be lifted up with pride and self-worth. Self no longer promotes itself. Self no longer strives to be the center of attention nor seeks recognition. Self no longer jockeys for the highest position nor strives for supremacy

---

[149] White, *Thoughts from the Mount of Blessing*, p. 14.

but considers others as better than self (see Phil. 2:3). To be crucified with Christ is to crucify the flesh with all its affections and lusts (see Gal. 5:24).

The call to live by the faith of Jesus is heightened by the call to afflict the soul on the day of atonement. This call is no less than the call to die to self by denying self. "This is to be a lasting ordinance for you: On the tenth day of the seventh month, you must *deny yourselves* and not do any work—whether native-born or a foreigner residing among you" (Lev. 16:29, NIV, emphasis added).

In the final atonement, death to self is made permanent and final. "He that is holy let him be holy still." The command to "take away their filthy garments… and give them a change of raiment" removes the sinful, corrupt Adamic self forever and gives place to the reception of Christ's selfless life and character within the soul. Sin dwelling in me, which is the principle of self-love, the root of all human sinning and the greatest hindrance to character perfection, is crucified once and for all and taken out of the way. At this stage, the believer is fully and permanently purified of sin. Hence, the announcement, "They are nevermore to be defiled by the corruptions of the world.… They are eternally secure from the tempter's devices."[150]

The Third Angel's Message and the Ark of the Covenant

The three articles enshrined in the ark of the covenant, namely, the tables of the covenant, the golden pot that had manna, and Aaron's rod that budded (see Heb. 9:5), were not deposited there merely to commemorate certain significant events in Israel's history. They are not to be regarded merely as sacred relics, preserved in the ark to remind everyone of God's miraculous interventions in Israel's glorious past. Rather, they serve a higher, loftier spiritual purpose.

In God's infinite wisdom and foreknowledge, these articles were preserved in the ark to serve as emblems of the experience of those who are demonstrating in their daily lives the purifying influence of the third angel's message—"the commandments of God and the faith

---

[150] White, *Prophets and Kings*, p. 591.

of Jesus." Through this, they show they have followed Jesus by faith into the Most Holy Place of the heavenly sanctuary.

Let us remember that God revealed to Israel His "glorious ideal of character in the command to build the sanctuary."[151] The articles and furniture in the sanctuary symbolize various stages of the Christian experience. The altar of burnt offering in the courtyard, for instance, represents pardon and justification for the individual as a result of faith in Christ's sacrificial death on Calvary (see Col. 1:20). The laver is a symbol of baptism and cleansing (see Acts 22:16).

Moving on to the first apartment, the articles found therein are symbols of a higher level of spiritual development, known as growth in grace or sanctification, a daily process. The table of showbread represents the Word of God, partaking of which results in spiritual growth (see John 6:53–56). The altar of incense represents prayer, which is the means of unrestricted communion with God (see Rev. 5:8; 8:3, 4). The candlesticks represent spiritual discernment and power for holy living (see Zech. 4:6). All three elements combined make the sanctification of character possible. Sanctification is provided as a benefit of Christ's continuous work of intercession in the first apartment of the heavenly sanctuary.

The Most Holy Place Experience

The ark of the covenant was the only piece of furniture found in the second apartment of the sanctuary. The three articles placed in the ark fitly represent the experience of those who are purified completely from sin and perfected as a result of demonstrating the third angel's message in their lives—keeping the commandments of God and the faith of Jesus. Keeping the moral law is represented by the two tables of the covenant or the Ten Commandments and faithfulness in the physical health laws is represented by the pot of manna. Only one article is left—the rod of Aaron that budded. This article amazingly represents the experience of keeping the faith of Jesus! It is easy to

---

[151] White, *The Desire of Ages*, p. 208.

see the rationale for the symbolism with the first two articles, but how does the rod of Aaron represent the faith of Jesus?

Aaron's rod was a dead, lifeless piece of wood, yet it was alive and bearing fruit! It is the most fitting symbol to represent the experience of those who are truly living by the faith of Jesus. "I am crucified with Christ" because the filthy garments have been removed and self no longer lives, "yet I live, yet not I, but Christ lives in me." The life lived is no longer the old life, but Christ's.

The rationale behind the placement of the three articles in the ark of the covenant in the second apartment of the sanctuary is now evident. These three articles beautifully and meaningfully sum up the experience of all who have embraced the third angel's message and are striving to demonstrate it in their daily lives. Seventh-day Adventists, who are called upon to "prophesy again before many peoples, and nations, and tongues, and kings" (see Rev 10:11), need to faithfully demonstrate this message in their lives before they can preach it effectively and with power.

The Third Angel's Message and the Pioneers

The history of the Seventh-day Adventist Church shows God has genuinely led that movement into the correct understanding and experience of the third angel's message. After much "anxious care" and diligent "study," discovering "link after link," the pioneers of this church became convinced that the charge to keep the commandments of God in the third angel's message called for a work of "Sabbath reform." This was in 1846.[152]

When the pioneers of the church understood the Sabbath truth that year, they realized they have been ignorantly transgressing the fourth commandment. They then abandoned Sunday and gladly embraced the Seventh-day Sabbath. Of this, Ellen White wrote, "In the autumn of 1846, we began to observe the Bible Sabbath, and to teach and defend it."[153]

---

[152] White, *Testimonies for the Church*, vol. 1, pp. 78, 79.
[153] *Ibid.*, 75.

In 1863, the health reform message was delivered to the remnant church through a vision given to Ellen White: "It was at the house of Brother A. Hilliard, at Otsego, Michigan, June 6, 1863, That the great subject of health Reform was opened before me in vision."[154]

Since then, article after article and book after book on health and temperance have been published to give impetus to the health-reform work God was calling His church to do. These publications include *Counsels of Diet and Foods, Healthful Living, Counsels on Health, Temperance, Medical Ministry, The Ministry of Healing, Christian Temperance and Bible Hygiene*, and others.

In 1888, the last component of the third angel's message was given to the church at the General Conference Session in Minneapolis, Minnesota, through Elders A. T. Jones and E. J. Waggoner. These men brought the message of righteousness by faith (i.e., the faith of Jesus) to the forefront of Adventist theology. That message was nothing but a gracious invitation "to receive the righteousness of Christ which is made manifest in obedience to all the commandments of God"[155]—both the moral and physical laws.

Conclusion

Thus, the Christian experience, specially tailored for the time of the end, is clearly spelled out in the three angels' message. These messages need to be understood as purifying messages designed to bring humanity back to God's original design—perfect conformity to His commandments. These messages need to be experienced daily as conviction, confession, conversion, coming out of spiritual Babylon, conformity to the moral law, conformity to the laws of the physical nature, and the crucifixion of self. It is the solemn duty of all Seventh-day Adventist Christians to daily demonstrate these truths in their lives in preparation for the final atonement and the judgment of the living.

---

[154] White, *Counsels on Diet and Foods*, p. 481.
[155] White, *Testimonies to Ministers and Gospel Workers*, p. 92.

The three articles deposited inside the ark of the covenant in the Most Holy Place represent the experience those who demonstrate the third angel's message in their lives will possess: obedience to all of God's commandments and living by the faith of Jesus. This truly amazing discovery of the connection between the third angel's message and the symbolism behind the three articles found in the ark of the covenant validates the correctness of the points presented in this study.

Furthermore, the fact that God had led the pioneers of the church historically into a step-by-step understanding and experience of the third angel's message validates the authenticity of the movement they founded. The Seventh-day Adventist Church is truly God's commandment-keeping remnant people for the time of the end. Every church member who realizes this will consider it a great privilege to be part of this movement of destiny and will be meticulously demonstrating the third angel's message in the life. They will be eternally grateful for the blessed, advanced experience God is offering them through the three angels' messages.

We close this chapter with the powerful statement below:

> The first, second, and third angels' messages are all linked together. The evidences of the abiding, ever-living truth of these grand messages, that mean so much to us, that have awakened such intense opposition from the religious world, cannot be extinguished. Satan is constantly seeking to cast his hellish shadow about these messages, so that the remnant people of God shall not clearly discern their import, their time, and place; but they live, and are to exert their power upon our religious experience while time shall last.[156]

---

[156] White, *Selected Messages*, book 2, p. 117.

16

"Thou Must Prophesy Again"

Idea in Brief: This chapter discloses Adventism's two-fold marching orders as depicted in Revelation 10: "eat the little open book" in the hand of the mighty angel and "prophesy again." These marching orders were activated when the once-sealed prophesies of Daniel relating to the cleansing of the sanctuary were unsealed in 1844. The "finishing of the mystery of God" on earth—the closing work of the gospel—hinges on how well these sacred orders are carried out by the church.

Sealed Up Until the Time of the End

The book of Daniel closed with these words: "But thou, O Daniel, shut up the words, and seal the book, even to the time of the end" (12:4). We are told the entire book of Daniel was not sealed up; only the prophecies that pertained to the last days were.[157] Hence, the prophetic truths related to the final ministration of Jesus in the heavenly sanctuary were effectively closed up until the time of the end. The understanding of these truths would not be possible until that time arrives. Daniel wrote that when the time of the end comes, many would "run to and fro" and "knowledge" of the prophecies that were once sealed up would "increase." Many would go back and forth in their Bibles to gain the precious understanding of the

---

[157] See White, *The Acts of the Apostles*, p. 585.

prophecies concerning the end-time closing work of Jesus in the heavenly sanctuary.

The Unsealing of Daniel's Sealed Prophecies

The time of the unsealing of the last-day prophecies of Daniel is proclaimed in Revelation 10. A mighty angel was seen coming down from heaven and standing before John with a little book in his hand, open, indicating it is the same book that had been closed and sealed up in Daniel's time. This powerful visitor from heaven came down near the end of the blowing of the sixth trumpet. He swore by Him who lives forever and created the heavens, earth, and everything therein, as he solemnly announced, "there should be time no longer" and "the mystery of God should be finished" (vs. 6, 7). He indicated the mystery of God is to be finished as the seventh trumpet is *about* to blow.

The mighty angel then instructed John to take the little book in his hand and eat it. After John did what he was told, he was commissioned to "prophesy again before many peoples, and nations, and tongues, and kings" (v. 11). Today, Adventism's marching orders are found in the command to "eat the little open book" and "prophesy again." The little open book contains the once-sealed truths related to Christ's final ministration in the heavenly sanctuary, and the command to prophesy again is the command to share these truths with the entire world.

> "
> Seventh-day Adventists are commanded to earnestly study the work and mission of Jesus in the heavenly sanctuary and proclaim these truths to the world. That is their present duty. Faithfulness to that commission is what brings the mystery of God to an end.
> "

In other words, Seventh-day Adventists are commanded to earnestly study the work and mission of Jesus in the heavenly sanctuary and proclaim these truths to the world. That is their present duty. Faithfulness to that two-fold commission is what brings the mystery of God to an end. When the mystery of God is finished, probation closes and the seventh angel blows his trumpet.

The Thematic Link Between Daniel 12 and Revelation 10

The close connection between Daniel 12 and Revelation 10 needs to be clearly seen. While these two chapters are thematically linked, they are, at the same time, thematic opposites. Daniel 12 deals with the sealing up of prophetic events relating to the last days, whereas Revelation 10 deals with their unsealing. The angel who instructed Daniel to seal up the prophecies relating to the time of the end was the same mighty angel who came to John to announce the time had come for those prophecies to be unsealed. The table below demonstrates that:

The angel of Daniel 12	**The mighty angel of Revelation 10**
His feet are upon waters of the river (v. 6)	His feet are on water and land (v. 2)
He holds up his hands and swears by heaven (v. 7)	He swears by the name of the Creator (vs. 5–7)
He makes an oath related to time (v. 7)	He makes an oath related to time (vs. 5–7)
He declares everything will be finished (v. 7)	He declares the mystery of God should be finished (vs. 5–7)

Once it is established that the mighty angel who stood before John is none other than the angel that instructed Daniel to seal the book, then it can be deduced that the little open book in his hand was the same book that was closed up and sealed until the time of the end. The mighty angel had come to John in Revelation 10 to announce that Daniel's sealed prophecies for the last days were now unsealed and available for study and investigation.

The timing of the mighty angel's coming in Revelation 10 also needs to be noted. He came to John as the sixth trumpet had nearly finished blowing, and the seventh is *about* to blow. The blowing of the sixth trumpet neared its completion with the fall of the Ottoman Empire on August 11, 1840,[158] after it had tormented the Byzantine

---

[158] See White, *The Great Controversy*, pp. 334–336 for a more detailed explanation of this date.

Empire (Eastern Rome) for a prophetic "hour, a day, a month and a year," a total of 391 years and 15 days (9:15). At this time, as the blowing of the sixth trumpet is coming to a close, the Millerite movement appears on the stage of action, proclaiming the first angel's message, "Fear God, give glory to him. . ." (see 11:13).

The mighty angel's announcement by an oath that "there should be time no longer" points to the termination of the 2,300-year prophetic timeline of Daniel 8:14. The ending of the longest time prophecy in the Bible clears the way for the finishing of the mystery of God.

The Mystery of God

What is the mystery of God? What is the finishing of the mystery of God? The Bible defines the "mystery of God" as the gospel of Jesus Christ. "Now to him that is of power to stablish you according to my gospel, and the preaching of Jesus Christ, according to the revelation of the *mystery*, which was kept secret since the world began" (Rom. 16:25, emphasis added). Paul also wrote, "That utterance may be given unto me, that I may open my mouth boldly, to make known the *mystery of the gospel*, for which I am an ambassador in bonds: that therein I may speak boldly, as I ought to speak" (Eph. 6:18–20, emphasis added). He called the gospel "the mystery of Christ" (Col. 4:3).

The Finishing of the Mystery of God in the Soul

The gospel is a silent, mysterious power; it is "the power of God unto salvation to the Jews first and then to the Greek" (Rom. 1:16). Its purpose is to expel sin from the soul. It possesses the ability to transform characters and lives so amazingly that even devils are baffled by it. It is to them an "incomprehensible mystery." [159] Ultimately, the gospel is to restore "the well-nigh obliterated image of God in the soul."

When the mystery of God is finished in the soul temple, the human agent will no longer reflect Satan's image, but God's. Christ's character is to be reproduced in humanity. "To whom God would make known

---

[159] White, *Testimonies to Ministers and Gospel Workers*, p. 18.

what is the riches of the glory of this mystery among the Gentiles; which is *Christ in you*, the hope of glory" (Col. 1:27). There will be no more spot, wrinkle, or any such thing to mar the character (see Eph. 5:27). At its fulfillment, the conscience is perfected, and there is no more consciousness, awareness, or memory of sin (see Heb. 10:1, 2). We are privileged to look forward with joy to the full maturity of the character as the mystery of God is finished in the soul.

> Angels of God, intelligences of heaven, are *watching the development of character*, and weighing the moral worth of the professed followers of Christ. Look up, look above the whirl of daily occurrences, and fix your eyes upon Him who never changes and you will endure as seeing Him who is invisible. You may look forward with joy to *the finishing of the mystery*.[160]

The Finishing of the Mystery of God on Earth

By extension, the finishing of the mystery of God is the culmination of the gospel work on earth. The goal of the worldwide gospel proclamation is to gather into one body both Jews and Gentiles, living together in Christian love and perfect harmony. After all, the gospel is "the power of God unto salvation to the Jew first and also to the Greek." Paul made it clear that the "mystery of Christ" calls for the Gentiles to be fellow-heirs and partakers of the gospel promise, as are the Jews (see Eph. 3:3–6).

Jerusalem of old was inhabited mainly by Jews who were at enmity with their Gentile neighbors. However, the New Jerusalem is to be inhabited by Jews and Gentiles who accept the invitation to become spiritual Israel, living together in perfect unity. This harmony demonstrates the power of the gospel (see Zech. 2:4–11). "Thus saith the LORD of hosts; In those days it shall come to pass, that ten men shall take hold out of all languages of the nations, even shall take hold of the skirt of him that is a Jew, saying, We will go with you: for we have heard that God is with you" (8:20–23).

---

[160] White, *Manuscript Releases*, vol. 5, p. 11 (emphasis added).

To reiterate, the finishing of the mystery of God is the closing of the great work of the gospel. "The prophecies which were fulfilled in the outpouring of the former rain at the opening of the gospel, are again to be fulfilled in the latter rain at its close."[161]

When the Mystery of God Is to Be Finished

The mighty angel of Revelation 10 explains the timing of the finishing of the mystery of God: "But in the days of the voice of the seventh angel, when he is *about* to sound, the mystery of God should be finished" (v. 7, NKJV, emphasis added). The mystery of God will be finished when the seventh trumpet is *about* to blow, not when it *begins* to blow, as the KJV version says.[162] In other words, the mystery of God will be finished right before the seventh trumpet is blown.

The blowing of the seventh trumpet is the signal that human probation is closed. When that final trumpet is blown, the mystery of God will have been finished. The work of salvation on earth will have been completed. Every case will have been decided for life or death in the courts above, and the heavenly sanctuary will have been cleansed.

---

[161] White, *The Great Controversy*, p. 611.

[162] The KJV of the text says, "But in the days of the voice of the seventh angel, when he shall *begin* to sound…" (emphasis added). The English word "begin" is unfortunately not the most accurate translation of the original Greek word used in the passage, *mello*, which literally means "about to." The Greek word *mello* is translated correctly in Revelation 10:4: "When the seven thunders uttered, I was *about to* [*mello*] write…" (emphasis added). John had not begun writing when the angel spoke to him. He was *about* to write. The Greek word *mello* is also properly translated in 8:13: "Woe, woe, woe, to the inhabiters of the earth by reason of the other voices of the trumpet of the three angels, which are *yet* [*mello*] to sound!" (emphasis added). In the text, the three woe trumpets have not yet begun sounding. They are *about* to sound. In 10:7, the seventh angel does not begin sounding the trumpet. Rather, he is *about* to sound it. There is a big difference. The seventh trumpet does not begin to sound until 11:15. When it does sound, the mystery of God will have been finished: "And the seventh angel sounded; and there were great voices in heaven, saying, The kingdoms of this world are become the kingdoms of our Lord, and of his Christ; and he shall reign for ever and ever." Hence, the seventh trumpet did not begin sounding in 1844, as some of our pioneers taught. Rather, it was *about* to sound. The kingdoms of this world did not become the kingdom of our Lord in 1844. That is still a future event. The kingdoms of this world do not become Christ's until the mystery of God is finished. The NKJV of Revelation 10:7 is used in this book because it uses the correct translation of the original Greek word *mello*.

"Thou Must Prophesy Again"

The blowing of the seventh trumpet, an event still future, signals the close of the work of Jesus in the heavenly sanctuary. He will have made His final atonement to cleanse His followers and blot out their sins. At this point, He changes His attire from priestly garments to kingly robes; He assumes kingly authority and rules with a rod of iron. Daniel referred to this time as follows: "And at that time shall Michael stand up, the great prince which standeth for the children of thy people: and there shall be a time of trouble, such as never was since there was a nation even to that same time" (12:1).

In Revelation 10:7, the seventh trumpet is *about* to blow. Probation is still open, and the mystery of God is not yet finished. The seventh trumpet does not actually blow until one gets to 11:15. "And the seventh angel sounded; and there were great voices in heaven, saying, the kingdoms of this world are become the kingdoms of our Lord, and of his Christ; and he shall reign for ever and ever." Jesus receives the throne of His ancestral father David, and His enemies become His footstool (see Luke 1:32, 33; Heb. 1:13).

The time we are living in is the short period of time when the seventh trumpet is about to blow. It is a time of relative peace to allow the mystery of God to be finished. As the seventh trumpet is *about* to blow, God has given the church a tiny window of time and opportunity to fulfill her commission: "eat the little book" and "prophesy again."

The seventh trumpet is about to blow, and trouble is brewing on the earth, "yet held in check," we are told, "so as not to prevent the work of the third angel."[163] The four angels from the four corners of the earth are commanded to hold the winds of strife so the servants of God can be sealed on their foreheads (see Rev. 7:1). In other words, a restraint is placed on evil until the mystery of God shall be finished during this time of relative peace.

Three things are to be accomplished during the time designated as "the finishing of the mystery of God": 1) the cleansing of the heavenly sanctuary from the defilement it had borne for centuries and

---

[163] White, *Last Day Events,* p. 143.

restoration to its original, pure, undefiled state; 2) the restoration of the image of God in the characters of His children to the state of sinlessness Adam had before the fall; 3) the vindication of the law of God against Satan's claim that it is impossible to obey.

The seventh angel is *about* to blow his trumpet, and all things are about to come to an end. The only reason why it has not sounded yet is because the mystery of God is not yet finished. As long as the mystery of God is not finished, the seventh angel does not blow his trumpet, and the evil kingdoms of this world do not become Christ's. The great controversy will keep getting prolonged! What can the church do today to hasten the finishing of the mystery of God?

A Two-fold Present Duty
There is a two-fold call to the church of Laodicea in Revelation 10 to eat the little open book and prophesy again (see vs. 8–11). This is present duty. Needless to say, the reason why the mystery of God is taking longer to finish is because of the indifference of His denominated people today with regards to these calls. Perhaps this indifference is due to a lack of understanding of what this duty involves.

"Take the Little Open Book and Eat It"
To "eat the little open book" symbolically means to study and assimilate the messages found in the book that is in the hand of the mighty angel. This little book contains the unsealed messages of Daniel relating to the time of the end: the cleansing of the heavenly sanctuary, the investigative judgment, and other related truths. The book is open in the hand of the mighty angel to show these messages are no longer closed up as before. Its contents are now open for investigation. The imagery of eating a book or scroll for understanding and spiritual nourishment is borrowed from the Old Testament:

> Moreover he said unto me, Son of man, eat that thou findest; eat this roll, and go speak unto the house of Israel. So I opened my mouth, and he caused me to eat that roll. And he said unto me, Son of man, cause thy belly to eat, and fill thy bowels with this roll that

I give thee. Then did I eat it, and it was in my mouth as honey for sweetness. (Ezekiel 3:1–3)

Thy words were found, and I did eat them; and thy word was unto me the joy and rejoicing of mine heart. (Jeremiah 15:16)

Jesus employed the same figure of speech when He stressed to His disciples the importance of studying the Word of God: "Whoso eateth my flesh, and drinketh my blood, hath eternal life; and I will raise him up at the last day. For my flesh is meat indeed, and my blood is drink indeed. He that eateth my flesh, and drinketh my blood, dwelleth in me, and I in him" (John 6:54–56).

The Spirit of Prophecy explains the matter of "eating" the word of truth in plain language: "We should eat the flesh and drink the blood of the Son of God; that is, carefully study the Word, eat it, digest it, make it a part of our being. We are to live the Word, not keep it apart from our lives."[164]

Therefore, it should come as no surprise to find many calls in the Spirit of Prophecy to study the sanctuary and related truths. These are nothing but repeated echoes of the call of the mighty angel of Revelation 10 to eat the little book. To reiterate, giving due diligence to the investigation of the subject of Christ's final ministration in the heavenly sanctuary is the present duty for every Seventh-day Adventist; it is their sacred responsibility; it is an absolute necessity.

Here is just a tiny sampling of such calls in the Spirit of Prophecy:

> The subject of the sanctuary and the investigative judgment should be *clearly understood* by the people of God. All need a knowledge for themselves of the position and work of their great High Priest.[165]
>
> We are in the great day of atonement, and the sacred work of Christ for the people of God that is going on at the present time in the heavenly sanctuary should be our *constant study*.[166]

---

[164] White, "Prepare to Meet the Lord," *The Review and Herald*, November 27, 1900.
[165] White, *The Great Controversy*, p. 488 (emphasis added).
[166] White, *Testimonies for the Church*, vol. 5, p. 520 (emphasis added).

The great plan of redemption, as revealed in the closing work of these last days, should receive *close examination*.... All need to become *more intelligent* in regard to the work of the atonement, which is going on in the sanctuary above.[167]

The sanctuary in heaven is the very center of Christ's work in behalf of men. It concerns every soul living upon the earth. It opens to view the plan of redemption, bringing us down to the very close of time, and revealing the triumphant issue of the contest between righteousness and sin. It is of the utmost importance that all should *thoroughly investigate* these subjects, and be able to give an answer to every one that asketh them a reason of the hope that is in them.[168]

As a people, we should be earnest students of prophecy; we should *not rest* until we become *intelligent* in regard to the subject of the sanctuary, which is brought out in the visions of Daniel and John.[169]

"Thou Must Prophesy Again"

God designed that the messages of salvation contained in the little open book that the church is commanded to eat should be shared with "many peoples, and nations, and tongues, and kings." This is the reason behind the call to "prophesy again." This call finds an end-time fulfillment in the proclamation of the three angels' messages. "And I saw another angel fly in the midst of heaven, having the everlasting gospel to preach unto them that dwell on the earth, and to every nation, and kindred, and tongue, and people, Saying with a loud voice, Fear God, and give glory to him; for the hour of his judgment is come" (Rev. 14:6, 7).

The three angels' messages are not to be proclaimed to the world by pen and voice only but daily demonstrated in the life as a witness to the efficacy and power of these messages. Beholding with a prophetic eye the finishing work of the gospel in the time of the end, Jesus

---

[167] *Ibid.*, p. 575 (emphasis added).
[168] White, *Evangelism*, p. 222 (emphasis added).
[169] *Ibid.*, pp. 222, 223 (emphasis added).

declared, "And this gospel of the kingdom shall be preached in all the world for a *witness* unto all nations; and then shall the end come" (Matt. 24:14).

Those who are faithfully obeying the call to prophesy again are represented as angels flying in the midst of heaven:

> The angels are represented as flying in the midst of heaven, proclaiming to the world a message of warning, and having a direct bearing upon the people living in the last days of this earth's history. No one hears the voice of these angels, for they are a symbol to represent the people of God who are working in harmony with the universe of heaven. *Men and women, enlightened by the Spirit of God, and sanctified through the truth, proclaim the three messages in their order.*[170]

Conclusion

In view of the unsettled state of affairs in the world today, it is clear that the seventh trumpet is ready to blow and probation is about to close! How much more trouble should God allow before His people will arouse from their spiritual lethargy and fulfill her divine commission? What the church has neglected to do now during times of peace, she will have to do in the most forbidding manner and under the most trying circumstances.

More than ever, the need to understand Christ's work in the Most Holy Place of the heavenly sanctuary is paramount and pressing. Without that essential knowledge, there will be no faith that will carry the hearts and minds to the second apartment of the heavenly sanctuary, where

> " In view of the unsettled state of affairs in the world today, it is clear that the seventh trumpet is ready to blow and probation is about to close! How much more trouble should God allow before His people will arouse from their spiritual lethargy and fulfill her divine commission? "

---

[170] White, *Life Sketches of Ellen G. White*, p. 429 (emphasis added).

"the Forerunner is for us entered, even Jesus, made an high priest for ever after the order of Melchisedec" (Heb. 6:19).

The "faith that is essential at this time," if present, will be demonstrated in loving obedience to the divine call to "prophesy again."

17

The Danger of Concession, Conformity, and Compromise

Idea in Brief: This chapter draws from the experiences of the early Christian church in Jerusalem, composed mainly of Jews at first, and makes an application of the warnings Paul wrote to them for the benefit of God's end-time church. As the Hebrew believers were in danger of compromising their faith for the sake of gaining temporal advantage, the commandment-keeping church of God today is in danger of doing the same.

The Hebrew Christians Warned

Aside from being a systematic discourse on the high-priestly work of Christ in the heavenly sanctuary, Paul's epistle to the Hebrews is invaluable because of the timely warnings it sounds against certain dangers the Christians in Jerusalem were facing. These warnings apply with equal force to contemporary Seventh-day Adventists, since the dangers the Hebrew converts faced in Paul's day are practically the same as what Adventists are facing today.

The warnings and appeals Paul wrote to the Hebrew converts in Jerusalem were not like those he wrote in his epistles to the churches in Asia, which were mostly made up of Gentile converts coming in from pagan backgrounds. For instance, to the troubled church of Corinth, Paul warned against indulging in pagan practices, such as eating foods sacrificed to idols, engaging in immoral practices like adultery, fornication, homosexuality, indulging perverted appetite through intemperance and drunkenness, practicing extortion, and other sins (see 1 Cor. 5:1, 11; 11:1–7).

In 1 Corinthians 6:9–11, Paul warned the believers that neither "fornicators, nor idolaters, nor adulterers, nor effeminate, nor abusers of themselves with mankind, nor thieves, nor covetous, nor drunkards, nor revilers, nor extortioners, shall inherit the kingdom of God." The Corinthian believers were also hurling lawsuits against each other in worldly courts. Against this unchristian practice, Paul protested (see vs. 1–6).

To the church at Colossae, Paul warned against adopting human philosophy, traditions, and the rudiments of the world (see 2:8). To the church at Philippi, Paul warned against disorderly elements, who "minded earthly things and whose god is their belly" (3:19).

The Hebrew Christian church at Jerusalem, on the other hand, needed no such warnings from Paul. After all, they were Jews. Instructed in the law of Moses, they were bound by high standards of faith and morals by the Torah, Mishna, and Halakha.

In Hebrews, Paul warned the converts against being indifferent, negligent, and spiritually careless. He warned them about drifting away from the truths they once heard and letting them slip. In short, Paul warned them against apostatizing, backsliding, and falling away from the truth.

> Therefore we ought to give the more earnest heed to the things which we have heard, lest at any time we should let *them* slip. For if the word spoken by angels was stedfast, and every transgression and disobedience received a just recompence of reward; How shall we escape, if we neglect so great salvation; which at the first began to be spoken by the Lord, and was confirmed unto us by them that heard *him*. (Heb. 2:1–3)

Neglecting that "So Great Salvation"

Paul's fellow believers in Jerusalem were in danger of neglecting that "so great salvation." He warned them that such negligence was

The Danger of Concession, Conformity, and Compromise

tantamount to forfeiting their salvation and being unable to escape the Lord's "just recompense of reward" for every "transgression and disobedience."

That great salvation they were neglecting and letting slip was predicated on two things. In chapter 2, Paul identified these as 1) Christ's work as Atoning Sacrifice on earth and 2) His continuous ministry as High Priest in the heavenly sanctuary.

Regarding Christ's work as Atoning Sacrifice, Paul wrote, "But we see Jesus, who was made a little lower than the angels for the suffering of death, crowned with glory and honour; that he by the grace of God should taste death for every man" (v. 9). He added, "Forasmuch then as the children are partakers of flesh and blood, he also himself likewise took part of the same; that through death he might destroy him that had the power of death, that is, the devil" (v. 14).

With regards to the second phase of that atoning ministry, Paul wrote, "Wherefore in all things it behoved him to be made like unto his brethren, that he might be a merciful and faithful high priest in things pertaining to God, to make reconciliation for the sins of the people" (vs. 17, 18).

Christ's Dual Atoning Ministry

Christ's sacrificial death and high-priestly ministry are the two great truths around which all Bible truths cluster. There is a perfect balance between these two phases of Christ's atoning work. They complement each other; one role cannot exist without the other. A priest cannot accomplish anything without a sacrifice, whereas a sacrifice without a priest to offer it is useless. Therefore, to marginalize one aspect of Christ's work is to marginalize both. To neglect one aspect is to neglect the other. One only needs to destroy one part of Christ's atoning work to destroy both.

Therefore, it goes without saying that to accept Jesus as personal Savior is to wholeheartedly believe in Him both as Atoning Sacrifice and Great High Priest. Unfortunately, Christians today somehow tend to accept one part of Christ's work while ignoring the other. Believers today tend to gravitate towards Christ's death on the cross while ignoring His work in the heavenly sanctuary as High Priest, which is just as vital and essential!

They say, "Everything we need for salvation was obtained at the cross." This understanding naturally leads to the conclusion that whatever Jesus is doing in the heavenly sanctuary does not add to one's salvation. This is how believers today neglect half of that great salvation that was first spoken by our Lord and confirmed unto us by those who heard Him.

Christians today are just as prone to neglecting that great salvation as the Hebrew Christians were in the time of Paul. Light on Christ's closing work as High Priest in the heavenly sanctuary, sealed up in Daniel's time, has now been unsealed. Therefore, there is no excuse for any current believer to plead ignorance on that vital subject. To disregard that truth is to neglect that great salvation. Paul's admonition to his fellow Hebrew believers applies to Christians today: "Therefore we ought to give the more earnest heed to the things which we have heard, lest at any time we should let them slip" (v. 1).

Revisiting Early Church History

How did the Hebrew Christians in Paul's day end up being on dangerous ground? What could possibly have led them to let slip the things they had heard and neglect that "so great salvation" to their souls' detriment? We need to look back at some history to understand why.

AD 31

The Jews who accepted Jesus as the Messiah banded together to form what was known as the "early apostolic church." They were few at first, numbering about 120 during that memorable upper room meeting, recorded in Acts 1:15. On the day of Pentecost, however, their numbers skyrocketed, and what used to be a tiny band of obscure believers suddenly became a mass of congregants with megachurch status! On that day, thousands heard the gospel preached by the

The Danger of Concession, Conformity, and Compromise

apostle Peter and were baptized. "Then they that gladly received his word were baptized: and the same day there were added unto them about three thousand souls" (2:41).

The thousands who were added to the church at that time were composed mainly of Jews from all over Asia, Europe, and Africa who had come to Jerusalem to celebrate Pentecost. Since then, many more were added to the church membership daily. "And the Lord added to the church daily such as should be saved" (v. 47). The thriving condition of the church at that time is noted in Revelation 6:2: "And I saw, and behold a white horse: and he that sat on him had a bow; and a crown was given unto him: and he went forth conquering, and to conquer."

Many of those who were added daily to the Jewish Christian church in Jerusalem were priests. "And the word of God increased; and the number of the disciples multiplied in Jerusalem greatly; and a great company of the priests were obedient to the faith" (Acts 6:7). Many more from the sect of the Pharisees also believed and were added to the church (see 15:5). Hence, the Christian church in Jerusalem, composed initially of a small, ragtag company of believing Jews, morphed into a large megachurch within a few short years.

AD 34

Meanwhile, Jewish sentiment had increasingly turned against the church in Jerusalem, resulting in persecution and, finally, the stoning of Stephen, the first Christian martyr, in AD 34. "And at that time there was a great persecution against the church which was at Jerusalem; and they were all scattered abroad throughout the regions of Judaea and Samaria, *except the apostles*" (8:1, emphasis added). The thousands in Jerusalem who had been added to the church daily no longer found the city a safe haven; these were all scattered abroad, "except the apostles."

It was not in God's order that thousands of believers should conglomerate in a single place. Therefore, He allowed trials and difficulties to come to the church at Jerusalem to fulfill her great

> *It was not in God's order that thousands of believers should conglomerate in a single place. Therefore, He allowed trials and difficulties to come to the church at Jerusalem to fulfill her great gospel commission: "But ye shall receive power, after that the Holy Ghost is come upon you: and ye shall be witnesses unto me both in Jerusalem, and in all Judaea, and in Samaria, and unto the uttermost part of the earth"*

gospel commission: "But ye shall receive power, after that the Holy Ghost is come upon you: and ye shall be witnesses unto me both in Jerusalem, and in all Judaea, and in Samaria, and unto the uttermost part of the earth" (Acts 1:8).

AD 50–57

As we all know, Saul himself was converted to Christianity during his unforgettable road trip to Damascus (see ch. 9). Saul, who later became Paul, was Christ's "apostle to the Gentiles" (Rom. 11:13). He fulfilled his office by making three missionary trips to Asia Minor and founded many churches there, which were composed mainly of Gentile converts.[171]

By the end of his third missionary trip to Asia, Paul decided it was time to visit Jerusalem and meet the apostles. Regarding that meeting, he reported his company was accepted well by the brethren in Jerusalem. "And when we were come to Jerusalem, the brethren received us gladly" (Acts 21:17).

Paul then proceeded to report the wonderful things God had wrought for the Gentiles through his ministry (see v. 18). To this, James and the elders of the church who were present replied, saying, "Thou seest, brother, how many *thousands* of Jews there are which believe; and they are all zealous of the law" (v. 19, emphasis added). We gather from this reply that the Hebrew Christian church in Jerusalem had once more flourished and achieved megachurch status during this time.

---

[171] Paul's first missionary journey is recorded in Acts 13:4–14:26 (circa AD 46–47). His second missionary journey is recorded in Acts 15:36–18:22 (circa AD 49–51). His third missionary journey is recorded in Acts 18:23–21:17 (circa AD 52–57).

Recall that twenty-five years or so before, only a handful of disciples were left in Jerusalem after it had been purged. What might explain this great change? Was there another Pentecostal outpouring of the Holy Spirit, resulting in thousands of conversions? If this were the case, it would have been noted in Acts. Since there is none, this supposition is highly doubtful.

Concession, Conformity, and Compromise

The tremendous spike in membership can only be attributed to one and only one explanation: the persecution had stopped! The unconverted Jews were no longer pursuing the Hebrew Christians for their faith in Christ. What phenomenon might explain the conciliatory change in the attitude of the unbelieving Jews towards the Hebrew Christians in Jerusalem at this time? The words of James, the leader of the Hebrew church in Jerusalem, explains it. The "thousands of Jews who believe" were "zealous of the law."

The immediate context of the passage tells us it is the law of Moses, the ceremonial law, that is in view here. This so-called "zeal for the law" meant submitting to the old-covenant rite of circumcision, subscribing to the ceremonial washings, and showing up at the temple, where animal sacrifices were still being offered. In short, the thousands of Jews who believed observed the old-covenant ceremonial law while professing faith in Christ as the Messiah and basking in the light of the new covenant.

The leaders of the church in Jerusalem knew that as long as they subscribed to the law of Moses and observed its rites and ceremonies, they were not looked upon so much as apostates from the Jewish faith. Thus, to avoid persecution and gain popularity among the unconverted Jews, the Hebrew Christians made concessions by accommodating the ceremonial law.

> The leaders of the church in Jerusalem knew that by non-conformity to the ceremonial law, Christians would bring upon themselves the hatred of the Jews and expose themselves to persecution. The Sanhedrin was doing its utmost to hinder the progress

of the gospel. Men were chosen by this body to follow up the apostles, especially Paul, and in every possible way to oppose their work. *Should the believers in Christ be condemned before the Sanhedrin as breakers of the law, they would suffer swift and severe punishment as apostates from the Jewish faith.*[172]

It appears that men of influence in the church at Jerusalem were themselves favorable to the practice of circumcision and made unwise concessions for the observance of the ceremonial law as a whole. At the Council of Jerusalem, held sometime in AD 50, many Hebrew converts to Christianity, especially from the sect of the Pharisees, taught that it was necessary to be circumcised and keep the law of Moses to be saved. "And certain men which came down from Judaea taught the brethren, and said, Except ye be circumcised after the manner of Moses, ye cannot be saved… But there rose up certain of the sect of the Pharisees *which believed*, saying, That it was needful to circumcise them, and to command them to keep the law of Moses" (Acts 15:1–5).

The disciples themselves yet cherished a regard for the ceremonial law, and were too willing to make concessions, hoping by so doing to gain the confidence of their countrymen, remove their prejudice, and win them to faith in Christ as the world's Redeemer.[173]

Many of the Jews who had accepted the gospel still cherished a regard for the ceremonial law and were only too willing to *make unwise concessions*, hoping thus to gain the confidence of their countrymen, to remove their prejudice, and to win them to faith in Christ as the world's Redeemer.[174]

In line with their policy to observe the ceremonial law to appease the Jews and avoid persecution, James and the elders in the church in Jerusalem advised Paul to take certain men with him and present

---

[172] White, *The Acts of the Apostles*, p. 404 (emphasis added).
[173] White, *Sketches from the Life of Paul*, p. 213 (emphasis added).
[174] White, *The Acts of the Apostles*, p. 405 (emphasis added).

The Danger of Concession, Conformity, and Compromise

themselves in the temple for purification (see Acts 21:20–36). They hoped that by openly showing regard for the ceremonial law, Paul himself might disarm some of the prejudice held against him by the Sanhedrin and the unbelieving Jews.

This unwise move, as we know, backfired and led to Paul's untimely arrest. We are told that James' advice to Paul to present himself in the temple "was not prompted by the Spirit of God and was the fruit of cowardice."[175] We are also told that Paul "was not authorized of God to concede" to what the leaders of the church of Jerusalem had asked; and "neither was it in harmony with his own teachings."[176]

Two Mutually Exclusive Systems of Faith and Practice

It was to the "thousands of Jews in Jerusalem who believed and were zealous of the law" that Paul wrote Hebrews. Love for their souls actuated him to issue the warnings and appeals we read in chapter 2 and other parts of the epistle. Paul made it clear that reverting to the Mosaic rituals meant apostatizing from the Christian faith; it meant neglecting that so great salvation that was first spoken by the Lord and confirmed by those who heard Him (see 2:3). It was equivalent to crucifying to themselves the Son of God afresh and putting Him to open shame (see 6:4–6). It meant casting away their confidence, which has great recompense of reward, and drawing back unto perdition (see 10:35–39).

The old and new covenants are mutually exclusive. One cannot profess faith in Christ while living under the terms of the old covenant. In Hebrews 8, Paul explained that the old covenant had been superseded by the new covenant and therefore possessed no more value. "In that he saith, A new covenant, he hath made the first old. Now that which decayeth and waxeth old is ready to vanish away" (v. 13). Therefore, conforming to the old Jewish rituals, such as circumcision, ceremonial washings, and the offering of sacrifices, constituted a denial of faith in Christ and His atoning ministry.

---

[175] *Ibid.*, p. 404.
[176] White, *Sketches from the Life of Paul*, p. 213.

Feeding on Milk and Not Solid Food

In Hebrew 5, Paul hit the nail on the head by pointing out the reason why the converts in Jerusalem found it easy to compromise their faith for the sake of gaining temporal advantage. The Hebrew Christians were not as familiar as they ought to be with the truths that pertained to their time. It is an accepted principle in life that the lower the value that is assigned to an object, the easier it is to discard that object. What is not valued is not cherished. The lower the usefulness of an object, the lower the value that is assigned to that object. The same holds true for truth.

Truths that are not understood are not deemed useful; therefore, they are not valued or cherished as much. Truths that are not cherished as much are given up if that is what it takes to gain temporal gain. The Hebrew converts were led to compromise the truths that pertained to their time because they failed to advance in the understanding of those truths.

> Called of God an high priest after the order of Melchisedec. Of whom we have many things to say, and hard to be uttered, seeing ye are dull of hearing. For when for the time ye ought to be teachers, ye have need that one teach you again which *be* the first principles of the oracles of God; and are become such as have need of milk, and not of strong meat. For every one that useth milk *is* unskilful in the word of righteousness: for he is a babe. (Heb. 5:10–13)

Unfortunately, the Jewish Christians in Jerusalem were "babes" or mere infants when it came to the understanding of the truths that pertained to Christ's work as High Priest in the heavenly sanctuary. Satisfied with feeding on milk instead of strong meat, they were woefully deficient in knowledge of the great work of atonement that began at the cross and continued in the heavenly sanctuary. Paul declared he had many things to say about Jesus, "called a high priest according to the order of Melchisedek," but had not been able to because they were "dull of hearing." They still had to be taught "the first principles of the oracles of God" when they ought to be teachers.

Accustomed all their lives to look to the Levites who officiated daily in the temple, they were slow to grasp the meaning of the passages of Scripture that pointed to Christ's work in the heavenly sanctuary as High Priest according to the order of Melchizedek. As a result, they were, in Paul's words, "[unskillful] in the word of righteousness."

If the Jewish converts had only been diligently studying the Scriptures and keeping up with advancing light, they would have possessed a robust understanding and greater appreciation of Christ's work of atonement in the heavenly sanctuary. They would have immediately realized that going along with circumcision and the practice of ceremonial rites in the temple constituted a denial of their faith in Christ as their merciful and faithful High Priest. Again, truths that are not understood fully are not valued, and truths that are not valued are easily given up when circumstances press it.

Likewise, contemporary Christians in general seem mostly ignorant of the work of Christ as High Priest in the heavenly sanctuary. Many are feeding on milk and not on solid food when it comes to this mighty pillar of truth of the Christian faith. Many are neglecting that part of that "so great salvation" about which Paul wrote because they will not come to grips with the truths that pertain to the present work of Jesus in the heavenly sanctuary.

Regarding this vital subject, we are told that those who live in the time of the end will have to step fast and endeavor to learn within a short time what the pioneers of the church took years to learn.

> It is too late in the day to feed with milk. If souls a month or two old in the truth, who are about to enter the time of trouble such as never was, cannot hear all the straight truth, or endure the strong meat of the straightness of the way, how will they stand in the day of battle? Truths that we have been years learning must be learned

in a few months by those who now embrace the Third Angel's Message.[177]

Preparing for the Coming Crisis

Paul's main intention in writing Hebrews was to take the eyes of his fellow believers in Jerusalem away from the temple and focus them on the work going on in the heavenly sanctuary. He not only understood the new covenant had superseded the old covenant; he also understood the temple in Jerusalem would be destroyed in a few years, bringing to naught the entire system on which, for many centuries, the Jews had been leaning on for spiritual strength and support. He knew the destruction of the temple in Jerusalem would result in utter despair for those whose eyes were still fixed on its rites and ceremonies. Hence, we have the writing of the book of Hebrews, with its warnings and appeals.

A crisis more severe than the destruction of the temple in Jerusalem in AD 70 awaits the remnant people of God in the last days. The mark of the beast is soon to be enforced, and their faith is about to be tried to the utmost. Unless they fully understand the work Jesus is doing for them in the heavenly sanctuary, they, too, will compromise their faith and be swept away in the popular current. They will make unwise concessions and conform to gain acceptability and compromise to avoid reproach and persecution.

Even now, some are drawing back unto perdition and denying the work going forward in the heavenly sanctuary, just because they do not comprehend it (see Heb. 10:39). Even now, there are those whose souls are not "anchored on the hope which is sure and stedfast, and which entereth into that within the veil; Whither the forerunner is for us entered, even Jesus, made an high priest for ever after the order of Melchisedec" (6:19, 20). They are babes and dull of hearing when it comes to that sacred truth.

---

[177] White, *Manuscript Releases*, vol. 1, p. 33.

The Danger of Concession, Conformity, and Compromise

Holding Fast and Not Drawing Back

During this time and the final crisis, our only hope is to hold fast and not draw back. Our only safety is to not cast away our confidence (see 10:23–27, 35–39). We cannot let the truths searched out through prayer and diligent Bible study by our pioneers slip out of our minds. Doing so would mean apostasy from the truth, neglecting that "so great salvation" and inviting the wrath of an offended God.

We are to be continually eating that "little open book" from the hand of the mighty angel and drawing fresh light and power from its sacred pages. We cannot afford to be satisfied with milk and despise solid food when it comes to an understanding of the truths the Lord has entrusted to us. Instead of being dull of hearing, we need to be advancing in the knowledge of Christ's work and mission for the time of the end.

> *We cannot let the truths searched out through prayer and diligent Bible study by our pioneers slip out of our minds. Doing so would mean apostasy from the truth, neglecting that "so great salvation" and inviting the wrath of an offended God.*

The announcement "Unto 2300 days then shall the sanctuary be cleansed" should be clearly understood by us as God's last-day church. That light needs to be cherished and enshrined in our hearts and minds. If not, it will be easy for us to give it up and go along with those who oppose it. There is no room for willful ignorance regarding the points that define our unique faith as Seventh-day Adventists.

18

The Danger of Abandoning Once-Cherished Light

Idea in Brief: This chapter looks back at the experiences of the Millerites during the Advent proclamation of 1840–1844 in connection with the parable of the ten virgins. As two classes of Adventists were formed during that time as a result of the Great Disappointment, two classes of believers will also be formed within the church near the close of time. These two classes of believers will parallel the ten virgins in the parable of Matthew 25, five of whom were wise and five of whom were foolish.

Present Truth Until the Close of Time

Matthew 25 contains two parables that stress the importance of being found ready when Jesus comes again: the talents and the ten virgins. The Spirit of Prophecy tells us one of these parables has a present and future import:

> I am often referred to the parable of the ten virgins, five of whom were wise, and five foolish. This parable has been and will be fulfilled to the very letter, for it has a special application to this time, and, like the third angel's message, has been fulfilled and *will continue to be present truth till the close of time*.[178]

---

[178] White, "The Righteousness of Christ," *The Review and Herald*, August 19, 1890 (emphasis added).

We are also told the parable of the ten virgins had an application in the experience of those who lived through the proclamation of the advent message in the summer and autumn of 1844:

> In the summer and autumn of 1844, the proclamation, "Behold, the Bridegroom cometh," was given. The two classes represented by the wise and foolish virgins were then developed,—one class who looked with joy to the Lord's appearing, and who had been diligently preparing to meet him; another class that, influenced by fear, and acting from impulse, had been satisfied with a theory of the truth, but were destitute of the grace of God.[179]

Today, those who profess to be waiting for the bridegroom to come in the clouds of heaven need to revisit 1844 and the ensuing years. They need to learn hard lessons from the experience of those who went through those historic times. They need to be especially familiar with the events that led up to the formation of two separate and distinct classes of Adventists within the ranks of the Millerites. This split within Millerism was due to the differences in beliefs involving three fundamental points of doctrine: the sanctuary, seventh-day Sabbath, and spirit of prophecy. These points continue to serve as demarcation lines separating members of Adventist communities today. The distinction between the wise and foolish virgins are also drawn along these lines.

The Wise and Foolish Virgins in the Summer of 1844

Back in 1818, William Miller concluded that Jesus could come to cleanse the earth with fire in 1844, at the end of the 2,300-year timeline of Daniel 8:14.[180] With respect to the Jewish calendar, the year 1844 spanned from the spring of 1843 to the spring of 1844. Hence, Miller predicted that Jesus could come to cleanse the earth with fire anytime within that span. Aware of the biblical teaching that

---

[179] White, *The Great Controversy*, p. 426.
[180] See *Ibid.*, p. 329.

The Danger of Abandoning Once-Cherished Light

"no man knoweth the day nor the hour when the Son of man cometh," he set no specific date for Jesus to come within that year.

Therefore, those who accepted Miller's prediction eagerly waited for the Savior to come. When the spring of 1844 passed and summer arrived, it became apparent that Miller's prediction had failed. The Millerites suffered a great disappointment—their first! During that time, two classes of Advent believers were formed, represented by the wise and the foolish virgins. The wise were those who "looked forward with joy to the Lord's appearing and had been diligently preparing to meet Him." The foolish were those who "were influenced by feeling and acted on impulse."

In the summer of 1844, the Millerites soon discovered a mistake in the reckoning of prophetic time. They found the decree by Artaxerxes, allowing the Jews to return to Jerusalem to rebuild its walls and streets, was not made in the spring of 457 BC, as previously thought, but in the autumn of that year. This discovery caused a huge stir among the disappointed Millerites. The same biblical evidence that led them to look for their Lord in the spring of 1844 now led them to expect Him in the autumn of that year.

The October 22 date on which the Lord was expected to come was based on the understanding that the cleansing of the sanctuary took place on the day of atonement, "the tenth *day* of the [seventh] month" (Lev. 16:29). That day fell on October 22, when comparing the Jewish and Gregorian calendars.

In the summer of 1844, the ecstatic Millerites took to the streets once more and proclaimed the joyful tidings, "Behold the bridegroom cometh, go ye out to meet him." We are told that "about fifty thousand withdrew from the churches"[181] and joined hands with them in their proclamation of the midnight-cry message of the parable of the ten virgins. However, October 22, 1844 came and went. The Millerites suffered yet another bitter disappointment during that time.

During that time, the parable of the ten virgins had another unique application. Two classes of Millerites, represented by the wise and

---

[181] *Ibid.*, p. 376.

foolish virgins, were formed. We shall now examine the circumstances that led to the formation of those two classes in the autumn of 1844.

The Aftermath of the Second Great Disappointment

The Great Disappointment of the autumn of 1844 was immediately followed by great confusion within the ranks of the Millerites. Many who had joined the movement out of fear and impulse, rather than conviction, immediately abandoned the movement and disappeared. Those who stayed had to deal with discouragement, disillusionment, and ridicule by neighbors and former acquaintances. Some set new dates for the second coming of Jesus. As these dates passed, more disappointments set in. Many strange doctrines were promoted; fanaticism and spiritualism infiltrated the group, bringing more confusion into the ranks of the Millerites, which had dwindled from about 50,000 to about 30,000 by this time.[182]

The Albany Conference of the Millerites in 1845

To address the serious issues facing the group and "maintain harmony and uniformity of teaching," the two leading men of the Millerite movement, Joshua Himes and William Miller, called for a conference of "Second Advent lecturers, and brethren who still adhere to the original faith."[183] This conference was held in Albany, New York, from April 29 to May 1, 1845.

This meeting became known as the "Albany Conference of 1845." The result of these meetings was the formulation of a statement of ten fundamental beliefs, which were published on May 1, 1845, in the official Millerite paper, *The Advent Herald & Signs of the Times Reporter*. These doctrines, which were unanimously passed by the conference and prefaced by the following paragraph from the doctrinal committee, are listed below in summary form:

"In view of the many conflicting opinions, unscriptural views leading to unseemly practices, and the sad divisions which have

---

[182] See White, *Early Writings*, p. xvii.
[183] See Schwarz, *Light Bearers*, p. 52.

been (hereby caused by some professing to be Adventists), we deem it incumbent upon us to declare to the world, our belief that the Scriptures teach, among others, the following":

1. **The coming of Christ is near**—even at the doors.

2. **Two visible comings of Christ**—the first visible coming at His birth by a virgin in the time of Herod and the second visible coming when He descends from heaven with the shout of a trumpet and with flaming fire to take vengeance upon them that know not God.

3. **The belief that the condition of salvation** is repentance towards God and faith towards our Lord Jesus Christ.

4. **The belief in righteousness by faith** as the basis of obtaining the promise made to Abraham and his seed, and not through lineage.

5. **The belief that the ministers of the gospel** should continue calling people to repent because the kingdom of God is at hand.

6. **The belief that the man of sin** (the papal power) would continue persecuting God's people until the end when it is consumed with the brightness of Christ's coming.

7. **The belief that the saints** do not enter into their inheritance or receive their crowns at death.

8. **The belief in the resurrection** of the just and the unjust; the bodies of the just will be resurrected at his coming and the wicked a thousand years later.

9. **The belief in a millennium** occuring between the two resurrections, the first and second resurrections.

10. **The kingdom of God** will be established when this earth is destroyed by fire and made new.

One will immediately notice many of these beliefs align with the Seventh-day Adventist Church's doctrines today. However, it is worth mentioning the above statement of fundamental beliefs did not include the teachings that make Seventh-day Adventism unique. There was no mention of a belief in the ministration of Jesus Christ in the heavenly sanctuary, the seventh-day Sabbath, or the spirit of prophecy.

Millerism Formally Abandons Sacred Truths

Two weeks after these meetings, on May 14, 1845, an article appeared in the Millerite paper, in which warnings were issued against those who a) claim "special illumination," referring to the dreams and visions of Ellen White, b) teach "Jewish fables," referring to the seventh-day Sabbath, and c) were advocating "new tests," or new teachings. By being opposed to any proposed new light, they barred various forms of fanatical teachings from gaining entrance inside the group.

Unfortunately, this action also effectively closed the door to any advanced discoveries that could come along in the prophetic exposition of the cleansing of the sanctuary of Daniel 8:14. Thus, by formal action, the Millerites turned away from the visions of Ellen White, the seventh-day Sabbath, and the discovery of new light on the sanctuary.

The Foolish Virgins in the Autumn of 1844

After the Great Disappointment of the autumn of 1844, the main body of the Millerites concluded that nothing significant occurred during that year. Admitting they had been totally wrong in their interpretation of the 2,300-day prophecy and the meaning of the cleansing of the sanctuary, they abandoned any effort to investigate the matter further. They simply decided to drop the ball on Daniel 8:14 altogether. They came to terms with their two disappointments by concluding that any further investigation into the subject of the cleansing of the sanctuary was no longer necessary.

By doing so, most of the Millerites failed to discover the truths that would have corrected their errors. By abandoning any further investigation into Daniel 8:14, they missed the light that would have illuminated the way to the Most Holy Place of the heavenly sanctuary. That new light would have helped them see Jesus in His final ministration before His second coming.

The majority of the Millerites who took this path became the class represented by the five foolish virgins. Not aware of Christ's change of ministration in the heavenly sanctuary in 1844, due to lack of understanding, they failed to possess the extra oil of truth that would have enabled them to follow the Bridegroom by faith into the marriage chamber in time for the marriage.

If the majority of the Millerites had only taken a different path from what they had formally taken—if they had only searched the Scriptures more diligently—they would have found the reason for their disappointments. Through a prayerful study of the Word, they would have discovered the light of the ministration of Jesus in the heavenly sanctuary and been honored by heaven as God's repository of sacred truth for the time of the end. They would have been able to follow Jesus by faith in His final ministration in the heavenly sanctuary and recognize the need to keep the commandments of God, including the Sabbath. They would have been able to see the importance of proclaiming the third angel's message, and the outcome of their labors might have been much different.

The Wise Virgins in the Autumn of 1844

While the main body of Millerites were having their meetings in Albany, New York, in 1845, three men were diligently studying their Bibles and revisiting the subject of the sanctuary and its cleansing in Daniel 8:14 at another place. These were Hiram Edson, O. R. L. Crosier, and Dr. Franklin B. Hahn. Contrary to the position held by the majority of the Millerites on this topic, these men decided to delve into the matter further. As a result of their diligent studies, they discovered the sanctuary that needed cleansing on the antitypical day of atonement was not the earth, but the sanctuary in heaven—not by fire, but by the blood of Jesus.

This renewed interest in the meaning of the cleansing of the sanctuary of Daniel 8:14 was inspired by Hiram Edson's vision of Jesus moving to the second apartment of the heavenly sanctuary, which he had as he was walking through a cornfield on October 23, 1844.[184] The results of these men's diligent studies were a fulfillment of the prophecy in Daniel 12:4: "many will run and fro" (in their Bibles), and knowledge (of the sealed prophecies of Daniel) would increase.

Crosier, a schoolteacher, was tasked by the group to put their discoveries on paper. Their studies were published in an article in the *Day-Star Extra* the following year. In 1847, Ellen White received a copy of Crosier's article and fully endorsed it as having divine authority:

> The Lord shew me in vision, more than one year ago, that Brother Crosier had the true light, on the cleansing of the sanctuary, etc.; and that it was his will, that Brother C. should write out the view which he gave us in the Day-Star, Extra, February 7, 1846. I feel fully authorized by the Lord, to recommend that Extra, to every saint.[185]

Crosier's articles on the sanctuary, published in 1846, included an explanation as to why the sanctuary to be cleansed in Daniel 8:14 was not the earth but the sanctuary in heaven, built by God Himself. His article spelled out the typological relationship between the earthly sanctuary and the heavenly sanctuary. He and his friends clearly understood the dual-phased ministration of Christ in the heavenly sanctuary. In his *Day-Star* article, Crosier also presented arguments against the popular ideas that Christ made a full and final atonement

---

[184] In Hiram Edson's own words that morning, "Heaven seemed open to my view, and I saw distinctly and clearly, that instead of our High Priest coming out of the Most Holy Place of the heavenly Sanctuary to come to this earth... at the end of the 2,300 days that he for the first time entered on that day the second apartment of that sanctuary; and that he had a work to perform in the Most Holy Place before coming to this earth" (Schwarz, *Light Bearers to the Remnant*, p. 59).

[185] White, *A Word to the Little Flock*, p. 12.

at the cross and began His ministration in the second apartment of the heavenly sanctuary upon His ascension in AD 31.

The truths that Hiram Edson and his friends discovered through diligent Bible study in 1845 clearly illuminated the way to the Most Holy Place of the heavenly sanctuary, where Jesus, our Great High Priest, is engaged in His closing ministration for the salvation of humanity. This truth regarding the change in Christ's ministration in the heavenly sanctuary was the extra oil needed to light the way to the marriage chamber, and all who possessed that light would be able to come into the wedding by faith.

The Sanctuary-Sabbath Conferences of 1848

In 1848, a series of meetings was held in different parts of the East Coast by a few scattered Adventists, numbering about fifty. This small number included James White, Ellen Gould Harmon, Joseph Bates, Hiram Edson, J. N. Andrews, Stephen Haskell, John Loughborough, and a few others.[186] These meetings were known as the "Sanctuary-Sabbath Conferences of 1848."[187] During that time, the delegates who were present nailed down eight fundamental doctrinal points:[188]

1. The dual-phased ministration of Christ in the heavenly sanctuary

2. Spiritual gifts in the ministry of Ellen White

3. The binding claims of the fourth-commandment Sabbath

4. Conditional immortality and soul sleep

5. The three angels' messages of Revelation 14

6. The timing of the outpouring of the plagues

7. The literal, visible coming of Christ

8. The final destruction of the wicked after the Millennium

---

[186] See White, *Early Writings*, p. xvii.
[187] See Schwarz, *Light Bearers*, pp. 65–67.
[188] *Ibid.*

It is clear from the list of fundamental beliefs above that Crosier's *Day Star Extra* article on the sanctuary, published a year before and endorsed by the Spirit of Prophecy, had a substantial impact on the formation of Adventism's core belief of the sanctuary service.

Also prominent on the list was the acknowledgment of the binding claims of the seventh-day Sabbath and the acknowledgment of prophetic gifts in the ministry of Ellen G. White. The very beliefs over which mainstream Millerism stumbled—the beliefs they refused to accept—became central pillars in the doctrinal makeup of a small minority of Advent believers who would later become the pioneers of the Seventh-day Adventist Church. Thus, by 1848, a tiny group of Sabbath-keeping Adventists had developed a system of truth far beyond anything the Sunday-keeping evangelical churches knew at that time.

These Sabbath-keeping Adventists gladly accepted the truth concerning Christ's change of ministration in 1844 and followed Him into the Most Holy Place of the heavenly sanctuary by faith. Hence, they were the class represented by the wise virgins in the parable; they were able to go into the marriage chamber because they were ready (see Matt. 25:10).

> In the parable it was those that had oil in their vessels with their lamps that went in to the marriage. Those who, with a knowledge of the truth from the Scriptures, had also the Spirit and grace of God, and who, in the night of their bitter trial, had patiently waited, searching the Bible for clearer light—these saw the truth concerning the sanctuary in heaven and the Saviour's change in ministration, and by faith they followed Him in His work in the sanctuary above.[189]

The Wise and Foolish Virgins in the Church Today

We are told the story of the ten virgins illustrates the experience through which the church will go just before Jesus comes.[190] What

---

[189] White, *The Great Controversy*, p. 427.
[190] See White, *Christ's Object Lessons*, p. 406.

then is the application of that parable to the church today? Who are the wise or foolish virgins in our midst today? Who will be found ready to go into the marriage chamber with the Bridegroom before the door of probation is forever shut?

The foolish virgins in the church today are those who are sadly repeating the same mistakes the Millerites made after the Great Disappointment of 1844. They were those who once rejoiced in the proclamation of the cleansing of the sanctuary at the termination of the 2,300-day prophecy of Daniel 8:14, but later on, abandoned it. As a result, they ended up rejecting the sanctuary, Spirit of Prophecy, and seventh-day Sabbath altogether.

The wise virgins in the church today are those "who through the testimony of the Scriptures accept the same truths [regarding Christ's change of ministration in 1844], following Christ by faith as He enters in before God to perform the last work of mediation, and at its close to receive His kingdom—all these are represented as going in to the marriage."[191]

Many Seventh-day Adventists today are sadly deficient in the knowledge concerning the sanctuary and related truths. Many consider these truths to be irrelevant. Many do not find these truths appealing and will, therefore, not spend time diligently studying them. Many only know bits and pieces of this core teaching of the church.

Many today are unknowingly placing themselves in the same class as did the Millerites, who, in the autumn of 1844, rejected these very truths by formal action and therefore failed to find their way to the marriage chamber, where the wedding of the Lamb is taking place.

Today, those who are not diligently studying the subject of the sanctuary are at risk of never finding their way to the Most Holy Place of the heavenly sanctuary by faith. They are failing to "enter within the veil, whither the Forerunner is entered." They are at risk of neither understanding the nature of the final work going forward there nor

---

[191] White, *The Great Controversy*, pp. 427, 428.

receiving any benefit from that work. Sad will be the lot of those not ready to enter the marriage chamber when the door is shut.

Testing Truths

Are we wise? Are we trimming our lamps—that is, studying the truths that reveal more clearly the work of atonement going forward in the second apartment of the heavenly sanctuary? Are we running to and fro in our Bibles, seeking to understand the truths that pertain to our time, just like our pioneers did?

The truths we need to understand and hold firmly today cluster around the same fundamental truths the Millerites rejected back in 1844: the sanctuary, Sabbath, and spirit of prophecy. These truths are *testing* truths. These truths define true Adventism. Are we willing to embrace these truths even though they are unpopular?

Arrayed in Fine Linen, Clean and White

Joy and gladness will be the lot of those who are found ready for the marriage of the Lamb. Having followed their precious Redeemer into the marriage chamber by faith, they will be given the wedding garment needed to be admitted to the marriage supper. "Let us be glad and rejoice, and give honour to him: for the marriage of the Lamb is come, and his wife hath made herself ready. *And to her was granted that she should be arrayed in fine linen, clean and white*: for the fine linen is the righteousness of saints" (Rev. 19:7, 8, emphasis added).

This "fine linen, clean and white" is the same white raiment the church of Laodicea is being invited to buy in Revelation 3:18. Receiving the white raiment is the benefit of Christ's final atonement in the Most Holy Place of the heavenly sanctuary. It is a gift, received by grace through faith. Imparting the perfect character of Christ to the believing soul in the final atonement is His closing work in the heavenly sanctuary.

> *Oh, let us strive with all the power God has given us to be classed among the wise virgins. It means everything to us!*

Referring to the time when Christ's work in the soul will be finished, resulting in the perfecting of the character, the prophet Daniel declared, "Many shall be purified, and made white, and tried; but the wicked shall do wickedly: and none of the wicked shall understand, but the wise shall understand" (12:10).

Oh, let us strive with all the power God has given us to be classed among the wise virgins. It means everything to us! "We have nothing to fear for the future, except as we shall forget the way the Lord has led us, and his *teaching* in our past *history*."[192]

---

[192] White, *Selected Messages*, book 3, p. 162 (emphasis added).

19

The Danger of Indolence

Idea in Brief: In this chapter, the experience God requires of and provides to those who will go through the time of Jacob's trouble is clearly spelled out. This experience, which no one possesses as of yet, is not to be confused with the experience believers now possess through righteousness by faith in Christ as their Substitute. This chapter presents arguments showing why the experience the saints now possess will not suffice in the time of trouble.

A Time of Trouble Such as Never Was

Daniel 12 speaks of a time of trouble that is unprecedented in all human history: "And at that time shall Michael stand up, the great prince which standeth for the children of thy people: and there shall be a time of trouble, such as never was since there was a nation even to that same time: and at that time thy people shall be delivered, every one that shall be found written in the book" (v. 1).

This time of trouble is unlike any other trouble that has swept the planet in the past because it occurs at the time when Michael, aka Jesus, stands up. The expression "stand up" in Bible prophecy means to take the throne and assume kingly power and authority. Referring to the rise of the last four kings of the Persian empire to power, the angel Gabriel said, "Behold, there shall *stand up* yet three kings in Persia; and the fourth shall be far richer than [they] all" (11:2, emphasis added). He also prophesied of the rise of the Greek emperor

Alexander the Great to power: "And a mighty king shall *stand up*, that shall rule with great dominion, and do according to his will" (v. 3, emphasis added).

The rise of the Roman emperor Augustus to power is described in the following words: "Then shall *stand up* in his estate a raiser of taxes in the glory of the kingdom: but within few days he shall be destroyed, neither in anger, nor in battle" (v. 20, emphasis added). This was fulfilled in the time of Christ: "And it came to pass in those days, that there went out a decree from Caesar Augustus, that all the world should be taxed" (Luke 2:1).

When Michael Stands Up

Finally, Jesus stands up, subdues all the kingdoms of the world, and establishes His everlasting kingdom. At the close of Christ's work as High Priest, He changes from priestly robes to the garments of a king and receives the throne of His ancestral father, David. That event coincides with the blowing of the seventh trumpet: "And the seventh angel sounded; and there were great voices in heaven, saying, the kingdoms of this world are become the kingdoms of our Lord, and of his Christ; and he shall reign for ever and ever" (Rev. 11:15). The enemies of Christ become His footstool (see Heb. 1:13). He "shall rule the nations with a rod of iron and tread the winepress of the fierceness of the wrath of God" (Rev. 19:15).

When Jesus is done with His work as Mediator in the heavenly sanctuary and assumes kingly power, human probation closes. Jesus no longer stands between His Father and guilty humanity, and there is nothing to stay the wrath of an offended God as it falls on the shelterless heads of the wicked elements of this world.[193] The four angels standing at the four corners of the earth are no longer bidden to hold the winds of strife and commotion from blowing onto the earth and sea (see Rev. 7:1). These images depicting the world's final crisis as human probation comes to a close all coincide with the great time of trouble described in Daniel 12.

---

[193] See White, *Early Writings*, p. 280.

The restraint placed on evil while Jesus ministered in the sanctuary above is, at last, removed. Consequently, the whole world is plunged into the scenario of indescribable chaos depicted in Daniel 12:1. "It is often the case that trouble is greater in anticipation than in reality; but this is not true of the crisis before us. The most vivid presentation cannot reach the magnitude of the ordeal."[194]

The Promise of Deliverance

Daniel said only those whose names are found written in the book (of life) shall be delivered at that time. Jeremiah was shown the horrors of the time of trouble yet saw certain people being saved out of it. "Ask ye now, and see whether a man doth travail with child? Wherefore do I see every man with his hands on his loins, as a woman in travail, and all faces are turned into paleness? Alas! for that day is great, so that none is like it: it is even the time of Jacob's trouble; but he shall be saved out of it" (Jer. 30:6, 7).

When probation closes, the cases of those whose names are not found written in the book of life are hopeless. "And whosoever was not found written in the book of life was cast into the lake of fire" (Rev. 20:15). Therefore, the all-important question to be asked at this point is, What sort of people do we need to be if our names are to be retained in the book of life and we are to be delivered in the time of trouble?

> The "time of trouble, such as never was," is soon to open upon us; and *we shall need an experience which we do not now possess* and which many are *too indolent* to obtain.... *In that time of trial, every soul must stand for himself before God.* "Though Noah, Daniel, and Job" were in the land, "as I live, saith the Lord God, they shall deliver neither son nor daughter; *they shall but deliver their own souls by their righteousness.*"[195]

---

[194] White, *The Great Controversy*, p. 622.
[195] White, *The Great Controversy*, pp. 622, 623 (emphasis added).

The Experience We Do Not Now Possess

If nothing else, the reason why we need to take the subject of the time of trouble seriously now is this: It is soon to open upon us. That word "soon" makes all the difference. This crisis, which is greater in reality than in anticipation, will not happen generations from now. It is just around the corner!

To be ready for the time of trouble, we are told, "we shall need an experience which we do not now possess." Ellen White also warned that this experience is something "many are too indolent to obtain." That part is sad! Many will not be able to obtain the experience they need to survive during the time of trouble because of indolence. There is no place in the book of life for the names of those who are spiritually indifferent and lazy.

We are not left guessing what this experience, which we do not now possess, is. The above statement explains, "In that time of trial, every soul must stand for himself before God." The experience, which we are told we do not now possess, is one in which we are able to stand *for ourselves* before God. This means being able to stand before God without leaning on the righteousness of a substitute!

To explain further what this means, White quoted Ezekiel 14:20: "they shall but deliver their own souls by their righteousness." Thus, it is clear that in the time of trouble, the saints will not be able to deliver themselves by hiding behind the righteousness of another.

In short, those who stand at that time of trial can no longer lean on Christ's imputed righteousness to cover their character deficiencies. Righteousness by imputation or proxy, while good during probationary time, will no longer work after Jesus finishes His work of ministration in the heavenly sanctuary and probation is closed. The saints will then need to have a righteousness or level of character development that does not require propping up through someone else's righteousness. The saints will need to have a righteousness of their own!

Having a righteousness of their own need not to be taken to mean God's people are to somehow attain to it through human effort, sufficiency, or creature merit. This is an impossibility. The fact is the experience of being able to possess a righteousness of one's own and stand for oneself in the time of trouble is not something anyone can legalistically produce. Rather, it is something received by grace through faith in Christ's final atonement in the heavenly sanctuary. What God requires, He Himself provides! "Take away the filthy and give them a change of raiment."

Being able to stand in the time of trouble without leaning on Christ's imputed righteousness does not equate to being left to fend for oneself. That conclusion is totally unwarranted, as being clothed with Christ's perfect righteousness in the final atonement means being filled with the latter-rain power—the fullness of the Spirit.

Since those who go through the time of trouble must stand before a holy God without hiding behind the *imputed* righteousness of Christ for deliverance, they are required to display a level of character development not seen in previous generations. They can no longer afford to have sin and defects of character in their lives; they must reflect the character of Jesus fully.[196]

The Experience We Now Possess

For centuries, Christ's followers have always leaned on His imputed righteousness for justification and acceptance. Faith in Christ as Substitute has obtained for them the righteousness they need to be approved by God, despite their sinful and defective state. This experience is called "righteousness by faith." Even now, through Christ's perfect righteousness, believers are "accepted *in the Beloved*" (Eph. 1:16). They are accounted "perfect *in Christ*" (Col. 1:28, emphasis added). "There is *now* no condemnation for those who are *in Christ Jesus*" (Rom. 8:1, emphasis added). "Therefore being justified by faith, we have peace with God *through our Lord Jesus*" (5:1, emphasis added).

The expressions "in the Beloved," "in Christ," and "through our Lord Jesus Christ" all presuppose a work of substitution. Righteousness by faith is predicated on the notion that Jesus substitutes His perfect righteousness for the sinner's unrighteousness so God can look at that

---

[196] See White, *Early Writings*, p. 71.

person as if he or she had not sinned.[197] Jesus presents His followers to the Father, clothed in the white raiment of His own character so their imperfections are no longer seen.[198]

In the experience of justification by faith, believers are accounted just and righteous, notwithstanding their imperfections of character. Through righteousness by faith, we deliver our souls by Christ's righteousness, not by our own. Jesus graciously imputes His perfect righteousness to us because we do not have it. This is why Paul could say, "And be found in him, not having mine own righteousness, which is of the law, but that which is through the faith of Christ, the righteousness which is of God by faith" (Phil. 3:9).

The righteousness believers obtain by keeping the law not being sufficient and meritorious, they have to rely on Christ's by faith. This is the experience believers in Christ now possess. It is based on the merits of His substitutionary righteousness, which they claim and possess only by faith.

Righteousness by faith in Christ is a blessed experience. Paul quotes the psalmist to describe the blessedness of one who is righteous by faith in Christ: "Even as David also describeth the blessedness of the man, unto whom God imputeth righteousness without works, *Saying*, Blessed *are* they whose iniquities are forgiven, and whose sins are covered. Blessed *is* the man to whom the Lord will not impute sin" (Rom. 4:6–8). Hence, through the blessedness of Christ's imputed righteousness, millions of believers of past generations are entitled to heaven even though they died not possessing a righteousness of their own.

The Problem with Substitution

Unfortunately, righteousness by faith in Christ's perfection will no longer suffice in the time of trouble. "In that time of trial, every soul

---

[197] See White, *Steps to Christ*, p. 62.
[198] "Through His sacrifice, human beings may reach the high ideal set before them, and hear at last the words, 'Ye are complete in him,' not having your own righteousness, but the righteousness that He wrought out for you. Your imperfection is no longer seen; for you are clothed with the robe of Christ's perfection" (White, *The Seventh-day Adventist Bible Commentary*, vol. 7, p. 907).

The Danger of Indolence

must stand for himself before God." The "borrowed" righteousness that saved millions of justified believers in previous generations will not be good enough for those who shall go through the time of trouble. Here's why: Substitution, like pardon and justification, is a benefit of Christ's continuous work of intercession in the heavenly sanctuary. It is available as long as Jesus ministers in the sanctuary, offering gifts and sacrifices for sin.

This is where the problem with substitution lies. It is good only as long as it lasts. The substitute righteousness obtained as a benefit of the sanctuary service will not always be available. In short, righteousness by faith in a perfect Substitute has an expiration date. The offer expires when Jesus ends His work of mediation in the heavenly sanctuary at the close of probation. When that time comes, the righteousness of Christ, which has justified defective believers for centuries, will no longer be available since the conferral of that righteousness requires the operation of a full-time intercessor in the heavenly sanctuary.

In the time of trouble, when there is no more intercession going on in the sanctuary, the saints are required "to stand *for themselves* before God" without a Substitute or Mediator. During that time, they will need a righteousness that is not borrowed, imputed, or pasted on, such as the one they now possess by faith. The saints will need a righteousness that is their own, enabling them to deliver their souls—no substitute needed. This is the experience they do not now possess.

Point of Clarification

Many are described as being "too indolent to obtain it," due perhaps to the presupposition that the proxy righteousness they now possess by faith will be good enough to deliver them in the time of trouble. This is a fatal delusion. It is based on the assumption that since Jesus

> Many are described as being "too indolent to obtain it," due perhaps to the presupposition that the proxy righteousness they now possess by faith will be good enough to deliver them in the time of trouble. This is a fatal delusion.

promised never to leave His people, then it must mean He will continue interceding for them in the time of trouble, imputing His perfect righteousness to them and making accommodations to cover their irredeemable character flaws.

Some go further in their erroneous presuppositions by adding that only the wicked will have no intercessor in the time of trouble—that the righteous ones will continue to enjoy the blessings of Christ's intercessory work in the heavenly sanctuary. The Spirit of Prophecy is quite clear regarding this point: "In that fearful time, after the close of Jesus' mediation, *the saints* were living in the sight of a holy God without an intercessor."[199] Not only the wicked, but even the saints, are to stand without an intercessor during the time of trouble.

To some, the notion there will be no more intercessor in the time of trouble is repulsive because it gives the impression that God's people will be left to fend for themselves during that time. The truth is when Jesus ceases His work of mediation in the heavenly sanctuary, it does not mean God's people will be left to look after themselves with no help from above. In reality, the saints will have nothing about which to worry in the time of trouble if they are fully reflecting the character of Jesus and no longer prone to sinning. They will be like a fortress impregnable to the assaults of Satan. They will have the seal of God on their foreheads, which will guarantee their protection and safety while thousands will be falling by their side. Their "bread and water will be sure" while the wicked will be perishing of hunger and thirst around them.

Clothed with latter-rain power, they will be able to perform the same mighty works Christ and His disciples did (see John 14:12). They will have the faith of Jesus, enabling them to depend entirely on God to keep all His commandments (see Rev. 14:12). Although they will no longer require *forgiving* grace, they will continuously be supplied with God's *empowering* grace to keep them from falling (see Titus 2:11, 12). Even though their prayers are not answered immediately, their relationship with God is such that they do not doubt the fulfillment of His promises.

---

[199] White, *Early Writings*, p. 280 (emphasis added).

Obtaining the Experience We Do Not Now Possess
With that said, how and when will the saints obtain that experience that they do not now possess and many are too indolent to obtain? Christ's perfect righteousness cannot be obtained legalistically or just by rigidly adhering to a works-oriented program. It will not be obtained by just striving to overcome every known sin. The truth is character perfection will not be obtained through the normal process of daily sanctification, which is the benefit of the daily service in the heavenly sanctuary. Character perfection is to be received as a *gift*, by grace through faith, courtesy of the final atonement Jesus makes just before He leaves the second apartment of the heavenly sanctuary (see Lev. 16:30).

The Righteousness of the Saints
In Revelation 19, a group of people is described as possessing a righteousness that is no longer just imputed and substituted. The garments of righteousness they have been borrowing from Jesus have become their own—theirs to keep forever. Righteousness by faith has become righteousness by sight. Christ's righteousness is no longer just shared with the saints but given away. It is rightfully called "the righteousness of the saints"!

What a cause of rejoicing, indeed, when this scenario becomes a reality! "Let us be glad and rejoice, and give honour to him: for the marriage of the Lamb is come, and his wife hath made herself ready. And to her was granted that she should be arrayed in fine linen, clean and white: for the fine linen is *the righteousness of saints*" (vs. 7, 8, emphasis added).

"The righteousness of the saints" is not a righteousness *produced* by the saints, but a righteousness *given* to the saints. "And to her was *granted* that she should be arrayed in fine linen." This garment of righteousness covers no spot, wrinkle, or any such thing, for in the command to "take away their filthy garments and give them a change of raiment," all the defects of character have been removed, not simply covered, and Christ's perfect character has taken their place. This is the perfection of character represented by "the fine linen, clean and white." The experience we do not now possess, we will possess in the final atonement. This experience will enable us to stand for ourselves before God when probation closes.

Buy of Me the White Raiment

This "fine linen, clean and white" is the same commodity Jesus is offering the church of Laodicea in the message, "Buy of me the white raiment" (3:18). What He is offering Laodicea to buy is not imputed or borrowed righteousness. That, she already possesses. What Jesus is graciously offering her is the righteousness she does not now possess. He is offering her the experience she needs to stand for herself without a High Priest in the sanctuary through the time of trouble. The questions are, Will she accept it? Is she willing to pay the price to obtain it? Is she willing to give up her filthy garments of sin and self-righteousness in exchange for that righteousness that will never fade or be corrupted?

Substitution's Greatest Problem

Righteousness by faith through a substitute is a temporary fix to the sin problem. God never intended substitution to be the final and permanent solution to the problem of sin. Here's why: Substitution prolongs the great controversy. As long as someone is leaning on Christ as his Substitute, Satan argues the law cannot be kept!

Substitution presupposes deficiency on humanity's part. In substitution, Christ's character stands in place of the believer's defective character. Substitution presupposes inability on a person's part to satisfy the demands of the law oneself. Therefore, Christ's obedience is credited to the believer. To Satan, this is proof that the law cannot be kept. Substitution allows him to present the argument that one is unable to satisfy the claims of the law on his or her own. He puts forth the argument that the only way a person is able to satisfy the demands of the law is through a substitute. Therefore, substitution is like a two-edged sword. While it benefits the fallen race, it also furthers the cause of Satan!

In their sinless state in the Garden of Eden, Adam and Eve needed no substitute. They communed with God face to face, with no mediator in between. They had no sin or character defects that needed covering by a perfect substitute. Therefore, they could stand for themselves before God and deliver their soul by their own righteousness.

The purpose of the final cleansing is to bring a people back to that position where Adam and Eve were before they fell. The perfecting of the character and the blotting out of sin in the final atonement are designed to make substitution totally unnecessary. When God points to the final generation and says, "Here are they that keep the commandments of God and the faith of Jesus," He is showcasing a group of believers who are standing for themselves before Him without the Great Substitute. They are perfect and righteous even as Christ is perfect and righteous. They demonstrate in their lives that humanity can satisfy the claims of the law without a substitute. This is what ends the great controversy.

The Danger of Indolence

"My people are destroyed for lack of knowledge" (Hosea 4:6). The church of Laodicea is in danger of not recognizing God's providential leadings at this time for lack of spiritual discernment. If she understood what His glorious design for her is as His last-day remnant church, there would be zeal in place of indolence, faith in place of unbelief, and deep repentance in place of impenitence. If she can come to grips with the unique truths God has entrusted to her as His repository of sacred truth for the time of the end, half the battle will have been won.

May the Lord be gracious to the church of Laodicea and make her see her blindness, misery, nakedness, and poverty of soul. May He give her the faith she needs so she can "buy" the experience she does not now possess. Only then will she be able to truthfully say, "I am increased with goods and have need of nothing."

> Why there is so little exercise of true faith, and so little of the weight of truth resting upon many professed believers, is because they are indolent in spiritual things. They are unwilling to make exertions, to deny self, to agonize before God, to pray long and earnestly for the blessing, and therefore they do not obtain it. That

faith which will live through the time of trouble must be daily in exercise now. Those who do not make strong efforts now to exercise persevering faith, will be wholly unprepared to exercise that faith which will enable them to stand in the day of trouble.[200]

---

[200] White, *The Spirit of Prophecy*, vol. 1, pp. 124, 125.

20

Three Levels of Human Perfection

Idea in Brief: This chapter looks into numerous statements made by Ellen White that seem to suggest perfection is attainable now simply by overcoming sin in the life, among other things. These statements are being used by some in the church to shoot down Adventism's classic Last Generation Theology, which promotes the concept of perfection through a future final atonement in the heavenly sanctuary. This chapter examines the merit of such statements and puts them in their proper place in the Christian experience, taking into consideration Ellen White's precise use of terms such as "character perfection" and "Christian perfection."

Character Perfection, Now or in the Future?

There are statements made by Ellen White that seem to suggest perfection is attainable today if certain things are done. Here is just a few of them:

> Perfection of character is attained through exercise of the faculties of the mind, in times of supreme test, by obedience to every requirement of God's law. Men in positions of trust are to be instrumentalities in the hands of God for promoting His glory; and in performing their duties with the utmost faithfulness they may attain perfection of character.[201]

---

[201] White, *Medical Ministry*, p. 168.

He teaches them that the perfection of character He requires can only be attained by becoming familiar with His Word. The psalmist declares, "The entrance of thy word giveth light; it giveth understanding to the simple."[202]

The completeness of Christian character is attained when the impulse to help and bless others springs constantly from within—when the sunshine of heaven fills the heart and is revealed in the countenance.[203]

Before the believer is held out the wonderful possibility of being like Christ, obedient to all the principles of the law.... Man's obedience can be made perfect only by the incense of Christ's righteousness, which fills with divine fragrance every act of obedience. The part of the Christian is to persevere in overcoming every fault. Constantly he is to pray to the Saviour to heal the disorders of his sin-sick soul. He has not the wisdom or the strength to overcome; these belong to the Lord, and He bestows them on those who in humiliation and contrition seek Him for help.[204]

The character of Christ is the one perfect pattern which we are to copy. Repentance and faith, the surrender of the will, and the consecration of the affections to God, are the means appointed for the accomplishment of this work.[205]

Through repentance, faith, and good works he may perfect a righteous character, and claim, through the merits of Christ, the privileges of the sons of God.[206]

As the Spirit of Prophecy quotes provided above show, it would, therefore, seem that perfection of the Christian's character can be obtained here and now, simply by exercising the following:

- exercising the faculties of the mind, and in times of supreme test by obeying every requirement of God's Law

---

[202] White, *The Seventh-day Adventist Bible Commentary*, vol. 3, p. 1143.
[203] White, *Christ's Object Lessons*, p. 384.
[204] White, *The Acts of the Apostles*, p. 532
[205] White, "*The Primal Object of Education,*" Review and Herald, July 11, 1882.
[206] White, *Sons and Daughters of God*, p. 10.

- performance of duties with the utmost faithfulness
- becoming familiar with His word
- when the impulse to help and bless others springs constantly from within
- persevering in overcoming every fault
- repentance, faith and good works

However, as shown in previous chapters, Ellen White also wrote that perfection of the character is something that is not obtained for the living until the "closing scenes of the great day of atonement," an event still future. She marked this event as occurring when "men will be required to render obedience to human edicts in violation of the divine law." As God's people approach that very time, they are, in fact, described as still wearing "filthy garments," meaning their characters are still defective and, therefore, less than perfect.

As they "afflict the soul and plead for purity of heart," the command is given: "Take away their filthy garments"; and the encouraging words are spoken: "and give them a change of raiment." Perfection of the character is attained when God's faithful remnant are clothed with Christ's glorious apparel, "nevermore to be defiled by the corruptions of the world," "eternally secure from the tempter's devices." Moreover, "their sins are transferred to the originator of sin."[207] This last statement is clearly a reference to the blotting out of sins from the books of record after Jesus has made His final atonement and perfected the characters of His people. Bear in mind again that this event is still in the future.

Other statements suggesting perfection is not obtained until sometime in the future are included below:

> When the decree goes forth and the stamp is impressed, their *character will remain pure and spotless* for eternity.[208]

---

[207] See White, *Prophets and Kings*, pp. 587–591.
[208] White, *Testimonies for the Church*, vol. 5, p. 216 (emphasis added).

> As the members of Christ's body approach the period of their final conflict *they will grow up into him, and will possess symmetrical characters*. As the message of the third angel swells to a loud cry, great power and glory will attend the closing work. It is the latter rain, which revives and strengthens the people of God to pass through the time of Jacob's trouble referred to by the prophets.[209]

What then, do we make of these seemingly conflicting sets of statements? If character perfection is attainable now, then the talk of Jesus making a final atonement and cleansing for His followers in the second apartment of the heavenly sanctuary is pointless. His closing ministration in the heavenly sanctuary need not even be taken seriously. The repeated calls in the Bible and Spirit of Prophecy to follow Jesus by faith in the heavenly sanctuary to receive the benefit from His final ministration become unnecessary.[210] The call to "afflict the soul" on the day of atonement becomes unnecessary and an exercise in futility.

The blotting out of sin ends up strictly being just a judicial act on God's part to erase records of sins in the books of heaven, having no impact whatsoever on the lives and experiences of God's people. This is the sad indictment of those who tend to focus more on what is happening with themselves than on what's happening in the heavenly sanctuary to gain perfection. For them, the work going forward in the second apartment of the heavenly sanctuary carries but little significance.

The questions we need to be seriously asking ourselves at this juncture are:

1. Is perfection attainable now or something to be obtained "in the near future," during the "closing scenes of the great day of atonement"?

---

[209] White, "Jacob and the Angel," *The Signs of the Times*, November 27, 1879 (emphasis added).
[210] For example, see *The Great Controversy*, p. 430; *Testimonies for the Church*, vol. 5, p. 575; *Maranatha*, p. 248.

2. Are the statements made by Ellen White saying that perfection is obtained at a future final atonement and cleansing less inspired than those that say perfection is attainable now?

3. How do we harmonize these seemingly conflicting sets of statements from the same source—the Spirit of Prophecy?

4. Is it possible there may be more than one level of perfection being referred to here?

Character Perfection and Sanctification

The main reason for the apparent confusion over the matter of how and when perfection is achieved is Ellen White's use of terminology. It will be helpful to know at this point that when she used the terms "character perfection" and "Christian perfection" in her writings, she was really describing what is known in the Christian experience as "sanctification," which is the lifelong, ever-advancing process of developing a holy, Christlike character. Here is a sampling of statements demonstrating such usage:

> Ample provision has been made that the people of God may attain *perfection of character*. The apostle says, "This is the will of God, even your *sanctification*." Let every individual draw for himself from the inexhaustible source of all moral and intellectual power, in order that he may work the works of righteousness.[211]
>
> While we are to seek earnestly for *perfection of character*, we must remember that *sanctification* is not the work of a moment, but of a lifetime. Said Paul, "I die daily" (1 Corinthians 15:31). Day by day the work of overcoming must go forward. Every day we are to resist temptation, and gain the victory over selfishness in all its forms.[212]

---

[211] White, "Exposing of the Brethren's Mistakes Reproved," *The Review and Herald*, November 30, 1897 (emphasis added).
[212] White, *Ye Shall Receive Power*, p. 353 (emphasis added).

One brother said that when he listened to the sermon impressing upon them the necessity of purity and *perfection of character*, he felt that he could not be saved; that his case was hopeless. But when it was stated that *sanctification* was not the work of a moment, but of a lifetime, he was encouraged, and determined that day by day he would pray and watch, and search the Scriptures; he would be an overcomer, gaining an experience daily, until he should become strong, and be able to be a blessing to others.[213]

Let the church become united in Christ Jesus in working for purity and *perfection of character*. There needs to be a practical *daily sanctification* of the spirit. Before one is prepared for Christ's coming there must be seen in the life the fruits of the Spirit.[214]

The apostle presents before the believers the ladder of *Christian perfection*, every step of which represents continual advancement in the knowledge of God, and in the climbing of which there is to be no standstill.... We are saved by climbing round after round, mounting step after step, to the height of Christ's ideal for us. Thus he is made unto us wisdom, and righteousness, and *sanctification*, and redemption."[215]

As the above quotes demonstrate, Ellen White placed "Christian perfection," "character perfection," and "sanctification" all in the same bag. This fact is extremely important to know. As far as she was concerned, these terms point to the same experience. Therefore, one will often find her referring to these terms interchangeably in her writings:

---

[213] White, *Historical Sketches*, p. 183 (emphasis added).
[214] White, "The Merced Campmeeting," *The Review and Herald*, September 12, 1907 (emphasis added).
[215] White, "Peter's Last Epistle and His Death," *The Review and Herald*, September 19, 1912 (emphasis added).

Three Levels of Human Perfection

Sanctification	Christian Perfection/ Character Perfection
The *Word of God is our sanctification* and righteousness because it is spiritual food. To study it is to eat the leaves of the tree of life.[216]	He teaches them that the *perfection of character He requires can only be attained by becoming familiar with His Word*. The psalmist declares, "The entrance of thy word giveth light; it giveth understanding to the simple."[217]
True sanctification means perfect love, perfect obedience, perfect conformity to the will of God. We are to be *sanctified to God through obedience to the truth*.[218]	*Obedience through Jesus Christ gives to man perfection of character* and a right to that tree of life.[219]
Sanctification is the result of *lifelong obedience*.[220]	*Perfection of character is a lifelong work*, unattainable by those who are not willing to strive for it in God's appointed way, by slow and toilsome steps.[221]

---

[216] White, *Evangelism*, p. 138 (emphasis added).
[217] White, *The Seventh-day Adventist Bible Commentary*, vol. 3, p. 1143 (emphasis added).
[218] White, *The Acts of the Apostles*, p. 565 (emphasis added).
[219] White, *The Seventh-day Adventist Bible Commentary*, vol. 1, p. 1088 (emphasis added).
[220] White, *The Acts of the Apostles*, p. 560 (emphasis added).
[221] White, *Testimonies for the Church*, vol. 5, p. 500 (emphasis added).

The only way to remain steadfast is *to progress daily in the divine life*. Faith will increase if, when brought in conflict with doubts and obstacles, it overcomes them. True *sanctification is progressive*.[222]

We need constantly a fresh revelation of Christ, a daily experience that harmonizes with His teachings. High and holy attainments are within our reach. *Continual progress* in knowledge and virtue is God's purpose for us.... Every day we may advance in perfection of Christian character.[223]

Enoch kept the Lord ever before him, and the Inspired Word says that he "walked with God." He made Christ his constant companion. He was in the world, and performed his duties to the world; but he was ever under the influence of Jesus. He reflected Christ's character, exhibiting the same qualities in goodness, mercy, tender compassion, sympathy, forbearance, meekness, humility, and love. His association with Christ day by day transformed him into the image of Him with whom he was so intimately connected. Day by day he was growing away from his own way into Christ's way, the heavenly,

Not with standing the corruption of that degenerate age, Enoch *perfected a Christian character*.[224]
Enoch and Elijah are the correct representatives of what the race might be through faith in Jesus Christ if they chose to be. Satan was greatly disturbed because these noble, holy men stood untainted amid the moral pollution surrounding them, *perfected righteous characters*, and were accounted worthy for translation to heaven.[225]

---

[222] White, *Messages to Young People*, p. 121 (emphasis added).
[223] White, *Gospel Workers*, p. 274 (emphasis added).
[224] White, *Christ Triumphant*, p. 52 (emphasis added).
[225] White, *Selected Messages*, vol. 3, p. 146 (emphasis added).

> the divine, in his thoughts and feelings.... His was a constant growth and he had fellowship with the Father and the Son. *This is genuine sanctification.*[226]

Character Perfection Is Attainable Now

"Character perfection," "Christian perfection," or "sanctification" is the level of character development that genuine believers of all ages have been privileged to have. The numerous statements quoted above indicate this high level of spiritual development may be attained now. Again, in Ellen White's words, "Ample provision has been made that the people of God may attain *perfection of character*. The apostle says, 'This is the will of God, even your *sanctification.*'"[227]

Character Perfection Is Relative Perfection

To continue the discussion, the following crucial point regarding Christian perfection/character perfection/sanctification must now be brought to light and stressed: This level of character development must not be confused with *sinless perfection*! Character perfection is relative perfection; it is not to be equated with sinless perfection, the highest level of spiritual development in which there are no more flaws, spots, or wrinkles in the character, and best of all, no more consciousness or memory of past sin (see Heb. 10:1, 2).

What is *relative* perfection, one might ask? It is simply this: when the believer is at the point in his or her spiritual walk where God expects him to be, taking into account the amount of light and privileges he has received, then he or she is deemed perfect in heaven's eyes. As the believer receives more light and exerts commensurate effort to live up to all that light, then that believer is considered perfect. Therefore, at every stage of character development where assimilated light and

---

[226] White, *In Heavenly Places*, p. 337 (emphasis added).
[227] White, "Exposing of the Brethren's Mistakes Reproved," *The Review and Herald*, November 30, 1897 (emphasis added).

other blessings produce corresponding fruit resulting in growth and spiritual maturity, perfection is involved. This principle is illustrated in the natural world.

> The development of the plant is a beautiful figure of Christian growth. As in nature, so in grace; there can be no life without growth. The plant must either grow or die. As its growth is silent and imperceptible, but continuous, so is the development of the Christian life. *At every stage of development our life may be perfect*; yet if God's purpose for us is fulfilled, there will be continual advancement. Sanctification is the work of a lifetime.[228]

Character Perfection Is Bible Perfection

Bearing in mind what relative perfection involves, one begins to understand why many Bible characters are noted as being "perfect" when, in reality, they were not. They were less than *sinlessly* perfect. Daniel, for example, was not sinlessly perfect, although he lived a sanctified life. Ellen White referred to Daniel as "an inspired illustration of true sanctification."[229]

In Daniel 9, at a very advanced age, the prophet still had personal sins to confess, along with the sins of his people. "And whiles I [was] speaking, and praying, and *confessing my sin* and the sin of my people Israel, and presenting my supplication before the LORD my God for the holy mountain of my God" (v. 20). Regarding that incident, in which the angel Gabriel appeared to Daniel while he was studying, fasting, praying, and making confession, Ellen White wrote, "Daniel humbled himself before God, to confess *his sins* and the sins of his people."[230]

Regarding Gabriel's subsequent appearance to Daniel in chapter 10, the Spirit of Prophecy expounds upon it:

---

[228] White, *Christ's Object Lessons*, p. 65 (emphasis added).
[229] *The Sanctified Life*, p. 52.
[230] In What Shall We Glory *The Review and Herald*, March 15, 1887 (emphasis added).

Three Levels of Human Perfection

When the prophet Daniel beheld the glory surrounding the heavenly messenger that was sent unto him, he was *overwhelmed with a sense of his own weakness and imperfection*. Describing the effect of the wonderful scene, he says, "There remained no strength in me: for my comeliness was turned in me into corruption, and I retained no strength."[231]

The patriarch Enoch, who also lived a sanctified life and walked with God for three hundred years, perfected a righteous character, along with Elijah.[232] Even then, he was not sinlessly perfect either, as the statement below shows:

> Enoch was a man of strong and highly cultivated mind and extensive knowledge; he was honored with special revelations from God; yet being in constant communion with Heaven, with a sense of the divine greatness and perfection ever before him, he was one of the humblest of men. The closer the connection with God, the deeper was *the sense of his own weakness and imperfection*.[233]

We are familiar with other Bible characters who are said to be "perfect" but were, in fact, perfect only in the relative sense. They were not necessarily *sinlessly* perfect.
For instance:

a. Job was accounted perfect by the Lord Himself at the beginning of the book (see 1:8) but repented of sin later on in the book (see 42:6).

b. Noah was perfect in all his generations (see Gen. 6:9) but sinned (see 9:21).

c. David's heart was said to be perfect, unlike that of his son Solomon, who was enticed into idolatry due to the baleful influence of his wives (see 1 Kings 11:4).

---

[231] White, *Steps to Christ*, p. 29 (emphasis added).
[232] See White, *Selected Messages*, vol. 3, p. 146
[233] White, *Patriarchs and Prophets*, p. 85 (emphasis added).

d. King Asa was perfect in all his days (see 2 Chron. 15:17) but sinned (see 16:1–11).

e. Jesus told the young ruler if he wished to be perfect right there and then, all he needed to do was sell his goods, give to the poor, and follow him (see Matt. 19:21).

f. Paul called the Philippian believers perfect at the same time he admitted they have not yet attained to it (see Phil. 3:12–15)

To repeat, character perfection (or Christian perfection or sanctification) is Bible perfection. It is the level of perfection that God's faithful people in biblical times experienced. It is a level of perfection that is, at best, relative. It must not be confused with sinless perfection.

"We Are Not Yet Perfect"

Four years before she died, Ellen White made a remarkable statement, in which she admitted she, too, along with her peers, was still imperfect. In short, perfection was still an experience they had not possessed.

> *We are not yet perfect*; but it is our privilege to cut away from the entanglements of self and sin, and *advance to perfection*. Great possibilities, high and holy attainments, are placed *within the reach of all*.[234]

Her call to "advance to perfection" is but an echo of Paul's appeal to the Hebrew Christians to leave the basic elements of faith and practice behind and advance towards perfection. "Therefore leaving the principles of the doctrine of Christ, *let us go on unto perfection*; not laying again the foundation of repentance from dead works, and of faith toward God" (Heb. 6:1, emphasis added). Were Ellen White and Paul calling the believers of their day to be *sinlessly* perfect? Not

---

[234] White, *The Acts of the Apostles*, p. 565 (emphasis added).

Three Levels of Human Perfection

necessarily. Theirs was a call to attain to Bible perfection, which is that "high and holy attainment, within the reach of all."

Their call to perfection ran parallel with Christ's own call to perfection in His Sermon on the Mount: *"Be ye therefore perfect, even as your Father which is in heaven is perfect"* (Matt. 5:48, emphasis added). This was nothing but a call to advance towards spiritual maturity, to the point where they love even their enemies. God exemplifies that love by letting the sun shine on both the good and the bad without condition. In other words, this was another appeal to advance towards Christian perfection or sanctification—better still, Bible perfection.

Sinless Perfection Waits Until the Final Atonement

Sinless perfection, as high and holy an attainment as it is, is *not* within the reach of all. Sinless perfection is reserved for the final generation—i.e., those who will be alive during the closing scenes of the great day of atonement, when Jesus gives the command to "take away their filthy garments… and give them a change of raiment." Previous generations of faithful believers never had the opportunity to experience anything beyond Bible perfection or sanctification for the simple reason that they were not exposed to the same amount of light the final generation has. In fact, that light was sealed up until the time of the end (see Dan. 8:26; 12:4).

Sinless Perfection, Better Than Character Perfection

Sinless perfection transcends relative perfection. It means more than just being spiritually mature and fully surrendered to God. It means attaining to "the measure of the stature of the *fulness* of Christ" (see Eph. 4:13, emphasis added). To be sinlessly perfect is to reflect the image of Jesus *fully*.[235] It is to have Christ fully formed within. As Jesus never developed a single character defect, those who attain sinless perfection through the final atonement will have no more

---

[235] See White, *Early Writings*, p. 71.

blemishes or wrinkles—no more plague spots of character. Not even the slightest memory of sin remains!

Sinless perfection is *permanent* perfection. "When the decree goes forth and the stamp is impressed, their character will remain pure and spotless for eternity."[236] At this stage of character development, the believer is ripe for the harvest (see Mark 4:26–29; Rev. 14:14–16).

Sinless Perfection, the Experience Saved for Last!

In perfecting the characters of His people, rendering them sinless, just before He leaves the Most Holy Place of the heavenly sanctuary, Jesus saves the best experience for last! The complete transformation of God's people during that event shows that the work Jesus began in their hearts, He is able to finish (see Phil. 1:6). In perfecting the characters of His people as such, Christ's power to amply, completely, and permanently reclaim from sin and save to the uttermost is put on display before the entire universe to the praise and glory of His name. Christ will be glorified and admired in His perfected end-time saints. Here, at last, is a company, called the 144,000, all beneficiaries of the final atonement and cleansing, prepared as an army, ready to stand the rigors, tests, and trials of the time of trouble without an intercessor.

Perfect at Every Stage

To summarize, there are three primary stages or levels of development in the Christian experience. At each stage, the believer is deemed perfect:

Level 1: Character perfection/Christian perfection/sanctification

- attained by persevering to overcome every fault, dying daily to self, advancing in the knowledge of God, living a life of service
- character is constantly maturing

---

[236] White, *Testimonies for the Church*, vol. 5, p. 216.

- not a permanent change
- relative perfection
- experience needed to prepare for the final atonement
- must be the believer's experience now

Level 2: Sinless perfection

- no more character flaws (see Eph. 5:27)
- sinful desires no longer cherished (see *The Great* Controversy, p. 623).
- no memory of any particular sin (see Jer. 50:20; *Selected Messages*, book 3, p. 135; *The Great Controversy*, p. 620).
- the experience of the 144,000 (see Rev. 14:5)
- complete and permanent change (see Rev. 22:11)
- this perfection only granted during the final atonement (see Lev 16:30; Zech. 3:1–5; *Prophets and Kings*, pp. 587–591)

Level 3: Nature perfection

- hereditary nature changed in the twinkling of an eye (see Phil. 3:21)
- sinless flesh or holy flesh is granted, meaning no more unholy, sinful desires, urges, and passions as in fallen flesh
- this perfection not granted during the final atonement; it waits until the second coming of Jesus

It is the genuine believer's great privilege to experience all of the above miraculous transformations of character and nature *in their order* by faith in God's redeeming grace. "First the blade, then the ear, after that the full corn in the ear" (Mark 4:28).

Bibliography

Ford, Desmond. *Daniel 8:14, The Day of Atonement, and the Investigative Judgment*. Casselberry, FL: Euangelion Press, 2018.

Froom, Leroy. *The Movement of Destiny*, Washington, DC: Review and Herald Publishing Association, 1971.

Holbrook, Frank B., ed. *Doctrine of the Sanctuary: A Historical Survey*. Silver Spring, MD: Biblical Research Institute, 1989.

———. *The Seventy Weeks, Leviticus, and the Nature of Prophecy*. Silver Spring, MD: Biblical Research Institute, 1986.

The KJV Study Bible. Grand Rapids, MI: Zondervan, 2002.

Martin, Walter R. *The Truth About Seventh-day Adventism*. Grand Rapids, MI: Zondervan Publishing House, 1960.

Schwarz, Richard W. and Greenleaf, Floyd. *Light Bearers: A History of the Seventh-day Adventist Church*. Nampa, Idaho: Pacific Press Publishing Association, 2000.

Singer, Isidore. *The Jewish Encyclopedia*. Vol. 2. London: Forgotten Books, 2017.

Smith, Uriah. *Daniel and the Revelation*. Nashville: Southern Publishing Association, 1896.

Strong, James. The Strongest Strong's Exhaustive Concordance of the Bible. Grand Rapids, MI: Zondervan Publishing House, 2001.

Whiston, William. The Genuine Works of Flavius Josephus, the Jewish Historian. London, 1737.

White, Ellen G. *The Acts of the Apostles*. Mountain View, CA: Pacific Press Publishing Association, 1911.

———. "An Appeal for Help." *Australasian Union Conference Record*, July 28, 1899.

———. "Christ the Medium of Blessing." *The Signs of the Times*, June 18, 1896.

———. *Christ's Object Lessons*. Washington, DC: Review and Herald Publishing Association, 1900.

———. "The Christian Rule in Deal." *The Signs of the Times*, February, 7, 1884.

———. *Christian Temperance and Bible Hygiene*. Battle Creek, MI: Good Health Publishing Co., 1890.

———. *Counsels on Diet and Foods*. Washington, DC: Review and Herald Publishing Association, 1938.

———. *The Desire of Ages*. Mountain View, CA: Pacific Press Publishing Association, 1898.

———. *Early Writings*. Washington, DC: Review and Herald Publishing Association, 1882.

———. *Evangelism*. Washington, DC: Review and Herald Publishing Association, 1946.

———. *Faith and Works*. Nashville, TN: Southern Publishing Association, 1979.

———. *The Great Controversy*. Mountain View, CA: Pacific Press Publishing Association, 1911.

———. "The Great Controversy. Between Christ and His Angels and Satan and His Angels." *The Signs of the Times*, November 27, 1879.

———. *Historical Sketches of the Foreign Missions of the Seventh-day Adventists*. Basle: Imprimerie Polyglotte, 1886.

———. *Last Day Events*. Boise, ID: Pacific Press Publishing Association, 1992.

———. *Life Sketches of Ellen G. White*. Mountain View, CA: Pacific Press Publishing Association, 1915.

———. *Manuscript Releases*. Vol. 1. Silver Spring, MD: Ellen G. White Estate, 1981.

———. *Manuscript Releases*. Vol. 5. Silver Spring, MD: Ellen G. White Estate, 1990.

———. *Manuscript Releases*. Vol. 21. Silver Spring, MD: Ellen G. White Estate, 1993.

———. "Notes on Travel." *The Review and Herald*, November 25, 1884.

———. "Our Duty and Responsibility," *The General Conference Bulletin*, October 1, 1896.

———. *Patriarchs and Prophets*. Washington, DC: Review and Herald Publishing Association, 1890.

———. "Peace in Christ." *The Review and Herald*, November 29, 1887.

Bibliography

———. "A Perfect Law." *The Signs of the Times*, July 31, 1901.

———. "Prepare to Meet the Lord." *The Review and Herald*, November 27, 1900.

———. "The Price of Our Redemption," *The Youth's Instructor*, June 21, 1900.

———. *Prophets and Kings*. Mountain View, CA: Pacific Press Publishing Association, 1917.

———. "The Righteousness of Christ." *The Review and Herald*, August 19, 1890.

———. *Selected Messages*. Book 1. Washington, DC: Review and Herald Publishing Association, 1958.

———. *Selected Messages*. Book 2. Washington, DC: Review and Herald Publishing Association, 1958.

———. Selected Messages. Book 3. Washington, DC: Review and Herald Publishing Association, 1980.

———. *The SDA Bible Commentary*. Vol. 6. Washington, DC: Review and Herald Publishing Association, 1956.

———. *The SDA Bible Commentary*. Vol. 7. Washington, DC: Review and Herald Publishing Association, 1957.

———. *Sketches from the Life of Paul*. Battle Creek, MI: Review and Herald, 1883.

———. *Sons and Daughters of God*. Washington, DC: Review and Herald Publishing Association, 1955.

———. *The Spirit of Prophecy.* Vol. 1. Battle Creek, MI: Seventh-day Adventist Publishing Association, 1870.

———. *Spiritual Gifts.* Vol. 1. Battle Creek, MI: Seventh-day Adventist Publishing Association, 1858.

———. *Steps to Christ.* Mountain View, CA: Pacific Press Publishing Association, 1892.

———. *Testimonies for the Church.* Vol. 1. Mountain View, CA: Pacific Press Publishing Association, 1868.

———. *Testimonies for the Church.* Vol. 3. Mountain View, CA: Pacific Press Publishing Association, 1875.

———. *Testimonies for the Church.* Vol. 5. Mountain View, CA: Pacific Press Publishing Association, 1889.

———. *Testimonies for the Church.* Vol. 6. Mountain View, CA: Pacific Press Publishing Association, 1901.

———. *Testimonies for the Church.* Vol. 8. Mountain View, CA: Pacific Press Publishing Association, 1904.

———. *Testimonies to Ministers and Gospel Workers.* Mountain View, CA: Pacific Press Publishing Association, 1923.

———. *Thoughts from the Mount of Blessing.* Mountain View, CA: Pacific Press Publishing Association, 1896.

———. *A Word to the Little Flock.* Washington, DC: Review and Herald Publishing Association, 1847.

———. "Ye are the Light of the World." *The Home Missionary*, July 1, 1897.

———. "Ye Are the Light of the World." *The Review and Herald*, September 21, 1897.

TEACH Services, Inc.
PUBLISHING

We invite you to view the complete
selection of titles we publish at:
www.TEACHServices.com

We encourage you to write us
with your thoughts about this,
or any other book we publish at:
info@TEACHServices.com

TEACH Services' titles may be purchased in
bulk quantities for educational, fund-raising,
business, or promotional use.
bulksales@TEACHServices.com

Finally, if you are interested in seeing
your own book in print, please contact us at:
publishing@TEACHServices.com
We are happy to review your manuscript at no charge.

www.ingramcontent.com/pod-product-compliance
Lightning Source LLC
Chambersburg PA
CBHW071146160426
43196CB00011B/2019